Dances with Sheep

Michigan Monograph Series in Japanese Studies
Number 37
Center for Japanese Studies
The University of Michigan

Dances with Sheep

The Quest for Identity
in the Fiction of Murakami Haruki

Matthew Carl Strecher

Center for Japanese Studies
The University of Michigan
Ann Arbor, 2002

*Open access edition funded by the National Endowment for the Humanities/
Andrew W. Mellon Foundation Humanities Open Book Program.*

Published by the Center for Japanese Studies, The University of Michigan,
202 S. Thayer St., Ann Arbor, MI 48104-1608

Library of Congress Cataloging in Publication Data

Strecher, Matthew.
    Dances with sheep : the quest for identity in the fiction of Murakami
Haruki / Matthew Carl Strecher.
        p. cm. — (Michigan monograph series in Japanese studies ; no. 37)
    Includes bibliographical references and index.
    ISBN 1-929280-07-6 (cloth : alk. paper)
    1. Murakami, Haruki, 1949—Criticism and interpretation. I. Title.
II. Series.

PL856.U673 Z86 2002
895.6'35—dc21
                                                              2001059866

This book was set in Bauer Bodoni.

This publication meets the ANSI/NISO Standards for Permanence of Paper
for Publications and Documents in Libraries and Archives
(Z39.48–1992).

Published in the United States of America

ISBN 978-1-929280-07-0 (hardcover)
ISBN 978-0-472-03833-6 (paper)
ISBN 978-0-472-12806-8 (ebook)
ISBN 978-0-472-90202-6 (open access)

To Mei, Victor, and Lizzie, who have endured with me.

Contents

Preface

> I wanted to turn my eyes to the past, and to reconstruct that past
> in a form that I could comprehend more easily.
> —Murakami Haruki, "'Monogatari' no tame no Bōken"

Murakami Haruki (b. 1949) first appeared on the Japanese literary scene
more than two decades ago with his novella *Kaze no uta o kike* (Hear the
Wind Sing, 1979). That work earned the coveted Gunzō New Writer's Award
and launched Murakami's career as a writer virtually overnight. Up until
that time (and for some time afterward) the author had been proprietor of
a popular jazz cafe called Peter Cat.

Since that debut, regard for Murakami has increased dramatically,
not only at home but throughout the world, as a writer of so-called
"postmodern" fiction, while a tremendous body of secondary literature has
been produced to explain (and in some cases, explain *away*) his success.
And while some critical essays on Murakami have been published outside
of Japan for non-Japanese audiences, the vast majority, naturally enough,
has been written by Japanese critics for Japanese audiences. Indeed, until
now there has been no book-length work of criticism on Murakami in the
English language that takes into account the growing body of his work
available in translation.

The present text is intended to help fill this gap. My goal in writing
it has been to produce a study sophisticated enough to do justice to the
complexities of Murakami's fictional world—it *is* complex—and be useful
to scholars of modern Japanese literature, on the one hand, and yet to keep
the level of discussion such that the book will be accessible to general readers, particularly those whose access to Murakami is through translated texts.

This, I strongly believe, is the correct approach to this author's work
in particular, because he himself has managed, as not many before him

have managed, to tread the tightrope that is still widely believed to divide "serious literature" and "popular fiction." Murakami's work is, in fact, both. As Yoshio Iwamoto wrote some years ago, despite the popularity of Murakami's texts, "[t]here is enough of the 'pure' and 'serious' about the work . . . to have held critics back from dismissing it merely as popular stuff—enough, it might be said, of the adversarial role against established norms of all sorts that the distinguished writer Kenzaburo Oe sees as the defining feature of 'pure literature'" (Iwamoto 1993).

But there is no sweeping aside the popularity of Murakami's writing; each successive novel and short story collection makes the bestseller lists in Japan, and often enough outside it, too (Murakami enjoys rock-star status in Taiwan and South Korea). The readership is diverse and enthusiastic, and ranges from high school students to college professors. Murakami himself has rarely expressed pretensions about being part of the "serious" literary crowd—though he unquestionably claims a significant role in contemporary Japanese writing—preferring instead to focus on the "story" as both the medium and the purpose of contemporary writing. This has been especially true in the case of his third novel, *Hitsuji o meguru bōken* (A Wild Sheep Chase, 1982), in which he claims to have put stylistic issues away for a while and concentrated instead simply on his task as a storyteller (Kawamoto 1985, 62). Such statements should be read, I think, primarily as a rejection of writing as "art," either as an effort to beautify the human condition, or to perfect humanity by aestheticizing it.

This does not mean, however, that Murakami's fiction is irrelevant to contemporary society. Quite the contrary, he would argue that it is art that is now irrelevant; in today's world, awash in the artificial images of television, advertising, and the mass media, of computers and "cyberspace," the story *is* our reality, and thus is the most direct means to reach the public. It was for this reason, as Alfred Birnbaum pointed out some years ago, that Murakami and other young writers—among them, Shimada Masahiko, Yamada Eimi, Murakami Ryū and Yoshimoto Banana—began to distance themselves from terms like "pure literature" (*junbungaku*) in favor of "fiction" (*fuikkushon*) (Birnbaum 1991, 1).

Others, looking at the broader picture of Japanese literary history, have pointed out that it is pure literature itself that has changed with the times, and that writers like Murakami Haruki have been part of this evolution from the beginning. Kawamura Minato argued quite recently, for instance, that both Murakami Haruki and Murakami Ryū, having debuted in *Gunzō*, were marked for pure literature from the start, but that they faced formidable resistance from the entrenched "old guard" of the Japanese literary establishment.

Both Murakami Haruki and Murakami Ryū began their careers with *Gunzō*, and thus came out as so-called "pure" writers at the outset. There was, of course, resistance to them. The more conventional writers and critics of pure literature—especially the older ones—certainly set themselves against them, but by then they had already won a place for themselves. (Kawamura and Osugi 2000, 133)

Of course, the same could be said of many young writers seeking to win acceptance by the literary establishment. The difference in Murakami's case is that he has never really actively sought the acceptance of the literary establishment at all, insisting instead that he simply writes what he wants, however he wants (Kawamoto 1985, 39–40). His decision to turn to writing, rather, was a result of his own internal need to understand the major events of his generation's past. "I wanted to turn my eyes to the past," he says of writing *Hear the Wind Sing*, "to reconstruct that past in a form that I could comprehend more easily" (Kawamoto 1985, 38).

Unquestionably, some of this impulse toward understanding remains in Murakami's writing to this day. Much of his interest in the world of multinational capitalism, in terrorism and violence, and most recently in the effects of PTSD (Post Traumatic Stress Disorder), especially related to the 1995 Kobe earthquake, and the AUM Shinrikyō cult's 1995 sarin gas attack in the Tokyo subways, is an attempt to make sense of these things to himself.[1] At the same time, both Murakami and his protagonists have matured enough over the past twenty years or so to develop some interest in helping others to understand better themselves and their world, too. Accordingly, in addition to his own fiction, the author's repertoire of writing today includes translations of major works of American fiction, numerous travelogues, two nonfiction works (discussed below) connected with the AUM incident, illustrated comic-type books, and even a "guidebook" to recent Japanese fiction for young readers. Clearly, he has diversified considerably since 1979.

Having said this, a word or two about the admittedly limited scope of the present volume is appropriate. I have deliberately ignored Murakami's travelogues, his translations of American authors, the guidebook to Japanese short fiction, and those works obviously written to appeal to the comic book readership among Japanese high school and college students. Instead, my study is focused almost exclusively on the author's fiction. My reasons

1. The matter of PTSD comes up in particular in a 1996 discussion between Murakami and clinical psychologist Kawai Hayao, published in *Sekai*, vol. 46, no. 621 (April 1996) as "'Monogatari' de ningen wa nani o naosu no ka."

for this are numerous, but foremost among them is my belief that we will find the most comprehensive expressions of Murakami's worldview, his *raison d'etre* as writer, in his original fiction—particularly his novels. Readers will also notice, no doubt, that some works are discussed in more than one chapter. This reflects my resistance to taking a chronological approach to Murakami, my rejection of the notion that his third novel, for instance, led naturally and inevitably to his fourth. I do not mean to deny that Murakami has developed and matured as a craftsman over the years, or that his ideas have not grown as a result of past experiences; but to read his works in a deterministic way would become, finally, a severe obstacle to our ability to discern the author's real methodology.

That methodology may be described as a kind of experimentation with genre, style, and theme. Sometimes he writes more than one work in a similar vein—there are, for instance, several works that explore the adventure formula, several romances, and so forth—but this does not mean that the latter work is necessarily more advanced than the former, the result of lessons learned before. This is, incidentally, what keeps Murakami's work fresh: his willingness to try new things, to go out on the occasional limb. Some of those limbs, admittedly, have broken off beneath him, but for the most part there is something worthwhile to be found in each of his novels. I have sought in this book to highlight these points, while using each novel, as appropriate, to outline Murakami's larger projects of probing the nature of identity, the unconscious, late-model capitalism, and the tropes of postmodernism. In so doing, and in keeping with my determination to include rather than exclude readers whose access to Murakami comes through translations, I have tried to direct my critical energies onto texts available (or soon to be available) in English.

Having come this far, however, I am compelled to note that the translations of passages from Murakami in this text are my own, and readers may well wonder at the seeming contradiction in my decision not to use the published texts for these analyses. There are several reasons for this. One is philosophical: my interpretations of Murakami's fiction are all based on close readings of the original texts, and I feel some anxiety about introducing a new "remove," to borrow an expression from Plato, between my critical eye and its object. This becomes particularly important where my readings are based on a single word or phrase, one whose significance to me may be a little different from that of another. In short, to do a close reading of a translated text is as much to interpret the translator as the author in some cases. I wished to avoid this. (It is worth noting that this concern did not seem so critical in dealing with other authors—Furui

Yoshikichi, for instance, or Shimada Masahiko, whose works are discussed more generally—and so I have quoted from translations in these cases.)

A somewhat more prosaic reason for using my own translations is a desire to preserve stylistic unity in my own text. That is to say, while the translations of Murakami's works—chiefly by Alfred Birnbaum, Phil Gabriel, and Jay Rubin—are generally both accurate and lively, the styles of the translators vary. Birnbaum, in particular, demonstrates in his early translations a tendency to experiment with accent and dialect, while Gabriel tends to use a more conversational style in his work than Rubin, and so forth. None of these stylistic differences necessarily take anything away from the text, but they do not always suit the style in which I have written the present text, and so I have solved the problem of stylistic unity by doing the translations myself, but citing the page numbers both from the originals and the translations, which will hopefully be of use to readers who use those texts.

I hope the translators named above will understand my motivations, and that readers will find this volume useful and interesting.

Matthew C. Strecher
Tokyo, October 2000

Acknowledgments

This book began, as so many do today, as a doctoral research project, and so my first and most fervent expressions of gratitude are to Jay Rubin at Harvard, and John Whittier Treat at Yale. I thank Jay for introducing me to Murakami's fiction, and later to the author himself, and for giving me sound advice and helpful encouragement right up to the completion of the present text. I offer thanks to John for guiding me in useful new research directions that somehow always managed to feed this project, and for his patience while teaching me the "language" of contemporary critical writing.

Many others have contributed, in direct or indirect ways. Michael Brown at Notre Dame and Steve Kohl of the University of Oregon both had useful comments on certain parts of this text that I happened to present on their campuses, and I appreciate their candor. I am grateful to former colleagues at Northern Illinois University—to Taylor Atkins, Katarina Barbe, Bill Harrison, and especially to Ray Tourville, all of whom showed kind interest in my work, throughout its progress and up to the point of completion.

Former colleagues and friends at the University of Montana also deserve mention: Phil West and Steve Levine at the Maureen and Mike Mansfield Center for finding excuses to send me to Tokyo, and for their very important friendships; Chris Anderson and Hayden Ausland for intellectual and moral support; to Michel Valentin for helping me to understand postmodernism—especially French postmodernism—better than I ever had before; to Gerry Brenner for his encouragement at key moments.

Here in Japan, I offer my gratitude to Kuroko Kazuo, whose voluminous work on Murakami has so obviously affected my own. Gratitude is also due to Masahiro Oikawa at Ritsumeikan University, who provided some of my first opportunities to present my work on Murakami to a Japanese audience, to Seiji Shibata in Shikoku, and to colleagues and administrators here at Tōyō University, who are too many to name here, but have always endeavored to help me with this project. Also here in Japan, I extend thanks to a very bright former student, Dan Sullivan, who took time out of an arduous schedule as a Monbushō research scholar to dig up the most recent texts for me while I was still in the U.S.. Of course, most of all I would like to thank Murakami Haruki himself, who made time to visit with me even when we both knew he could ill afford it. His contribution has been invaluable, though he himself may downplay its importance.

Finally, thanks goes to my family, who have suffered through this project with me for years; to the anonymous readers who took the time to read my work carefully and offered extremely useful comments; and to the editors at the Center for Japanese Studies at the University of Michigan, particularly Bruce Willoughby, whose patience and diligence has made this project genuinely fun.

Parts of chapter one originally appeared in "Beyond 'Pure' Literature: Mimesis, Formula, and the Postmodern in the Fiction of Murakami Haruki," *Journal of Asian Studies* 57.2 (May 1998): 354–78, and are reprinted with permission of the Association for Asian Studies. Portions of chapter two originally appeared in "Magical Realism and the Search for Identity in the Fiction of Murakami Haruki," *Journal of Japanese Studies* 25.2 (summer 1999): 263–98, and are used with permission.

Note: All Japanese names appear in Japanese order, that is, surname first (e.g., Yokoo Kazuhiro).

Abbreviations

AGCD   *Kami no kodomotachi wa mina odoru* (All the gods' children dance). Tokyo: Shinchōsha, 2000.

DDD   *Dance, Dance, Dance.* Translated by Alfred Birnbaum. New York: Vintage, 1995.

DM   *Dream Messenger.* By Shimada Masahiko. Translated by Philip Gabriel. Tokyo, New York, and London: Kodansha International, 1989.

EV   *The Elephant Vanishes.* Translated by Alfred Birnbaum and Jay Rubin. New York: Knopf, 1993.

HBW&EW   *Hard-Boiled Wonderland and the End of the World.* Translated by Alfred Birnbaum. New York: Vintage, 1991.

KMTN   *Kokkyō no minami, taiyō no nishi* (South of the border, west of the sun). Tokyo: Kōdansha, 1992.

MHZ   *Murakami Haruki zensakuhin, 1979-1989* (Complete works of Murakami Haruki, 1979-1989). 8 vols. Tokyo: Kōdansha, 1991.

NK   *Nejimakidori kuronikuru* (Wind-up bird chronicle). Tokyo: Shinchōsha, 1994-96.

SBWS   *South of the Border, West of the Sun.* Translated by Philip Gabriel. New York: Vintage, 2000. Originally published by Alfred A. Knopf, 1999.

SK   *Supūtoniku no koibito* (The Sputnik sweetheart). Tokyo: Kōdansha, 1999.

WSC   *A Wild Sheep Chase.* Translated by Alfred Birnbaum. New York: Plume, 1989.

WUBC   *The Wind-Up Bird Chronicle.* Translated by Jay Rubin. New York: Knopf, 1997.

Introduction

The Cultural Milieu of Murakami Haruki

"Murakami Haruki writes in Japanese, but his writing is not really Japanese. If you translate it into American English, it can be read very naturally in New York."
　　　　　　　—Ōe Kenzaburō, "The Novelist in Today's World"

It is fitting to begin this book with Ōe's paradoxical statement above, for paradoxes about Murakami Haruki abound. He is a "serious" writer, yet one with a widely popular readership. He writes in Japanese, but as Ōe says above, his writing is "not really Japanese"; rather, its language disturbs Japanese native speakers, who find something vaguely off-center, almost foreign in it.[1] His works are usually set in Japan but could almost as easily take place abroad.

　　Part of the reason for this, as pointed out by virtually every critic who has ever dealt with Murakami, lies in his fondness for images of popular culture familiar to the Western world. Readers can hardly miss the frequent invocation of Western cultural icons—the Beatles, John F. Kennedy, McDonald's, Budweiser. But does this make Murakami "un-Japanese"? Is it really fair to say that these images, though they originate in Euro-American culture (primarily American), have not become Japanese (in the sense of being internalized by the Japanese) by now? Jürgen Stalph (1995) suggests that the reason Western audiences—German readers in his case—respond to Murakami so well is the fact that these images replace more tradi-

---

1. See, for instance, Katō 1988, 104–28. He argues, among other things, that Murakami was the first Japanese writer to use terms previously thought quintessentially Japanese in such a way as to lend the atmosphere of American "hard-boiled" fiction to Japanese writing. See also Numano 1989, 144–57, esp. 147, 155–57. He analyzes the "Americanness" and "Japaneseness" of Murakami's prose.

1

tionally "Japanese" ones. But then we are compelled to ask, are the Beatles more German than Japanese? Is Kennedy more familiar to Londoners than Tokyoites? Is there something more exotic about Japanese drinking Budweiser than there might be, say, for Canadians?

Questions such as those above, however we respond, reveal that something strongly ethnic and regional remains in our reading of world cultures, and that this clouds our reading experience with expectations that may be out of place, or at least out of date. Such stereotyping may be inevitable, yet it becomes increasingly difficult to cling to such regional thinking while attempting to embrace the new "international" literatures being produced by younger writers throughout the world. Still, stereotyping also has its value: it forces us to confront and to interrogate what we might term the "cultural simultaneity" of the contemporary world, which means, in the context of today's cultural productions, that the world is getting smaller.

MURAKAMI ABROAD

It is important to bear this point in mind when discussing Murakami, because his emergence at this particular moment in our cultural history is no accident. To phrase this another way, we might say that the emergence of a writer like Murakami would not have been possible without the unique combination of certain events in the world, both cultural and historical. Murakami's type of "non-Japanese Japanese literature" could only have been produced (a) near or after the end of the Cold War, (b) in the atmosphere of cultural curiosity fostered by the so-called "postmodern moment," and (c) during a time when Japan reached a peak both in its economic and cultural influences worldwide. One could say that the success of a writer such as Murakami was a predictable, even inevitable development, and ultimately necessary to bring Japanese literature into a synchronic relationship with the rest of the industrialized world.

Indeed, a look at how Murakami's work has fared in this country during his twenty-year career is revealing. In 1985 Alfred Birnbaum published his excellent translation of the author's 1982 novel, *Hitsuji o meguru bōken*, as *A Wild Sheep Chase*, and "Murakami Mania" was born. Four years later *Sekai no owari to hādo-boirudo wandārando* was published in English as *Hard-Boiled Wonderland and the End of the World*, and the mania grew. Both works sold well and were praised widely by the American critics, and Murakami could claim true international stardom.

No doubt Birnbaum found it easier to find publishers for his translations of Murakami's later works, and yet by the time his version of *Dansu*

dansu dansu (Dance Dance Dance) came out, "Murakami Mania" was all
but over. By the early 1990s, much of the excitement had worn off, and
while it appears that Jay Rubin's outstanding translation of *Nejimakidori
kuronikuru* (The Wind-Up Bird Chronicle) has outsold *A Wild Sheep Chase*,
much of the initial excitement at finding a fresh Japanese author has long
since worn off. One would be well advised, however, not to read too much
into this. While critical interest in the academy might be expected to remain reasonably strong, the tastes of the public readership at large are
notoriously capricious, perhaps rightly so, as readers are not bound to defend their reading selections.

It might therefore be argued that Murakami Haruki has had his
moment in the sun, that his work now remains only to be catalogued and
analyzed by scholars, should they deem it worthy, and placed within the
overall scheme of Japanese literary history. This is not to say that Murakami
will produce no more great works; indeed, his best works may well be yet to
come. But certain intangibles inform the reception of any writer overseas:
does his work mesh with the overall popular concerns of the culture into
which it is introduced? Is there general interest in the author's native culture overseas, and is his work therefore likely to gain favorable attention as
a result (a matter usually related to economic concerns as much as anything else)? Does his work translate well into the target culture as well as
language, and therefore "make sense" to readers there?

The year 1985, or more generally the period from the early 1980s
through the early 1990s, was unique in terms of combining all three of the
factors above over a long enough period of time to permit Murakami's smooth
and effective transmission into American and European cultures. To begin
with, the 1980s were, for all intents and purposes, the "Japanese decade,"
economically and culturally. Japan's "bubble economy," along with the
unprecedented strengthening of the yen against other world currencies,
permitted an almost unlimited Japanese expansion of business and industry into markets throughout the world.[2] This expansion was matched by a
national policy, no doubt influenced by Japanese awareness of post-World
War II mistrust on the part of former enemies, of spreading a benevolent
version of Japanese culture (as opposed to the "Greater East Asia Co-Pros-
perity Sphere" of the 1930s–1940s) throughout the world. Japanese em-
bassies and consulates throughout the world labored to make cultural information and funding available to virtually anyone interested in studying
or teaching about Japan. Many in the field of Japanese studies remember

2. For more on Japan's rise to economic preeminence in the 1980s, see Williams 1994.

this as a time when new Japanese programs sprang up all over the United States, many funded by Monbushō or the Japan Foundation.

In terms of cultural appropriateness, Murakami was also fortunate to be writing at a time when world cultures seemed to be coming together, rather than moving apart. *A Wild Sheep Chase* came out in America at the very height of the so-called postmodern moment, a moment that, like the student movements of the late 1960s, seemed to carry with it certain universal characteristics among the industrialized cultures of the world: a preference for multiplicity and plurality over singularity; a strong sense of suspicion toward "reality" as a concept, particularly in its representation through language; the blurring of cultural borders with the advent of faster, cheaper, and more reliable modes of communication; and a new phase in capitalist production that brought new and sophisticated modes of fetish consumerism to the postindustrial marketplace.

Of course, historically the postmodern has made the most sense in the context of the post-Cold War, at which point the vast, totalizing binaries of world regionality—Soviet Bloc versus the West (including many in the East and Middle East!)—were finally deconstructed. The result was the establishment of a new, paradoxical era of hope and unease: hope in the fact that the cold "war" was over; unease for the fact that détente, though grim, was (equally paradoxically) the only thing shielding the world from nuclear annihilation. As Baudrillard notes wryly, "The East's great weapon is no longer the H-bomb, but Chernobyl" (1994a, 39). It was at this point, at the level of global politics as well as culture, that our understanding of such basic terms as "good" and "evil" was swept into oblivion, replaced by an atmosphere of doubt and confusion.

MURAKAMI'S "INTERNATIONAL STYLE"

This cultural confusion—some would simply term it a new cosmopolitanism—is reflected clearly in Murakami's language. Dispensing with the inherent subtleties of Japanese—implied subjects and the like—Murakami prefers to be blunt. One is rarely in doubt about what is happening, or to whom. Indeed, his work may provide the most translatable Japanese texts ever to appear on the international scene, and this is one of his most unique characteristics. It is not merely the author's liberal use of the first-person pronoun "I" (*boku*) that lends his style a foreign flavor (literary Japanese avoids overuse of pronouns, except where clarity is at stake); it lies also in his use of foreign images and idioms. So much does Murakami's Japanese seem to reflect awareness of Western languages, in fact, that Stalph (1995,

105) has declared it to be almost seamless when rendered into them.

What permits Japanese and non-Japanese readers alike such unmitigated accessibility to Murakami's "voice" as a writer? One suspects it lies in his intimate, somehow personal way of describing things as though they were matters that anyone would understand immediately from his own experience. The world he describes is at once personal and yet shared, unique yet commonplace. We can almost always understand what Murakami tries to show us by relying on our historical pasts. One can almost hear him say, "Surely you understand what I mean from your own similar experiences." Perhaps this is the real source of the intimate connection that seems to form almost instantly between the narrators of Murakami works and those who read them. Much of the author's popularity seems to come from his ability to make the reader feel what he himself is feeling, the mark of any good writer or poet.

But as I noted above, Murakami's international style and translatability are as much a matter of his—any Japanese's—knowledge of "things un-Japanese" as of linguistics. Few could miss the predominance of Western cultural artifacts that turn up in Murakami's writing. Stalph argues that this is precisely what has gained the author such a wide following in Germany, for "he shows German readers a Japan they never knew. In his novels and stories we find no kimono, no refined Eastern aesthetics, no profound Japanese spirit closed off in mysterious darkness . . ." (Stalph 1995, 105). In short, Murakami makes no pretense of being heir to Tanizaki Jun'ichirō, Kawabata Yasunari, or even more recent Japanese literary spokesmen such as Ōe or Abe Kōbō who, along with Mishima Yukio, are considered by many to have been Japan's first truly international writers.

This internationalism, too, has caused a certain disquiet on both sides of the Pacific, and at all levels of critical thinking. We see it in major critics and writers like Ōe, who fears that, in the era of Murakami, Japanese literature is losing its cultural specificity; in well-placed scholars such as Masao Miyoshi, who sees Japanese literature becoming cheapened by writers like Murakami; and even in newspaper critics searching in vain for something more recognizably Japanese in contemporary Japanese literature. Herbert Mitgang, a critic for the *New York Times*, complained in 1993 that the author's works failed to convey any real sense of cultural identity at all:

> I wish the characters in "The Elephant Vanishes," his new book of short stories, wouldn't spend so much time at McDonald's, lighting up Marlboros, listening to Bruce Springsteen records and watching Woody Allen movies as a prelude to romance. Just when

you're ready for some wisdom from the Orient, the author serves up a Big Mac. (Mitgang 1993)

It is difficult not to be irritated by the undisguised Orientalism expressed in the statement above, and yet Mitgang's impression of Japan, no doubt born of several vigorous readings of James Clavell's *Shōgun*, is worth noting seriously for two reasons: first, it reveals something significant about the popular readership of Japanese literature in this country, and second, because it is echoed by critics far more sophisticated than Mitgang. Even Ōe's complaint above, I believe, is not unrelated to the kind of desire—even expectation—for traditional cultural specificities demonstrated in Mitgang's statement.

Yet, a look at Murakami's international readership reveals an interesting paradox: even as critics from Mitgang to Ōe decry the "un-Japanese" style of Murakami's writing, this is precisely what the majority of his readers around the world find so attractive. I noted above that Murakami's work succeeded in the United States in the mid-1980s because America was at that time receptive to Japanese culture. This is true not only of Japanese culture but of East Asian culture in general, as may be seen in the popularity of entertainment novels such as Clavell's *Shōgun, Tai-Pan,* and *Noble House,* to say nothing of the more vulgar works by Eric van Lustbader (*The Ninja, The Miko, Black Heart*), and other popular books that dealt with stereotypical impressions of the Far East. Indeed, the trend began even earlier, in the 1970s, and only bloomed in the 1980s.

But if this is what the typical American reader of popular fiction really wanted, then why would he or she be interested in a writer from Japan who writes as though he were not Japanese? The answer is, quite simply, that Murakami broke into the international scene at a particularly opportune moment: a point when Japan was often in the news, and therefore gaining the interest of mainstream Americans, but also a moment when anachronistic views of Japan—quaint visions of a nation filled with esoteric philosophy and a love of ancient things—were augmented by a more realistic acknowledgment of Japan as a modern world superpower. This more realistic perception of Japanese culture was fueled primarily by the generation of intellectuals that developed the field in the 1970s, a generation capable of seeing Japan as other than a defeated former enemy.

However, the "Japan Boom" of the 1980s was also the result of a young generation eager to take part in both the cultural and the economic opportunities that East Asia offered at the time. Two major characteristics marked this new generation: first, a greater degree of skepticism toward authority, no doubt inherited from the student generation of the 1960s.

One attributes much of this to the increased vigilance of the press following the Nixon presidency; for better or worse, Americans, like the press, were determined not to be taken in again by anyone. Hence, where our elders were molded by Watergate and Vietnam, we were baptized in the 1980s by the Iran-Contra scandal and Reaganomics.

Second, but of equal importance, was the powerful desire on the part of younger Americans to celebrate and embrace cultural diversity, to break down the great binaries that had until then divided the planet into highly distinct geopolitical units—East versus West, Warsaw Pact versus NATO, and so forth. No doubt this new attitude resulted from the rejection of forty years of the political ideology of mistrust that marked the Cold War era. At the very least one could say that the generation just reaching maturity in the early 1980s had little desire to carry on the politics of mistrust that led to the disastrous conflicts in Vietnam and Afghanistan. There can be little question that these conflicts undermined the truth-value of political ideologies such as "Democracy" and "Communism." By 1980 young Americans, at least, were less interested than ever in maintaining such divisions. This was registered in our rejection of the hard-line anti-Soviet stance that marked the early years of the Reagan presidency, our approval of the challenge to Mikhail Gorbachev to tear down the Berlin Wall. The subsequent collapse of the Warsaw Pact was unquestionably a sign that, culturally, at least, people had grown weary of division and sought instead a kind of worldwide simultaneity of culture.

The technology of the time, of course, was also responsible for this shift in attitudes. For the first time in our history, technology made it possible for us to be, almost literally, in more than one place at the same time. One thinks of the famous "Live Aid" concerts of 1985, held simultaneously in New York and London, and as if to emphasize the trans-Atlantic connectivity of the event, Phil Collins performed first at New York, then took the Concorde to Heathrow to perform on the London stage, both of his performances beamed by live satellite to the other site. It is worth noting that on each stage Collins played the same songs, announced with the same quips ("This is the other song I know on the piano," etc.), thus enhancing the illusion that live audiences on both sides of the Atlantic were simultaneously viewing the "same" performance (in duplicate), while television audiences, catching the live broadcast on the relatively young MTV network, "shared" the experience via satellite.

With this shrinkage of distance, both geographic and cultural borders grow indistinct. It should come as no surprise, then, that a writer like Murakami, who more than any other Japanese writer embodies non-culture-specific literary expression, should have found a receptive audience both in Europe and the United States in the 1980s.

Such are the conditions of the postmodern, and for precisely this reason expressions of postmodernism have elicited both thrill and resistance. Murakami's literature certainly created a stir outside of Japan, where, along with Yoshimoto Banana, he contributed to a brief but intense revival of interest in Japanese writing in the mid-1980s throughout the world, culminating, one might say, in the awarding of the Nobel Prize for literature to Ōe in 1994. But by far the most intense scrutiny of Murakami literature has taken place in Japan, where the sheer volume (if not always the quality) of critical writing on him suggests that he is considered more than a passing fancy by his Japanese audience.

CRITICAL RESPONSES TO MURAKAMI IN JAPAN

A remarkable variety of secondary writing on Murakami Haruki exists in Japan, and the number of essays and separate volumes devoted to him increases yearly. Some of the more exceptional works come from literary and intellectual historians such as Kuroko Kazuo (1990, 1993) and Karatani Kōjin (1990b), both of whom have been instrumental in situating Murakami in the general history of postwar Japanese literature. Others, such as Kazamaru Yoshihiko (1992) have made contributions to our understanding of the cross-generational reception of Murakami's fiction. Katō Norihiro and Kawamoto Saburō have both approached Murakami as a contemporary, and their works focus on the author's role as a potential spokesman for the younger members of the defunct Zenkyōtō movement of the late 1960s, a movement that ended inconclusively when, one by one, the various political justifications for a left-wing opposition in Japan were eliminated.

Still others, particularly members of the older generation of writers such as Ueno Chizuko and Ōe Kenzaburō, have been ambivalent about Murakami's work and rise to fame. Ueno described Murakami's 1987 bestseller *Noruwei no mori* (Norwegian Wood) as "epoch-making" for the strongly contemporary sensation of the book's passive hero. A fellow commentator, Ogura Chikako, on the other hand, claimed that the hero's egotism had made her sick.[3] Ōe, meanwhile, although acknowledging that Murakami has brought welcome attention to Japanese literature in ways that he himself has not, feels that Murakami represents a trend among Japanese writers away from literary expression, critical thinking, and intellec-

---

3. Both comments come from Ueno Chizuko et al. 1992, 257–58.

tual responsibility (Ōe 1989). Ōe's concerns, it should be noted, while often directed against Murakami's works, may be more broadly applied to Japanese postmodern literature in general, which, according to him, represents a massive break, a catastrophic rupture, between contemporary writing and the dialectical literature of the postwar written between 1945 and 1970 (which he identifies as *junbungaku*, or "pure literature"); "any future restoration of *junbungaku*," writes Ōe, "will be possible only if ways are found to fill in the wide gap that exists between Murakami and pre-1970 postwar literature" (Ōe 1989, 200).

But in the main, Japanese secondary literature on Murakami, though voluminous, is often less than satisfactory. With few exceptions, the bulk of such writing focuses on simple (or, occasionally, astonishingly complex) interpretive pieces on individual works.[4] Few scholars in Japan have concerned themselves with the historical and theoretical groundwork that underlies the author's narrative strategies, or the broader question of why a writer such as Murakami is necessary to Japanese literature.

What we do regularly find in Japanese critical writing on Murakami are lists of "influences" on the author, which yield only questionable results. One may well point out that Murakami's parents were both teachers of Japanese classical literature and grammar in public schools, that he read primarily American paperback fiction in high school, that his influences include Truman Capote, Raymond Carver, John Cheever, Richard Brautigan, Kurt Vonnegut Jr., Raymond Chandler, and J.D. Salinger. This offers us one portrait of the author. But when we confront the additional obvious and diverse influences of Ōe Kenzaburō, Edogawa Rampo, Ueda Akinari (a mid-Edo writer of supernatural tales), and of genres from classical and medieval Japan (particularly Noh drama), these "influences" become a jumble and do not show us a clear portrait of Murakami's development, but the more realistic picture of the complexity of the author's thinking.

Rather than concerning ourselves too much with what Murakami read as a student, it seems probable that more is to be gained from examining who reads Murakami, and why. This is another aspect of Japanese criticism that has been fairly widespread, and that does reveal some interesting facts about the author's work.

Some of those drawn most to the author's early works, 1979–82, were members of Murakami's own generation—those born in the first ten

---

4. One thinks, for instance, of Katō Norihiro's heroic attempt to chart the nineteen days over which *Hear the Wind Sings* and to draw attention to the temporal gaps he perceives between the "real" world of the protagonist and the "spirit" world of his alter ego, "Rat." See Katō 1996b, 36–49. More will be written on this novel in chapter two below.

years of the postwar era, who reached adulthood between 1965 and 1975. The reasons for this are not too difficult to find: these early works deal with the shared experience of growing up amid the increasing affluence of the 1950s and 1960s, of witnessing—and later participating in—the various counterculture movements that had been active since the beginning of the postwar, and finally, of watching those movements fall silent in the face of an increasingly systematized, controlled society after 1970. Such readers, encountering the cultural markers of the time—particularly the popular bands of the time such as Deep Purple, the Beatles, and the Rolling Stones— could hardly have failed to recall the demise of the student counterculture movements in Japan known as Zenkyōtō, a movement in which many college-age Japanese grounded their identities as young adults. The collapse of the various counterculture movements shortly after 1970 was a traumatic experience that Murakami's first three major works—*Kaze no uta o kike* (Hear the Wind Sing, 1979), *1973-nen no pinbōru* (Pinball, 1973; 1980), and the above-mentioned *A Wild Sheep Chase*—permitted them to revisit, reexamine, and reevaluate. Such a reevaluation may well be a part of what Baudrillard (1994) points out as our endless fascination with reconstructing the past as we approach the *fin de siècle*. In it lies our "mania for trials," our obsession with escaping the judgment of the twenty-first century by frantically rewriting the preceding one.

But I think it is more than this. The desire for closure of the 1960s is also grounded, and not only in Japan, in the common perception of a collective failure. This is not dissimilar to efforts to "confront" the Vietnam War, another great failure, to understand what the experience meant to those who were there. In both Japan and the United States, especially, much literature has been devoted to understanding the counterculture movement, particularly because it disappeared so suddenly, and its members, for the most part, seem to have abandoned their youthful idealism so completely. Tim O'Brien, an American contemporary of Murakami's known for his writings on the Vietnam War, writes fearfully about his generation's atrophy:

> What happened to them? All of us? I wonder about the conse-
> quences of our disillusion, the loss of energy, the slow hardening
> of a generation's arteries. What *happened*? Was it entropy? Ge-
> netic decay? And who among us would become a martyr, and for
> what? (1985, 127)

The same could just as easily be asked of the masses of Japanese "radicals" who swarmed into the streets in 1969 brandishing staves (*gebabō*), then abandoned radicalism and joined mainstream culture only a year later. It was not so much that the student radicals grew up and joined society—most eventually do—but the suddenness of the transformation that seems to bewilder Japanese writers and critics.

One of the more prolific of these is journalist Kawamoto Saburō, who focuses on Murakami's role as a spokesman for the last generation to experience the fervor of the counterculture movements. Describing his powerfully empathetic reading of *A Wild Sheep Chase*, Kawamoto writes of the sense of wandering that his generation has endured since the end of the 1960s:

> Reaching the part where the protagonist goes to Hokkaido, it occurred to me that here was another person who was *searching* for something. That was part of what drew me into the Murakami world. Finally, in that strange "other world" amidst the forests of Hokkaido, the protagonist meets his friend, after all those years. Quietly he asks him, "You're dead, aren't you?" Reading that, I found myself shedding unexpected tears. (Kawamoto 1986, 45)

Kawamoto's heavily sentimental reading experience was probably not uncommon among members of that generation, who recalled in *A Wild Sheep Chase* their own days on the front lines of Zenkyōtō, a movement whose use of mass violence peaked in 1969, followed by an evident loss of interest among its participants by the spring of 1970. This is exactly the historical moment in which Murakami seems the most interested. It was, in Kawamoto's view, a time when people disappeared, and old friendships were broken.

> From the end of the 1960s through the beginning of the 1970s a lot of our friends really *did* disappear like Rat. . . . There were times that, like Murakami's protagonist, I wanted to go out and find them. I, too, wish to ask, "Where have you all gone?" (Kawamoto 1986, 56)

Katō Norihiro, another contemporary, chastises the author mildly for romanticizing and thus obscuring the harsh reality of the 1960s, but at the same time compares Murakami's approach in writing *A Wild Sheep Chase* to Francis Coppola's approach to making *Apocalypse Now*: "Coppola said of *Apocalypse Now* that he aimed at producing a film that would 'give the audience a sense of the fear, insanity, sensations, and moral dilemmas of the Vietnam War.' But somewhere in the midst of doing this, 'the film began to take on a life of its own.'"[5] This is, according to Katō, an apt de-

---

5. Katō 1986, 72. Katō comments further on Coppola's work and quotes Murakami on the subject (1996a, 56–61).

scription of *A Wild Sheep Chase* as well, for "its attempt to portray the era of political radicalism embodied in terms like 'Zenkyōtō' and the 'Red Army'" ultimately "turns *A Wild Sheep Chase* into a nonsensical novel" (1986, 71–72).

But Katō does not mean by "nonsense" that the novel defies our attempts to read it; rather, he refers to the "distortions" (*yugami*) imposed upon the historical narrative by Murakami's creative processing of his memories of that period, that is, quite literally the psychology of textualizing the past. Such "distortions" are, of course, what make the experience of reading *A Wild Sheep Chase* (or almost any other Murakami novel) potentially very disturbing: one is taken by surprise by the historical narrative—what I shall later term "historiographic relief narrative"—that lurks beneath and grounds the surface text. It is for this reason also that Kawamoto is able to call *A Wild Sheep Chase* "a totally *un*political novel by a totally *un*political writer, that nevertheless makes us think constantly about the politics of that era," despite the fact that "neither the term 'Zenkyōtō' nor 'revolution' (*kakumei*) ever appears in the text" (1986, 56).

Whereas Kawamoto and Katō, among others, are excited by Murakami's abstraction of the Zenkyōtō period, however, another group of readers, only a few years younger, latched onto Murakami's writing at precisely the same time, but for very different reasons. This is the readership described by Kazamaru Yoshihiko, who defines his generation as "people born around or a little before 1960," who "dreamed of escaping the System, and just wanted to get through the 1970s without anyone bothering them" (Kazamaru 1992, 204). Obviously, this initial desire for withdrawal comes about partly as a result of the failure of Zenkyōtō. Displaying the scorn of the young toward the failures of their elders, Kazamaru goes on to note that "we thought all those Zenkyōtō activist types were complete morons" (ibid.).

Essentially, this generation appreciates Murakami for his portrayal of what Nakano Osamu terms the "indecisive lifestyle" (*hikettei no jinsei taido*), ideally suited to those who "linger in some middle ground where they can go on living indecisively forever" (Nakano 1989, 41). For purposes of contemporary literature it is a particularly important readership, however, for this was the first generation to abandon the idealism that had been feeding Japan's (indeed, the world's) counterculture movement, and to face the issue of identity in the near absence of political resistance. They were the first to accept the (state) ideology grounded in affluence, and to commit their resources, energy, and futures to that ideology. Most important of all, while it was the first generation to do all this, it was by no means the last. In fact, I would argue that the appeal of Murakami's writing—especially among readers aged twenty to thirty (Murakami and his protagonists age, but his readership does not!)—continues precisely because the identity crisis in Japan to which the author's work has always spoken so directly is not solved; it remains unchecked, or worse.

Interestingly, Kazamaru's definition of this readership has the effect of placing Murakami into a rather awkward historical position, his literature interposed precariously between the high-minded idealism of Ōe, Oda Makoto and (rather more cynically) Kaikō Takeshi, and the political lethargy of the post-1970 generation represented by Kazamaru himself. This, I believe, is an apt description of the author's works in general; light, humorous, and to return to Katō's expression, often seemingly "nonsensical" (kōtō mukei), yet never without a certain idealistic and ideological grounding. It is why Murakami literature appeals to such a wide variety of readers (as, say, Ōe's does not), yet is wholly satisfying to none.

What better description could there be for a postmodern writer? The characterization I offer here is not limited merely to Murakami Haruki but might be applied to the majority of postmodern writers working after 1970, and indeed to the postmodern moment in general. Andreas Huyssen (1986) in particular has written convincingly of the year 1970 as a "great divide" that stands between the politically charged modernist (or avantgardist) works of writers from the 1920s until the end of the 1960s, and the "nonconfrontational" literature—one is tempted to use the term "tolerant"—of the post-1970 period. Huyssen goes so far as to deny that postmodernism even existed before 1970, because in his definition, postmodernism is "largely affirmative . . . [having] abandoned any claim to critique, transgression or negation" (Huyssen 1986, 188).

This definition of the postmodern is, on the surface, at least, concordant with that of Linda Hutcheon, whose various analyses remind us, however, that terms like "critique" refer to methodology more than they do to purpose. In this context, Huyssen's use of the term "affirmative" should be understood to mean that virtually any literary methodology is tolerated: "transgressions" of genre, of style, even of disciplines (literature and history, for instance) are acceptable; "critique" of previous literary models is avoided; and nothing is "negated," nothing cast aside or completely replaced. Pastiche here replaces the classic model of the dialectic: thesis, antithesis, and finally synthesis.

The postmodern also implies multiplicity, the rejection of "totalizing" or "centered" narratives (which, whether historical or fictional, are supposed to be universal), in favor of multiple, often peripheralized ones, thus undermining not only the disciplinary divides but those of factuality and veracity.[6] The matter of Truth (singular, centered) is cast aside in favor of *truths*, often noncomplementary, conflicting, even paradoxical in relation to one another. This is not, however, to suggest that postmodern literature is either noncritical nor depoliticized in its perception of the world(s) it describes; quite the reverse, postmodern discourse of the type Hutcheon and Huyssen describe is overtly political, for it always highlights the textuality—the linguistic grounding—of the realities encountered, then self-consciously critiques the validity of the interpretive strategies employed to make meaning out of them.

On the point of overt political literature, however, Murakami has from the very start remained a controversial figure. Critics and scholars are widely divided, and even apologists for Murakami are often uncertain what to make of texts that appear to eschew politicization, yet are ultimately about the politics of contemporary society. Kuroko Kazuo, whose authorship of several book-length studies on Murakami suggests his belief in the author's importance to contemporary Japanese writing, is nevertheless clearly concerned that Murakami's popularity portends a decline of interest in critical social issues that should concern all Japanese—particularly, pollution, discrimination, nuclear weapons, and Japan's relationship with other Asian countries.

> While we cant about the dullness of contemporary writing and the weakening of 'pure literature,' Murakami sells four million copies of *Norwegian Wood*, and Yoshimoto Banana's works are grabbing the attention of hundreds of thousands of readers. What can one say, except that the era of radically changing values is reflected in the world of literature as well as everywhere else? (Kuroko 1990, 14)

What are these "radically changing values" of which Kuroko writes? To begin with, they include the gradual rejection of—or perhaps more passively, flight from—"reality as it is," and an appropriately resistant stance toward that reality, in favor of a reductionist tendency, a simplification, that draws the conflicts of the modern world in such broad terms that they can no longer threaten us. Adopting an essentially formalist stance toward the function of the literary text, Kuroko argues that in the era of Murakami and Yoshimoto, all sense of "differentiation" (*ika*), what Viktor Sklovsky

6. See Lyotard 1984 for his seminal argument concerning totalizing narratives.

called *ostranenie*, has been eliminated from Japanese literature.[7] Instead, we find the passive acceptance of the status quo. Kuroko, rather disgustedly, compares the experience of reading Murakami and Yoshimoto to that of reading comic books on a crowded train. Interestingly, the root of this phenomenon, in Kuroko's mind, would seem to be the increasing diversity that is so central to the postmodern ethic expressed by Huyssen above.

> The "differentiation" seen in literature both during the Meiji period and in the postwar is losing its validity in the contemporary age of diversification. In other words, the spirit of resistance toward contemporary society that one found in the writers and their works of modern and postwar literature is no longer strongly discernible. The pleasure one experiences while reading Murakami Haruki or Yoshimoto Banana, then, is probably very similar in nature to what one feels while reading a comic book or the sports page on a crowded train. (Kuroko 1990, 16)

Kuroko goes on to argue that writers like Murakami and Yoshimoto appeal to modern young readers purely because they afford a sense of "relief," rather than forcing them to confront the world from a new perspective, the function of literary differentiation as the Formalists used the term.

In the course of this argument Kuroko quotes from Ōe Kenzaburō's critical writings, in which Ōe describes himself, along with other postwar writers, as taking an "active stance" (*nōdōteki na shisei*) toward the world, as opposed to Murakami, whose attitude toward society is intentionally passive (*judōteki*).[8] "'The special characteristic of Murakami literature is the author's determination to avoid an active stance toward society, or indeed, toward the environment nearest to his own personal lifestyle,'" writes Ōe (Kuroko 1990, 33), who concludes that Murakami, along with other passive writers of the same generation, represents the end of socially critical, politically activated literature in Japan—for him, in other words, "pure literature" itself.

Such a viewpoint is revealing in its assumption to know what "political" literature is, and how it must be expressed. It is certainly interesting to note in this regard the authors Kuroko cites as overtly political writers, for it places into relief just how much of a shift has occurred, if not in values then at least in expression, in the past two decades. Using as his

---

7. "Differentiation" in Formalist terms refers to the practice of making the familiar world appear new and unfamiliar through innovative artistic presentation. For more on *ostranenie*, see Sklovsky 1991 (orig. pub. 1929).
8. The Ōe text quoted by Kuroko is "Sengo bungaku kara kyō no kyūkyō made" (1986).

principal criterion an author's willingness to confront, portray, and differentiate "reality," Kuroko lists as his major examples Oda Makoto, Tatematsu Wahei, Inoue Mitsuharu, Hikari Agata, and Kaikō Takeshi.

What is it that these writers have that Murakami, in Kuroko's opinion, does not? The answer, it would seem, is a passion for the large, tangible, contentious issues that plague contemporary industrialized societies throughout the world: war, nuclear weapons, hunger, gender and racial discrimination, urbanization. There can be no question that these issues are real, observable, supported by (often brutal) empirical evidence, and critically important to the continued existence of humankind. Against this, on the other hand, Murakami presents a different kind of issue, one with which Kuroko is obviously impatient: the disillusionment and disaffection of his generation. Murakami presents the crisis of identity among those who partake of a society that achieved affluence while they were still children. It is not difficult to understand why this identity crisis irritates many intellectuals, particularly those who concern themselves with the issues of real survival. Against the exploitation of third world Asia—exploitation that feeds Japanese affluence—what does it matter that young Japanese can find no purpose in their lives beyond the mindless consumption of goods and services? One might conclude that young Japanese of the past two decades are simply spoiled.

There is no simple response to this argument. Yet it must be pointed out that Murakami's interest in the issue of identity is not wholly dissimilar to those of some of the authors Kuroko so obviously approves of. Whereas writers like Hikari, Tatematsu, and Inoue deal with matters that suggest literal threats to survival—poverty, urbanization, nuclear contamination, and so forth—in his examination of the contemporary identity crisis Murakami, too, approaches very real threats to survival, and on a similar scale. What, for instance, will be the long-term effects of a national identity based on consumerism? Faced with the strain of the erasure of spiritual or political ideological grounding due to modernity, and the failure to install any suitable ideology in its place (aside from consumerism), how long will it be before contemporary Japanese crack under the strain? Murakami forces us to confront an important philosophical question: Which is more dangerous, the threat of nuclear contamination, or the threat of a vacuous society drifting aimlessly, desperately seeking a meaningful means of self-expression?

The answer has already become manifest. The rise of the so-called "new religions" (*shin-shūkyō*) in Japan suggests, among other things, that more than a few contemporary Japanese have not found sufficient self-definition in ordinary social mechanisms—work, community, family. Ōe has written in a recent novel of the potential of such religious groups to "ground" those unwilling or unable to accept prefabricated definitions of what it means to be a member of Japanese society, but he also hints at the potential for group hysteria, even group violence or suicide, as a result of excessive devotion to a charismatic leader (Ōe 1989). This indeed became a reality when Asahara Shōkō led the AUM Shinrikyō cult to commit mass murder in the Tokyo subways in 1995. And while this kind of violence is hardly typical of the various "new religions" that have sprung up in Japan in recent years, Murakami warns us, as Ōe seemed to do, that without efforts to help people find alternatives to the mainstream definition of the contemporary Japanese, more such incidents are inevitable (Murakami 1998, 12).

This is the political angle in Murakami's work, and it is becoming increasingly obvious that his approach is not only socially and politically relevant to contemporary Japan, but applicable to most industrialized societies in the world, where similar catastrophes of identity are taking place. If we seek to understand the resonance of Murakami's literature in the United States, for instance, we have only to look at recent headlines, from street violence to shootings in public schools, synagogues, churches and public offices. Neither victims nor perpetrators of these incidents are professional criminals; they are ordinary people in crisis. Human beings have not become more violent; however, we may be more aware of the lack of spiritual and ideological grounding in our culture, and begun to respond negatively to it. If we seek a relationship between contemporary literature and contemporary life, this is it.

Viewed in this context, especially in post-1970 Japan, one begins to understand the importance of Kazamaru Yoshihiko's generational self-definition above. His age group was the first, after Murakami's own, to confront the question of its own identity in the political vacuum of the post-1970 era, and found itself naturally drawn to the Murakami universe because of it. There is no question that the author's work, from the earliest to the most recent, has been particularly focused on the peripheral, the unusual, the disaffected. Murakami's "heroes" are more commonly *anti*-heroes who would rather watch from the sideline, stay out of the way, than involve themselves in the conflicts of society.

THE DISAFFECTED HERO

Kuroko describes contemporary Japan as a "Walkman society," and laments that it becomes increasingly difficult to find young Japanese willing to do anything together anymore (1990, 14). True to this spirit, the Murakami "hero" is always portrayed as a self-absorbed loner. As Kawamoto points out, despite having a job, "in the course of his work the protagonist interacts as little as possible with society" (1986, 48). Clearly this phenomenon, what Marilyn Ivy (1993, 250) has termed as the "'micro-ization' of the nuclear family into constituent monads (individuals) . . .", has become endemic to society. Murakami's heroes are not unique; they are representative of their readers, of each successive generation that has had to confront its identity in a society grounded (perhaps solely) in "a coordinated effort on the part of industry and the mass media to create a permanent body of mass consumers" resulting in "a new social atmosphere of materialism and self-absorption which gradually progressed to smaller and smaller social 'units,' ending with the individual" (Ivy 1993, 250). As will be shown below, however, the extent to which that "individual" understands itself beyond its role in the contemporary atmosphere of materialism is highly problematic. Murakami's fiction suggests that materialism—what will later be examined in terms of Jameson's "late-model capitalism," or as "rapid capitalism" in the author's own texts—has indeed destroyed the *soul* of the Japanese, preventing them from interacting with one another beyond (or outside of) that system.

This is, perhaps, the inevitable result of a world that has lost so much of its oppositionality. The collapse of counterculture in Japan and the West between 1970 and 1975 was only the beginning; Baudrillard may have said it best when he pointed out that the collapse of the Warsaw Pact was the final denouement of meaningful political activism, perhaps of meaning itself. Not coincidentally, he also describes this as the end of modernity (or in art, of modernism, avantgardism, etc.), and the beginning of the postmodern, the absorption of oppositions into simultaneity.

> Dissidents cannot bear a thaw. They have to die, or else become president (Walesa, Havel) in a sort of bitter revenge which, at any event, marks their death as dissidents. . . . When the Eastern bloc societies catch up with their dissidents and absorb them, it is the end of modernity, as it is when Western society catches up with and absorbs its avantgardes. In the East and the West, the Idea is finished. The organic consensus marks the dawning of post-modern societies, non-conflictual and at one with themselves. (Baudrillard 1994a, 41)

But this is no Utopia, nor does Baudrillard wish for us to imagine that it is. Rather, we have entered an era of unmitigated mediocrity, of tolerance and hyper-relativism. Concepts like "right" and "wrong" no longer ground our belief systems; or rather, we now lack the critical energy to face these concepts in a decisive manner. This phenomenon did not begin with the collapse of the Warsaw Pact, however; it began with the end of the Vietnam War, the disgrace of the Nixon presidency, and the subsequent decline of the counterculture movements throughout the world after 1970. The "absorption" of which Baudrillard writes, in fact, aptly describes the absorption that befell the Japanese Zenkyōtō activists between 1970 and 1972, turning them into an integral part of the system they had spent their youth attacking. Honda Katsuichi writes similarly of this period as the beginning of a gradual shift on the part of the left, eventually to converge with the right (Honda 1993, 93).

Postmodern culture is also, however, not about a "nonconflictual" society. Rather, as we see in every Murakami text and in reality itself, a severe conflict within the self—perhaps a more dangerous conflict, after all—results from the lack of an external adversary. In simplified terms, when "us versus them" becomes simply "us," then it becomes paradoxically difficult to define what "us" means. This is echoed in Honda's castigation of the Japanese press, whose function of checking up on the government has long since been discarded, fatally undermined by the media's partnership with the political center. "The mass media's connection to the powers that be is a frightful thing indeed. Given the tendency of power to corrupt, it is necessary for journalism to continue to criticize the powerful almost as a matter of course. There cannot be a coincidence of interests" (Honda 1993, 219). Arguing that the media has been corrupted, transformed into a mere tool of government, Honda likens Japan to a Soviet-type state, and claims that there is no division of power in Japan today (Honda 1993, 219–20).

Within such a context, Murakami's heroes have little choice but to create a new mode of dissidence, to proclaim their difference while proclaiming their solidarity with others who spend their existence, paradoxically, being "isolated together." This is the madness of contemporary urban society, whose peculiar paradigm is the kind of loneliness one can only experience among twenty million people. Murakami's protagonist has been called in some contexts *jiheiteki*—a medical term meaning "autistic," but in this context closer to the expression "self-absorbed" used by Ivy above. This is basically true, and it is indeed alarming how little he interacts. However, I am inclined to be a little skeptical of Kawamoto's contention that, as a result, "there is no scent of life about the Murakami hero" (1986, 46). Quite the reverse, Murakami's narrator is all too real; he is emblematic, perhaps more than any literary character today, of what it means to live in urban Japan at the end of the twentieth century. It might be more accurate to say that there is no scent of life in contemporary urban Japan.

Kawamoto's critique is far from unique. Kuroko, Katō, Karatani, and Ogura all find something ominous and in some cases arrogant in the aloofness of the Murakami hero. Even Aoki Tamotsu, who otherwise tries to find something positive in the protagonist's refusal to interact with society—a form of stoical self-control, an attempt not to impose on the sovereignty of others—is shaken by the degree to which the Murakami hero avoids human contact (Aoki 1985, 15–16). Yet here, too, is the extent to which contemporary society is "nonconflictual." As Katō writes in a recent essay:

> The hero is unable to lose himself. He has his own world, but cannot open it up to other people. As a result, people come to his "room," but, as if it were a motel, when their time is up they find an exit and leave.
> What is the hero's problem? He cannot leave his world. He is shut away inside of himself. This is why he has "never harmed anyone," nor is he ever "harmed by anyone." (Katō 1996a, 141)[9]

This, as both Katō and Aoki would agree, is a personality that will never interfere with another, thus never enter into conflict with other members of society so long as it is left alone. But I think Aoki and Katō would also agree—as would Baudrillard—that this lack of conflict constitutes certain risks, for the conflicts that were external—directed at an other—are now internalized, ticking bombs hidden from view. The so-called society of tranquility and heterogeneity is only a facade, concealing invisible tensions, discernible only through their occasionally explosive effects.

If this tells us anything about the postmodernism of Murakami Haruki, it is that he acknowledges the most commonly understood characteristics therein—affirmation, multiplicity, nonconfrontation—and to a point he sees in them the potential for liberation of expression, new modes of looking at the world. At the same time, however, the postmodern for Murakami fails to liberate the human spirit on the social level, and in this sense the author does not celebrate its effects, but rather (not unlike Jameson) laments them, creating a portrait of contemporary society that is virtually apocalyptic—an apocalypse for identity.

As I will argue at greater length below, the crisis of identity in Japan is both historical—and demonstrably so—and aesthetic. In terms of

---

9. Karatani (1990b) makes virtually the same point in his description of the "transcendent subject" in "Murakami Haruki no 'Fūkei,'" in *Shūen o megutte*.

historical reality we can say that the trend of events from 1970 onward toward stability, heterogeneity, peace and prosperity (marked by the end of the Vietnam War, and later the Cold War), systematically obviated the need, even the possibility, of meaningful political counterculture. In terms of aesthetics, we may say that the expression of these realities has taken on new, multiple forms that are tolerant of former differences; genres are transcended, styles mixed, former oppositions deconstructed.

One might add in this regard that representation becomes a critical issue, and that this, in the context of multiplicity, is one area that remains politically charged. That is to say, as we open the door to a multiplicity of realities (or histories, narratives, always plural), we admit simultaneously that reality itself is a construct, a question of representation, of textualization. Thus postmodern literature, including Murakami's, is not, and *cannot be* nonpolitical. Ultimately it comes down to a matter of what is represented, how, and why.

At the same time, I feel that one further step is required in approaching the issue of "reality" (or reali*ties*) in the Murakami text. It is not enough simply to say that the decisions made about which realities to narrate or how to do so is at issue. Rather, in order to approach the rich textures of Murakami's literary universe, and to appreciate the controversy it generates, we must be prepared to consider "reality" itself in less concrete terms.

CONCLUSION, OR A BEGINNING

Roland Barthes reveals something important about his conception of reality in *Image–Music–Text* (1977): he declares it to exist, free and autonomous, separate from our attempts to represent it meaningfully. Using the initial example of the newspaper photograph, Barthes differentiates this image from others—paintings, texts, and so forth—as a "denotative" message, one that escapes codification by virtue of its near identification with the reality it portrays. In other words, it presents a virtually perfect, direct representation of "reality" with little or no gap between the two.

> Certainly the image is not the reality but at least it is its perfect *analagon* and it is exactly this analogical perfection which, to common sense, defines the photograph. Thus can be seen the special status of the photographic image: *it is a message without a code*; from which proposition an important corollary must immediately be drawn: the photographic message is a continuous message. (Barthes 1977, 17; italics in original)

Of interest here is Barthes' clearly evident assumption not only that reality exists, which few would deny, but that it exists meaningfully outside the context of culture, language, and interpretation. At the core of this statement is an ontological question that has become more hotly contested in recent years: what is the ontological status of images, or even realities, as we see them "in nature"? Barthes's prejudice—perhaps a nostalgic one—for an external, autonomous, precultural reality is revealed when he writes, "What does the photograph transmit? By definition, the scene itself, *the literal reality*" (1977, 16-17; my italics). But this raises what are, today, virtually unanswerable questions: What is this "literal reality"? If by "literal" we take Barthes to mean "reality *as it is*," then how do we know how it really is? How can we consider, and thus *know* "reality" in ontological terms *not* bound up in language, and, by extension, bound up in interpretation, in culture?

Barthes is not alone in his assumption of an external reality. Baudrillard (1988), too, reveals nostalgia for the era of the "real," for "unmediated access to reality" (Hutcheon 1989, 33). Describing "three orders" of reality, the first marked by "cyclical reversal, annulment," the second by the "real" of the political economy, the third by hyperreality, "a nostalgic resurrection of the real," Baudrillard (1988, 119–48) asserts at least the possibility of a (now long defunct) presymbolic mode of reality in which signs were closer to—perhaps even identical to—their referents. This argument also lies at the heart of *Simulacra and Simulation* (1981), in which Baudrillard rather wistfully writes of the "liquidation of all referentials," the shattering of the relationship between the real and the imaginary, the real and its concept. "It is all of metaphysics that is lost. No more mirror of being and appearances, of the real and its concept" (Baudrillard 1994b, 2). In other words, one could, theoretically, see *and comprehend* the world around one without necessarily being bound by the cultural conditioning of one's experiences, filtered through cultural ideologies. He suggests implicitly, then, that "reality," theoretically, at least, could once have been "known" in a precultural, prelinguistic mode, something echoed by Jacques Lacan in his own discussions of the prelinguistic subject, as well.[10]

But again, the crucial ontological question comes into play: What is the "real" except a series of interpretations, linguistic readings and writings, the processing of images via individual or collective memory, experience, and history? I prefer Hutcheon's (1988, 1989) contention that reality

10. Lacan's conception of the realm of prelinguistic existence will be dealt with in chapter three below.

can never truly be apprehended meaningfully without representation, acknowledging the inevitability of politicization through perception and interpretation. Thus, we are again compelled to ask, *how* is something to be represented, *who* decides such questions, and what might the political stakes be? Writing in direct response to Baudrillard, Hutcheon asks,

> Have we ever known the "real" except through representations? We may see, hear, feel, smell, and touch it, but do we *know* it in the sense that we give meaning to it? In Lisa Tickner's succinct terms, the real is "*enabled to mean* through systems of signs organized into discourses on the world." (Hutcheon 1989, 33)

There are, of course, Japanese theorists—most prominently Karatani Kōjin—who have resisted arguments such as this as belonging to a specifically "first world" mentality concerning the postmodern. In fact, as Alan Wolfe (1989) argues, Karatani is bothered by the notion that the Japanese postmodern should be thought the same as that of the West, where issues such as representation emerge from the deconstruction of the signifier, of the subject, and the subsequent proliferation of mistrust toward language. Japanese postmodernism, on the other hand, is marked by its *lack* of resistance toward the deconstruction of previously grounded concepts like "subjectivity" and "signifier."

> Karatani's effort to identify a Japanese postmodern leads him to discover those elements of the Japanese "native tradition" which distinguish it from its Western counterpart, to erect a Japanese cultural generality which would account for this "difference." In what might appear to be a quasi-neonativist fashion, Karatani turns this "lack of resistance" into its opposite, a distinctively Japanese, and hence anti-Western notion of modernity, an "empty structure of power." (Wolfe 1989, 229)

There is no denying the validity, to a point, of critiquing the applicability of concepts like deconstruction in Japan where, lacking the same ideologies that fed Western intellectual development, there may indeed be no center (God, the Ideal, the subject etc.) to deconstruct. It may even be true, as Wolfe argues, "that Japan is not just postmodern: it is above all a part of the Western postmodern" (1989, 230). At the same time, I think it remains important not merely for us to understand Japanese postmodernism in the context of the Western, but also to examine recent expressions of the postmodern in the West in the context of the "nonresistant" postmodernism described by Wolfe (and through him, Karatani) above.

For instance, when Karatani argues that the Japanese postmodern is marked by "nonresistance," I suspect he has in mind a phenomenon very similar to that described by Ōe in "Japan's Dual Identity" (which appears in the same volume with Wolfe's essay), that Japanese intellectuals of today are unwilling or unable to engage critically successive cultural theories as they are imported, one by one, into Japan. Instead, like so many throw-away items, each theory is "consumed" (in books, in the mass media, in the classroom), then thrown away as the consumer sees fit. Whereas Ōe tends to see this as a kind of rupture, a failure on the part of younger intellectuals to retrace the steps of postwar *literati* such as Sakaguchi Ango, Tamura Taijirō, or, more recently, himself, Karatani seems more inclined to argue, with some justification, that the ideological groundwork for making sense of Western culture theory, and challenging and resisting it, simply does not exist in Japan. "In Japanese society, where there was no 'resistance' to this movement, concept like absence of the subject or decentering do not have the intensity they might have in France" (Wolfe 1989, 229).

At the same time, we should be cautious about accepting uncritically Karatani's contention that Western postmodernism is always marked by resistance. Rather, as I shall argue in the chapter that follows, the "resistance" that Karatani identifies as a defining characteristic of Western postmodernism might be viewed more in historical terms than geographic. That is to say, one is tempted, as Andreas Huyssen (1986) has done, to identify this "resistance" with an earlier phase of postmodernism, one that developed in the 1960s, yet whose very "resistance" against the traditions of high modernism led to its canonization in the 1970s as yet one more form of Art. In such an instance, the *lack* of resistance that Karatani maintains to be a unique characteristic of Japanese postmodernism could be viewed as definitive of the later phase of the postmodern that has been persistently nonconfrontational with regard to previous theoretical paradigms (Huyssen 1986; Hutcheon 1988). I think, in fact, that one could point to the writings of Ōe himself, and certainly to the surrealist experiments of Abe Kōbō, as representing the earlier phase of the postmodern, which was by no means "nonresistant" to modernist paradigms; one could, turning to the West, equally identify the writings of Richard Brautigan or Ian Watson as representative of the "nonresistance" of the later phase of postmodernism.

At this stage, however, I do not wish to move too far away from the subject at hand, which is "reality" as a construct. More important is that the question of the "real" be understood here as part, at the very least, of Murakami's own interrogation of postmodern. It is his own texts that require us to do so, for, as I shall argue below, particularly in the second chapter on "magical realism," the world for Murakami's protagonists almost always takes on the characteristics and dimensions of "text," of words, thus of interpretation and subjective perception. It is necessary to confront this issue in order for the present discussion of Murakami to be truly meaningful, for, as will be seen, Murakami's conception of reality, while often entertaining, is rarely innocent, rarely free of the politics of representation. If we may say that "reality" is always slightly off-center in the Murakami universe, we are forced to conclude that its eccentricity is always the result of its having been interpreted—often unconsciously—by the protagonist, the narrator, or the author himself.

At the same time, it is important to note that while the politics of representation are concerned with the realities of contemporary society, ideology and power, as noted above, for Murakami these issues spring from highly internalized, individual sources. The conditions confronted in Murakami fiction are perhaps endemic to society, but always we perceive them in his work through the rarefied gaze of his retiring antiheroes, whose realities are equally individualized. Despite his passivity and self-enclosure, the Murakami protagonist does not merely watch the world "as it is"; he *invents* it, piece by piece, character by character. The world is itself a "text"—*tada no kotoba*, or "just words," as one of his protagonists expresses it—and depends for its shape and structure on the protagonist's interpretive strategies.[11] It does not especially matter if the people and things he encounters are "external" to himself or generated from within his mind; he interprets, and therefore "constructs," them all. Nothing escapes this textualization. This is why the notion of an external, autonomous "reality" that may be recreated in analogue, such as Barthes suggests above, is alien to the Murakami universe. And if some find such an approach to reality too fanciful, even irresponsible, one is compelled to point out that subjectively perceiving and interpreting the world through the cultural signs of language is neither more nor less than what each of us does every day.

At stake here is not simply the portrayal of modernity (or postmodernity), but the redeclaration of the individual subject. When the Murakami hero resuscitates a lost friend by recasting the memory of him into an image he can apprehend in the "conscious" world, he commits an act of personal recovery, recouping lost memories, regaining elements of his own historical past. At the same time he connects his friend—identifies him, so

---

11. The phrase occurs in Murakami's 1980 short story, "Binbō na obasan no hanashi," in *MHZ* 3:55. I am indebted to Jay Rubin for bringing this phrase to my attention.

to speak—with a particular historical moment, and certain (selective) events, political, historical, and cultural, that constitute that moment. Such an act is intensely political, for it implies an alternative, the selection or creation of "reali*ties*" that may well run counter to the dominant "reality." Yet it is also essentially a humanist undertaking on the individual level. Indeed, if we seek the *raison d'être* in the author's work, it must be the recovery of the repressed individual in Japan's vaunted "homogeneous culture," one constituted by collective (bestowed) memories rather than individual ones. It is the revitalization of the human subject in the "system" of Japanese society. It is the rehumanization of the anonymous worker bee in Japan's industrial-economic machine. And if these issues seem out of date, Murakami directs our attention to numerous recent catastrophic examples of what happens when human beings are denied a mechanism by which to express themselves as individuals, or to locate and select an alternative "system" by which to define themselves.

Ultimately, the realities that are revealed in the Murakami text are of an intensely personal nature, as indeed we are encouraged by the author to view *all* realities. The relationship between these subjective realities and identity itself thus becomes clear, insofar as our grasp of the reality around ourselves is always historical: we are constituted as subjects according to our experiences via culture, and thus how we envision, interpret, and finally *know* the realities that surround us—and also ourselves as subjects—is finally the result of this relationship between culture and experience. However, this leaves us with the unnerving realization that "reality" can never be any more actual than "text," that both are subjective, dependent upon culture. Without this subjective perception, "reality" may as well not exist, for it is meaningless outside of a linguistic and cultural context.

What is needed, then, is an understanding of "reality" as construct, one that acknowledges the culturally contextual notion of the real and the objects that make up the real. Such an understanding is not intended to undermine the actual existence of reality itself, obviously, but rather to underscore the contingency of any real knowledge of that reality upon cultural, linguistic (con)textualization. Such an understanding would certainly permit us a more meaningful view of Murakami's narrative landscape, whose primary purpose seems to be to remind us simultaneously of our reliance on culture and language to define reality and our place in it, and also of the risks of giving ourselves over wholly to what culture often passes off as "reality," external and autonomous to ourselves. Rather, Murakami cautions us that, adrift in a sea of consumerism, we are gradually forfeiting our ability—perhaps even our right—to judge such matters for ourselves.

Chapter One

Mimesis, Formula, and Identity

> "I climbed the ladder of Murakami's *A Wild Sheep Chase*, expecting an uplifting experience. But when I looked through the tiny binoculars suspended from the ceiling, I found the words, 'FUCK YOU.'"
>
> —Katō Norihiro, "Jihei to Sakoku"

True to its postmodern grounding, the literature of Murakami Haruki is not about genre, but it is about genre transgression. It is not about formula, but the abuse of formula. It is not about "pure" literature, but about how the earlier borders between "pure" and "mass" literature can be overcome. It is not about reality and unreality, but something that lies outside the matrix, Baudrillard's "hyperreality"; not about subjectivity and objectivity, but intersubjectivity.

This highlights one of the central facets of Murakami's writing—his penchant for playing with the borders such as those above—and it seems to excite a fair amount of controversy. Such "border jumping" takes a variety of forms. At times Murakami writes something very like the "historiographic metafiction" described by Hutcheon (1988, 1989), thus challenging the borders between the genres of fiction and history writing. Almost always he concerns himself with the borders between the conscious and the unconscious, the real and the unreal, the magical and the commonplace.

I shall deal with each of these elements in its proper place in later chapters. For the present I would like to examine Murakami's experiments with genre and style, not to "place" the author within the spectrum of "pure" and "mass" literature—though certainly some comment on this point is in order—but to illuminate how he uses the structural tools of style, formula, and mimesis to exploit his reader's expectations. As we shall see, such exploitation is always ironic, and always political, thus providing an important underpinning to the author's work.

As noted briefly in my introduction, a number of critics in Japan have argued that Murakami fails to take contemporary society and its dilemmas seriously enough. One could say that his talent as a storyteller has contributed to this controversy, for his works somehow seem to lack the severity, the density, the sheer *difficulty* of those by some of his predecessors — notably, Ōe and Nakagami Kenji. Similar arguments, one might add, have been made comparing American writers such as Thomas Pynchon and Raymond Carver.

Yet arguments such as this lead us to the inescapable conclusion that some of the resistance to Murakami, at least, is grounded in simple literary snobbishness. Murakami's prose is easy to read, comparatively easy to translate, and rarely hides behind much of the ambiguity, the mystery for which Japanese literature has traditionally been so renowned. It lacks the density of language that marks Ōe's work and that makes it, comparatively, quite difficult to read, even for Japanese.

To conclude, however, that Murakami's work lacks critical importance amidst other Japanese literature because its language is clear, because it is readable, or because it entertains, is simply absurd. Certainly there are areas of the author's writing that are subject to criticism: he is repetitive, almost to the point that one may predict what will happen; his protagonists are so lethargic at times as to be maddening; occasionally, as with the recently published work, *The Sputnik Sweetheart* (Supūtoniku no koibito, 1999), the reader simply despairs of yet *another* sentimental love story. In between these less interesting works, however—and sometimes within them—we find an undercurrent that is far more disturbing—one that seeks to expose weaknesses in contemporary Japanese society and its authoritarian ideology. Most of the two million-odd Japanese who bought and read *Norwegian Wood* were probably too taken by the story of tragic love to pay much attention, but even in that novel lurks a dark subtext of political power, state ideology, and resistance.

What I shall argue in this chapter is that even the concept of the literary formula (or the transgression thereof) is not free from political concerns, particularly those connected with morality and state ideology. Rather, every text, as will soon become clear, represents either an affirmation or a challenge to the ideological paradigm that dominates the culture in which it is written. This is not news, but it does permit—in fact, it requires—us to look carefully at literature normally deemed "popular" from a newly politicized angle. This need becomes even more acute when we study the literature of a writer like Murakami, whose literature is admittedly very popular, yet whose use of the formula that engenders that popularity is an ironic device that, in the end, challenges rather than affirms the dominant ideology.

What is "formulaic" literature? In a nutshell, one may say that it is literature that creates a set of expectations in the reader—what will shortly be termed the "moral fantasy" of the work —and then sets out to fulfill those expectations. But the very existence of those expectations suggests the constant presence of a system of thought, of a common morality, a cultural ideology that supports the codes to be presented in the text. There can be no fulfillment for the reader of formulaic fiction unless author and reader are operating on common ground with regard to what is expected. The history of "popular" and "serious" literature (terms that will very shortly be problematized) is really about such fulfillment or non- fulfillment, the enactment or breach of the implied contract between author and reader.

Murakami Haruki, however, puts the literary formula to a more subversive use. Writing explicitly within the confines of literary formulas—detective and romance—Murakami sets up the kinds of expectations with his readers that normally attend such fictional forms, only to shatter them in the end.

What is his purpose in doing this? Several motives suggest themselves. His juxtapositioning of what would appear to be opposing impulses—the predictable and the unpredictable—could be read as a gesture toward pastiche, a celebration of the liberating effects of the postmodern aesthetic that permits him to write a serious text in terms accepted by and accessible to an extremely wide readership. We might also view his use of this paradoxical structure as a challenge to the structural binary that supports divisions between "pure" and "mass" literature in Japan (*junbungaku* and *taishūbungaku*, respectively), in order to undermine the "absolute" identities of either, even of the term "literature" itself. Finally, it can be read as a gesture of hostility, not merely toward dominant ideological paradigms in society, but also toward those who live within (and thus tacitly acquiesce to) those paradigms. Perhaps Katō Norihiro has put his finger on this third possibility when, writing of *A Wild Sheep Chase*, he contrasts the experience with the story about how John Lennon met Yoko Ono:

> When Lennon entered the room there was a ladder, and a small pair of binoculars suspended in black canvas from the ceiling. Having looked through them, he says,
> "In tiny letters I saw the word 'YES.'
> "Seeing that, I understood the positive attitude of this artist. I felt saved. When I went up the ladder and looked through the

binoculars, it didn't say 'NO,' or 'FUCK YOU.' It was 'YES.'"
    I climbed the ladder of Murakami's *A Wild Sheep Chase*, ex-
pecting a similarly uplifting experience. But when I looked through
the tiny binoculars suspended from the ceiling, I found the words,
"FUCK YOU." (Katō 1986, 66)

A sophisticated literary scholar, Katō is certainly not so naive as to expect
from a novel like *A Wild Sheep Chase* a happy ending, the neat closure of
the mystery, or the restoration of truth and justice in the world. What he
does expect, and perhaps rightly so in a novel that at least subliminally
takes on the 1960s, is an experience that leads to a fuller comprehension of
the events that shaped his life, rather than simply the final message that it
all meant nothing. Yet this, too, is part of the reality that Murakami wishes
to convey. Katō is probably correct if he senses a vague, perhaps unac-
knowledged hostility on the author's part; but I am more inclined to say
that Murakami has it right, and that it is Katō who indulges in fantasy
here: a fanciful desire for "closure" of the 1960s.
    Most readers probably do not think this far when they read Mura-
kami's novels, though one is also inclined to doubt that his popularity is
due solely to an entertaining style. Rather, as noted in the introduction
above, readers find something familiar in the soft-spoken, nonjudgmental
protagonist, nearly always presented in the first-person singular familiar
("Boku"). Murakami's works give readers the impression of a serious fiction writer who expresses himself in a distinctly *un*-serious manner. That is
to say, he writes in an engaging, entertaining, easily-read style in the tones
of an elder brother, pointing out the pitfalls of life to his readers, but a
sturdy message typically lies beneath this. The Murakami protagonist is
comfortingly ordinary: shy, reserved, slightly bored, uncertain of his purpose in life, perhaps doubtful that any such purpose exists. He is intelli-
gent, but not intellectual; educated, but not pedantic; introverted, but not
neurotic, certainly not melancholy or schizophrenic. Few would be tempted
to compare the Murakami hero to those of Sōseki, Ōgai, Akutagawa, or
even more recent writers such as Mishima or Ōe. For all the protagonist's
self-absorption, his movements are still more obvious, less cerebral, than
was common in Japanese literature until recent years. One does not have
the impression of reading a text written as art; its entertainment value is
too high for that, its language too transparent. If one might compare the
verbally dense style of Ōe to that of Pynchon, one might compare Murakami's
to that of Raymond Carver, not coincidentally one of his favorite writers.
    This is not to suggest, however, that Murakami's experiments with
the formulaic literary style place him into a category with contemporaries

such as Kataoka Yoshio, or Akagawa Jirō, both of whom write prolifically, but whose works tend to be almost indistinguishable from one another. Such authors clearly write for volume, quantity rather than quality, and form the lowest common denominator in the literary world. Mainly because their works show so little variation, both Akagawa and Kataoka are able to produce with tremendous speed, and to sell prodigiously, for they limit themselves for the most part to what has succeeded in the past.

Of course, to compare Ōe to Akagawa is similar to comparing Thomas Pynchon to Jackie Collins, and too simplistically polarizes the nature of the Japanese literary landscape today. I do not mean to suggest anything of this sort as a map of that landscape. Rather, my purpose is to argue that Murakami, perhaps more than any other writer, from Yoshimoto Banana to Shimada Masahiko, seems to succeed not merely in interposing himself at the centerpoint between these two extremes, but in drawing the two poles together to the point that they seem to converge within his work. That is to say, he appears to utilize the linguistic simplicity of Akagawa, or of Kataoka Yoshio, while at the same time concealing a far more critical subtext, one whose object is not all that dissimilar to those targeted in works by more overtly "serious" or "political" authors such as Ōe, or Tatematsu Wahei.

Like most authors, Murakami's work stands somewhere between the inventive, experimental texts of Ōe, and the highly formulaic, entertaining yet monotonously uniform novels of Akagawa Jirō. Unfortunately, his reliance on a simplistic language, hiding little or nothing from the reader, often obscures the seriousness of his literary contribution. The frequency of his use of the first-person pronoun "I" rivals that of English, despite a tradition of avoiding such self-reference, even in the culture that invented the *watakushi-shōsetsu*, or "I- novel." Murakami is also fond of using expressions from English, translated literally into Japanese (such as *sore ijō de mo nai shi, sore ika de mo nai* for "neither more nor less"), as well as repeating himself almost to the point that one can predict each instance of his most commonly recurring phrase, *Boku ni wa wakaranakatta*: "It wasn't clear to me." As noted above, his Japanese translates smoothly into foreign languages, partly because of its simplicity, and partly because of its reliance on foreign (or foreign-sounding) idioms. One finds there none of the fondness for the mysterious, or the pedantic, or the obscure, as is so often said of the prose of Kawabata, Mishima, or Ōe.

Of course, Murakami is not unique in this sense; he shares this fondness for simplicity and an international atmosphere in his language and setting with many of his contemporaries: Takahashi Gen'ichirō (b. 1951), Shimada Masahiko (b. 1961), Shimizu Yoshinori (b. 1947), and

Murakami Ryū (b. 1952), to name a few of the more successful. Katō argues that Murakami's "internationalization" of Japanese literature is rivaled primarily by Takahashi, whose linguistic style, like Murakami's, lends a foreign flavor to his use of expressions hitherto considered quintessentially Japanese (1988, 107). Certainly one could point, furthermore, to the frequent foreign settings of Yamada Eimi and Shimada, both of whom like to set part or all of their works in cosmopolitan cities like New York with no particular sign of exoticism. One could also look at the evidently "hybrid" characters of Shimizu Yoshinori, who live in cities like Tokyo and New York, yet whose nationality is far from clear. Like these authors, Murakami experiments with language, genre, realism and fantasy, in order to explore the outer limits of postmodern expression. Murakami may be unique among his peers, however, for his remarkable ability to bring an insightful understanding of the literary formula to his experiments with genre, demonstrating a knack for reproducing the structures of such texts, while at the same time maintaining a less overt seriousness that lies beneath these formulaic structures. Ironically, it is probably his very success at reproducing such formulaic structures that has contributed to his lack of acceptance by some Western scholars of Japanese literature.

THE FORMULAIC STRUCTURE

Between 1969 and 1976, John Cawelti constructed a Structuralist critique of the terms "serious" and "popular," ultimately abandoning both in favor of the less loaded "mimetic" and "formulaic." His strategy was to sidestep the traditional value judgments that accompany the former set of terms, and explore how virtually *all* literature falls within a continuum between the two extremes of the inventive and the conventional.

> Of course, the mimetic and the formulaic represent two poles that most literary works lie somewhere between. Few novels, however dedicated to the representation of reality, do not have some element of the ideal. And most formulaic works have a least the surface texture of the real world... (Cawelti 1976, 13; cf. Cawelti 1969, 381-90).

"Mimesis" as it is used here is not limited merely to the mirroring of life's events, but extends to elements within the narrative that reflect the conditions of everyday life. Uncertainty, fear, loose ends and confusion are all components of "real life," and as such these lend the air of reality to the mimetic work. The suspension of these elements, and the subsequent creation of a limited fantasy world, form the beginnings of the literary formula, which typically consists of a combination of universal truths, or archetypes, combined with culturally specific elements that create relevance for the intended audience within that culture. Hence, the "high mimetic hero" (v. Northrop Frye 1957) will be fitted with the trappings of the specific culture in which he or she appears. A useful comparison might thus be drawn between the American Western adventure, with its archetypal cowboy hero, and the Japanese Samurai tale. The "universal" elements between the two are quite similar: the hero is empowered with characteristics such as courage, conventional morality, and a belief in his duty and potential to redress evil. In both types of story the hero's task is to eliminate some specific evil or threat, and then to move on to the next crisis.

Cultural specificities, on the other hand, are quite different. Both types of story—the Western and the Samurai epic—are culturally relevant to their intended audiences, but would be far less so to outsiders. A Japanese might be confused, for instance, at the injunction against shooting a man in the back, while Americans usually find Japanese ritual suicide (*seppuku* or *hara-kiri*) incomprehensible. Cultural specificities such as these touch something fundamental in the audiences that witness them, affirming basic ideologies within the culture.

What links formulaic expression across cultures is the predictability of the ending: the hero succeeds in accomplishing that which is deemed by the audience to be morally right. There may be a last surprise—the final, sudden shot fired at Clint Eastwood at the end of *For a Few Dollars More*—but the end should bring about the death of the enemy, along with the clear understanding that the hero has not been wasting his time. War stories, another subgenre of the adventure tale, illustrate this point especially well. The more formulaic examples, such as *The Sands of Iwo Jima*, or *The Green Beret*, have in common their portrayal of the hero as a "good guy," who fights in the open, with honor, outnumbered by hordes of treacherous (or merely faceless) enemies. Such works usually serve most effectively as war propaganda, and their audiences may reasonably expect that the heroes will either survive the battle, gloriously successful, or fall tragically (but heroically) dead. Either way, the clear and ever-present message of such a tale is that the struggle matters, that it is worth the price paid.

Intertwined with the predictability of the formula is the first and most important imperative set out by Cawelti: that the "moral fantasy"—a belief or ideology essential to the society in question—will be upheld by the conclusion of the story. Naturally, that moral fantasy will differ not only from culture to culture, but from one genre to the next: most detective fiction values discovery and rationality over mystery and ambiguity; romance esteems the precedence of true love (or even monogamous marriage, not too many years ago) for the heroine, in place of sexual or career fulfillment; spy fiction, prior to the demise of the Warsaw Pact, emphasized free world democracy over communism.

On the other side of this equation stand films like *Platoon*, *All Quiet on the Western Front*, Philip Caputo's novel *A Rumor of War*, Norman Mailer's *The Naked and the Dead*, or Joseph Heller's *Catch-22*, in all of which heroism, where it exists, is overshadowed by the realistic emphasis on the ugliness and absurdity of war. The formulaic war tale glorifies the sacrifice of the individual hero, while the mimetic (or ironic) one shows the realities, either on the battlefield itself or in the absurdity of armed conflict.

The predictability of the formula suggests several things: first, that the world in which the action takes place will be removed sufficiently from the real world so that the reader or viewer is permitted to suspend his disbelief during the course of the story. In other words, the audience must be able to enter the universe of the story—be it film, text, or television—with a minimum of fuss, accepting the story on its own terms. At the same time, this condition serves to reduce to manageable levels the stress generated in scenes of extreme violence or horror: when faces start melting in *Raiders of the Lost Ark*, the viewer must be able to retreat into the real world, where such things do not (normally!) occur. The formulaic writer, thus, must create, master, and manipulate the worlds he or she creates, so that readers are both convinced and *not* convinced.

THE FORMULAIC MURAKAMI

Murakami works within the structural confines of the literary formula most visibly in his three most successful novels to date: *A Wild Sheep Chase* (the original title is *Hitsuji o meguru bōken*, An Adventure Surrounding Sheep), *Hard-Boiled Wonderland and the End of the World*, and *Norwegian Wood*. Although the plots of these novels differ greatly, all maintain sufficient ties to formulaic structure to instill the reader with the expectation of predictability. Indeed, Murakami clearly encourages this response in his readers through the titles of the first two novels, while the third plays on a song from the Beatles' album, *Rubber Soul*.

A Wild Sheep Chase is thoroughly different from anything Murakami had written to this point. Gone—or at least fading rapidly—is the brooding atmosphere of his first two novels, the pervasive, deathly boredom, and most of all, the lackadaisical mulling about by the protagonist. The work may begin at rest, but it does not remain so for long. The protagonist, a cool, detached character who owns an advertising agency and describes himself as "dumb to the world," is in fact the quintessential model of the hard-boiled detective, masking remarkable characteristics behind a facade of simplicity. His adversary in the story is a right-wing figure known only as "the Boss," the head of a powerful syndicate which is neither government, business, industry, nor media, yet which somehow holds all of these powers at its disposal. The Boss is, it would seem, a manifestation of the postmodern state described earlier: hidden, elusive, and unaccountable. As one of his henchmen describes it,

> "We built a kingdom," said the man. "A powerful underground kingdom. We subsumed various entities, political, financial, mass media, the bureaucracy, culture, all sorts of things you wouldn't have imagined. We even took in elements that were hostile to us. Everything, from those in power to those against them. Most never even noticed they had been subsumed. In other words, we had a tremendously sophisticated organization." (*MHZ* 2:154; *WSC* 118)[1]

At the heart of this organization stands the Boss, but even his power source is steeped in mystery. The theory professed by members of the Boss' clique is that he draws power from a magical sheep, credited with empowering/guiding other famous despots in history such as Genghis Khan. Perhaps because the sheep is of questionable reality, however, the Boss himself remains unseen throughout the story. With characteristic irony, Murakami creates in the Boss the symbol of a power syndicate that is neither government, business, nor industry, yet controls all of these. In other words, his "organization" emblemizes the postmodern state, while he himself would seem to symbolize the powerless emperor.

The plot of *A Wild Sheep Chase* revolves around the protagonist's quest for the mysterious sheep from which the Boss gains his power. His interest is not an idle one; his original involvement with the sheep comes via a close friend named Rat, who sends him a photograph of the sheep with the request that it be given a lot of exposure. Having followed these

---

1. All translated passages from Murakami's work are my own. As noted in the preface, excellent and reliable translations for most of Murakami's novels are available in the United States, and my decision to use my own translations is strictly in the interest of maintaining a uniformity of style between my text and quoted passages. Hereafter citations from original texts for which translations are easily obtained will be followed with correspondent page citations from those translations.

instructions, the entire world of the Boss's elusive state organization suddenly threatens to come down on the protagonist's shoulders, and by extension onto Rat's as well. He is pressured to reveal the means by which he obtained the photograph of the sheep, but refuses to do so out of the desire to protect his friend. As an alternative, he is offered the chance to go and find the sheep himself, and this he elects to do, though he makes it clear to his adversaries that his decision to play along is not inspired by any fear for himself; indeed, his own safety lies, as he himself notes, in his mediocrity. "I'm a no-name guy without social credibility, sex appeal, or talent. I'm not even young anymore. I'm always saying stupid things that I regret later on. In other words, to borrow your expression, I'm a mediocre person. What else have I got to lose? If you can think of anything, tell me" (*MHZ* 2:178; *WSC* 139).

Cawelti notes that the hero of "hard-boiled" detective fiction normally shows this kind of rebellious stance toward authority, not merely to express his contempt for the powers-that- be (though this is often the case), but to demonstrate a personal, moral commitment toward the crime and/or criminal. In doing so, he asserts his independence, and preserves a motivation that is more powerful—certainly more personal—than the "classic" detective's (i.e., Sherlock Holmes's) abstract, academic desire for a solution. The "classic" detective's detachment is alien to his "hard-boiled" counterpart, whose involvement with the case is critically linked to his identity as a person and a professional.

> Since he becomes emotionally and morally committed to some of the persons involved, or because the crime poses some basic crisis in his image of himself, the hard-boiled detective remains unfulfilled until he has taken a personal moral stance toward the criminal. (Cawelti 1976, 143)

The protagonist's speech, then, is not mere bravado. Rather, his rebellion is a thematic device necessary to demonstrate his independent, self-interested stance toward the crime.

With the trademark Murakami twist, however, the crime in this case is as "virtual" as the criminals themselves. There is no actual murder, no body, no weapons of any kind. The protagonist is simply threatened with his own erasure from society, with the implied understanding that his friend Rat will suffer the same fate. The result is unchanged, however: Murakami's hero is forced out of his initial state of inertia and launches into the excitement of the quest vigorously.

One is, however, never out of this "virtual" state in the Murakami text, even when he clearly appropriates the hard-boiled detective framework. The postmodern landscape that Murakami creates is rich with questionable realities and rests upon the superimposition of a fantasy-like world onto a more mimetic one. His sidekick in the chase is a plain young woman whose sole distinction seems to be the power and beauty of her ears, the mere sight of which causes everything from orgasms to heart failure. More importantly, however, as the symbolism of her ears suggests, she possesses psychic powers that prod the protagonist in the right direction in his search for the sheep. It is she who leads the chase to Hokkaidō, and specifically, to a mountain lodge from which the photograph of the sheep was taken.[2]

Once at the lodge, events occur in quick succession. The sidekick conveniently disappears, having fulfilled her function; heavy snow sets in, threatening to trap the protagonist in the lodge until the spring, and by extension threatening any successful outcome for his mission, the deadline of which is now only a month away; and a bizarre new character known as the "Sheepman" (Hitsuji-otoko) enters the narrative. Similar in his function to the girl with the ears, the Sheepman exists to provide a line of communication between the protagonist and the sheep; at the same time, one soon realizes that it provides his link to Rat, as well, for the Sheepman (as his name suggests) is a superimposition of Rat onto the sheep. Through the Sheepman, the protagonist arranges a final meeting with his friend, who explains the mystery of the sheep—its purpose, its method in selecting a "host," and its ultimate fate. What makes Murakami's explication scene a little different is that Rat is, by this time, dead and buried.

> "I hanged myself from the beam in the kitchen," said Rat.
> "The Sheepman buried me next to the garage. Dying didn't hurt, by the way, in case you worry for me or anything. Not that it matters."
> "When?"
> "A week before you got here." (*MHZ* 2:350-351; *WSC* 280)

2. Kawamoto Saburō (1986) and Yokoo Kazuhiro (1991) have both pointed out the allegorical connection between this mountain lodge and the hostage incident on Mt. Asama of 1972, in which former student activists-turned-terrorists, after killing a number of their comrades, barricaded themselves in a remote mountain villa with hostages for several days. The incident, which cost the life of one police officer, received widespread media coverage in Japan, and has been seen by some Japanese culture critics—Kawamoto and Katō Norihiro—as a real and symbolic end of the "Sixties" in Japan. Yokoo (1991, 16-17) goes so far as to compare the "death" of the Zenkyōtō movement on Mt. Asama to the death of Christ on the cross.

It is difficult to know what to make of a mystery that ends with the specter of the victim (or one of them) coming back to explain how it all happened. In addition to shifting the focus from the protagonist's ability to reason the mystery out for himself, Rat's supernatural appearance actually undermines the moral fantasy, according to which truth and clarity should triumph over mystery and doubt. Such a denouement can only be seen in an ironic sense, as our anticipation of the solution is haunted constantly by lingering doubts as to whether Rat, the Sheepman, the Man in Black, or the sheep, actually exist outside the protagonist's mind.

In this sense, and perhaps only in this sense, *A Wild Sheep Chase* bears some close methodological connection to other, less formulaic Murakami texts, in which the paranormal is free to operate in a surface text, grounding a more concrete, mimetic subtext. Precisely what that subtext *is* remains open to speculation and interpretation, but given the adversarial relationship between Rat, a kind of Sixties retro-hippie, and the Boss, representing the ultra- sophisticated, mechanical and technological state, it is difficult *not* to conclude that Murakami parodies the struggles of the various Japanese student movements of the 1960s—particularly the violent, self-destructive stage extending from 1968 to 1970 known as Zenkyōtō— against an unresponsive government in his subtext. Moreover, by setting *A Wild Sheep Chase* in 1978, the author seems willing to explore the potential for similar, more contemporary conflicts on the surface level of the text. But his point is not simply a nostalgia trip, shedding pointless tears over the death of the 1960s, or the student movement; rather, he simultaneously provides a dark, mimetic narrative depicting the mainstream state of today as more powerful, indeed, deadlier than ever. The adversarial relationship between the protagonist on the one hand, and the Boss and his power syndicate on the other, allegorizes the potentially lethal relationship of Japan's mass society and its slippery, unaccountable power structure, an entity that will be discussed at greater length in the chapter that follows. Against such an opponent, what real hope can there be for a satisfyingly conclusive ending?

For Murakami, who once professed an intense dislike for the pat, final page revelations that are a definitive part of the formulaic detective story,[3] this unsatisfying ending is perhaps inevitable. It is also, however, a definitive example of his resistance to the ideological demands of formulaic fiction, or cultural ideology in general, and thereby suggests at least the

3. Interview with Murakami Haruki, October 22, 1994.

potential for the use of the most conventional of literary forms in a resistance mode, rather than one of cultural reaffirmation.

HARD-BOILED LYRICISM

The dualism implicit in *A Wild Sheep Chase*, pitting the real against the imaginary, the contrived against the realistic, is given a more concrete structural expression in Murakami's next major novel, *Hard-Boiled Wonderland and the End of the World*. In this novel, which earned the author the Tanizaki Prize, two "worlds" are contrasted: one known as the "hard-boiled wonderland," and another, described in more lyrical language, referred to as the "end of the world." These two parallel texts are both narrated by Murakami's usual first-person singular "I," but they are distinguished in that the protagonist of the hard-boiled landscape uses the more formal pronoun "Watashi," while that of the more lyrical passages goes by the informal "Boku."

But this is only the beginning of the duality that forms the most striking feature of this novel. The protagonist known as "Watashi" describes to us a cyberpunk world that is urban and harsh, filled from end to end with dangers both seen and unseen. The world known to "Boku," on the other hand, is rural (known as "the Town"), filled with golden unicorns, a fearsome Gatekeeper, and a librarian for whom the protagonist feels some vague romantic attachment. As we eventually realize, however, these two places are in fact not opposites; rather, they represent the world interpreted, constructed (and thus textualized) via different modes of consciousness. It is not difficult to see that the world that most closely resembles our own, save for a variety of mechanical innovations, is that seen through "Watashi's" eyes, representing the conscious mind, whereas the more fantastic landscape described by "Boku," with its supernatural beasts and dreamlike qualities, represents the protagonist's unconscious perception. He is able to move between these two worlds via a series of implanted switches in his brain, but within this mechanism lies the central conflict of the novel: the protagonist is doomed to remain trapped forever in the end of the world, for the switches in his brain are on the verge of mechanical meltdown. Faced with the threat of permanent unconsciousness, he struggles desperately to preserve his life as he knows it, and thus the "moral fantasy" goal of this novel is twofold: to explicate the mysterious, and to thwart death.

Hard-Boiled Wonderland and the End of the World is, if anything, even more overtly hard-boiled than *A Wild Sheep Chase*, chiefly by virtue of its setting, the protagonist, and the nature of his quest. The protagonist of the "hard-boiled" sequences in this novel appears from the beginning as a tough, cocksure operator, but he is neither perfect nor superhuman. He is a *keisanshi*, or "calcutec,"[4] whose job is to use the mechanical implants in his brain to encode and decode secret information, much as a computer does from a floppy disk, except that his encoding is entirely unique; only he can read or write the code. His work, known as "shuffling," is performed for an organization known as "the System" (*shisutemu*, written with the kanji for *soshiki*). Its structure is not altogether dissimilar to that of the state as expressed in *A Wild Sheep Chase*. As the hard-boiled wonderland protagonist says, "the System was originally in private hands, but as it grew in importance it took on a quasi-governmental status" (*MHZ* 4:55; *HBW&EW* 33). Opposed to this protagonist and others like him are *kigōshi*, "semiotecs," information pirates who will stop at nothing—including torture and mutilation— to extract information from their victims. In such an environment, his uneasiness is not out of place, but his susceptibility to fear and anxiety on the job are also typical of the hard-boiled detective, for they cover up certain extraordinary qualities that set him apart from others. Like the protagonist of *A Wild Sheep Chase*, he is characterized by a sense of rebelliousness and marginality, and his principle talent is dealing with unusual—especially dangerous—situations.

The marginality of such a hero manifests itself in a variety of ways, but primarily it is expressed as hostility toward the authorities and mainstream society in general that seems to function effectively within Murakami's less-than-glamorous portrayal of the Japanese state. His protagonist in the "hard-boiled" sequences regularly takes matters into his own hands. He bypasses official channels to take on his present job, lies to his superiors, and works at his own pace, without the benefit of his liaison officer. This is, of course, not without risks, the most critical of which is a lack of trust between himself and his organization. At one point a superior officer from the System even promises to "terminate" the protagonist (in the most final sense of the word) if it is discovered that he is working for the other side, declaring that "'we are the state. There is nothing we cannot do'" (*MHZ* 4:217; *HBW&EW* 160).

This portrayal of the System/state as all-powerful, omniscient, and dangerous, is typical of Murakami's literature, but more importantly for the formula, it locates an evil presence throughout the urban landscape of

---

4. The terms "calcutec" and "semiotec" are borrowed from Birnbaum's very clever translation of *keisanshi* and *kigōshi*, respectively.

Tokyo. Evil in this scenario is no longer simply an aberration, but attains a sense of normalcy, against which the hero's marginality stands out as a rebellious yet wholesome good. Nor is the presence of the state the only source of terror in the protagonist's world; indeed, far greater terrors lurk behind the clean facade of megalopolitan Tokyo. Not only do the streets crawl with semiotecs, prepared to gouge out a calcutec's brains to obtain the information they contain, but beneath the ground lurk even more hideous creatures: the *kurayami*, or "INKlings," monsters who feed on human flesh, whose network of control extends throughout the Tokyo subway tunnels, as suggested by the protagonist's discovery of a businessman's shoe in chapter twenty-nine. This sinister characterization of the city as a beautiful shell, teeming with evil and danger, is a defining characteristic of the hard-boiled setting, for it underscores the notion that the evil lurking in society is not isolated psychopathy, but an endemic feature of the modern (or in this case, postmodern) social structure, in which the attractive modern allure of the urban landscape is replaced by a dark, pervasive sense of danger. In such a landscape, according to Cawelti, we find "empty modernity, corruption, and death. A gleaming and deceptive facade hides a world of exploitation and criminality in which enchantment and significance must usually be sought elsewhere" (Cawelti 1976, 141).

This structure seems to suit Murakami's own purposes particularly well, as he continues to point not only to the irony of the isolated individual in a city of over twenty million inhabitants, but also to the power of the late-capitalist consumerist state to strip the individual of his identity, and replace it with an artificial, externally constructed identity designed for optimum state control. As in *A Wild Sheep Chase*, the state is both ever-present, yet slippery and difficult to pin down. It is everywhere and nowhere. Even the task with which the protagonist is initially entrusted—to "shuffle" data privately for an aging scientist— turns out to be a pretense, for the old scientist is actually an ex-employee of the System, and his real purpose is to follow the results of an experiment he did on the protagonist himself some years earlier for that organization. It is from this experiment that the hero now faces the possibility of permanent imprisonment in his own subconscious and is thus very personally involved in the task at hand.

It should not be supposed, however, that the opposition of "the Town" to the urban landscape in this novel suggests that the setting within the protagonist's unconscious is perfectly pastoral. Rather, the Town is a perfect (or nearly perfect) mirror of the urban nightmare of Tokyo itself, viewed through different lenses of perception. It is guarded by a fearsome Gatekeeper, whose home is filled with all manner of bladed weapons, the constant sharpening of which forms his chief occupation. Precisely what he does with these weapons is clear when the protagonist first enters the Town's enclosure and is told he must surrender his shadow—which, we eventually come to understand, houses his conscious mind, his will, and his memories. Without it he will be trapped, unable to think or act, in the Town deep within his unconscious mind. The Gatekeeper who carves the shadow away with a keenly honed knife may thus be identified clearly as the unconscious manifestation of the System/state and its various control mechanisms. The same menacing potential for violence thus exists in the Town as in the urban streetscapes of Tokyo.

The juxtaposition of this seemingly mild, yet deceptively dangerous landscape, with the high-tech world of the "hard-boiled wonderland," makes for engaging reading, and at the same time raises interesting philosophical questions for the reader. What, for instance, are the real stakes in this story? Does perpetual existence in the unconscious arena constitute living, or does the protagonist face a form of death at the end of the story? The matter is further complicated by the fact that much of the landscape at the "end of the world" is not actually a product of his own cognition, but rather a fabrication created by the old scientist, drawing on his past experience as a film editor (*MHZ* 4:382; *HBW&EW* 263). What is the ontological status of a man entirely divorced from his conscious identity, entrapped in an artificially constituted approximation of his inner self? The world into which the protagonist is finally placed is little more than a clever virtual reality, a pastiche of computer-generated images organized according to the professional and artistic tastes of the scientist, rather than the protagonist himself. Thus this final world, lacking any possibility of choice or self-determination, represents a very real threat of death to the protagonist's individuality.

All of this brings the moral fantasy back to the fore. Once again, by virtue of the style and structure of the text, the reader may reasonably expect that the mystery in this novel will become clear, and indeed, everything *is* revealed by the old scientist at the end of the work. The essence of what is revealed, however, is that there is no hope for the protagonist. Because the old scientist's subterranean laboratory has been destroyed during the course of the novel, there is no longer any hope of reversing the damage. Technology, completely abused, has brought the protagonist beyond the point of hope.

By the end of the novel, as in *A Wild Sheep Chase*, all is explained, but nothing is solved. The story permits the fulfillment of the moral fantasy attached to the detective formula, but the larger moral fantasy—victory over death—has in the final run been subverted, or at least left ambiguous. Had the author written *Hard-Boiled Wonderland and the End of the World* in a more conventional vein, the protagonist of the hard-boiled sequence would surely have found and used some means of rescuing himself, proving once and for all his own superiority, and the primacy of life (consciousness) over death (unconsciousness). In doing so, moreover, he would presumably also preserve whatever sense of individual identity that remained to him. This, however, is not what Murakami elects to do. Instead, his protagonist settles for what appears to be the middle ground between state control and individual autonomy; because it exists entirely within the construct of his artificial unconscious, however, even this seeming "autonomy" cannot but strike us as hollow.

Though dualistic in structure, as *A Wild Sheep Chase* is dualistic, the subtext of *Hard-Boiled Wonderland and the End of the World* is somewhat more complex. We may conclude that Murakami portrays a futuristic world, but with the exception of certain technology not yet available, it seems that the "hard-boiled wonderland" is not so different from present-day reality. He portrays a setting that is at once technologically removed from the reader, yet frighteningly familiar in its portrayal of the dominant, mainstream culture. Brain implants, "shuffling," INKlings, and a maze of subterranean caverns crisscrossed beneath downtown Tokyo provide the cyberpunk icing to a postmodern cake, but the conflict itself, centered on information wars, the objectification and commodification of knowledge, the concretization of thoughts and memories, are all part of an ongoing trend observable in the real world. One thinks of advancements, especially from the 1980s on, in sophisticated computer equipment; floppy disks, CD-ROMs, and computer "memory" might all be viewed as physical manifestations of abstract concepts such as knowledge and information that have become commonplace in the contemporary era. The literal objectification of knowledge and memory is given peculiar expression by the old scientist early in *Hard-Boiled Wonderland and the End of the World*, when he asserts his theory that the skulls of animals retain the thoughts and memories of the animals they used to be. According to this theory, once a technique is discovered by which to recover such information, there would no longer be any need to torture prisoners for information; one could simply kill them, clean the skull, and retrieve the data (*MHZ* 4:50; *HBW&EW* 29).

Yet in presenting the objectification and appropriation of the memory, of perception and finally the physical self as a mere vessel for the storage and transportation of information, is Murakami showing his readers a world of science fiction, or one of actuality? Once again we are confronted with the suggestion that the so-called "fantasy" world is in fact not so divorced as we might like to imagine from the "real" one. What are the larger implications of a social and economic system that turns information (among other things) into a commodity to be bought, sold, or in this case, stolen? The focus on the power and value of information seen in *Hard-Boiled Wonderland and the End of the World* is by no means a peculiarly postmodern phenomenon, but it is especially pronounced in the postmodern moment, and perhaps at no other time in history has the importance of information been such an integral part of everyday life. In many ways this situation is foretold in *A Wild Sheep Chase*, in which the power of the Boss comes from control of political, industrial, and most importantly, media interests. The principal source of his power seems to be information, the key commodity of the postmodern moment. Marilyn Ivy astutely draws attention to the commodification of information as signaling the dawn of this important era.

> In this contemporary postmodern era, the virulence of capital has turned everything into pure commodified signs. National borders give way as information circulates at blinding speeds. Mass media, television, and advertising create "hyperreal" space, a space of "simulation.". . . The problem of knowledge as an informational commodity comes up repeatedly in Japanese texts devoted to analyzing the postmodern condition. (Ivy 1989, 24–25)

One hardly need add that whoever controls the means of disseminating this information holds a considerable source of power. The "texts" noted by Ivy are the semianthropological works of public figures such as Asada Akira and Isozaki Arata, but a growing number of recent novelists—Takahashi Gen'ichirō, Shimada Masahiko, Murakami Ryū—are also writing fiction (in general, somewhat less censorious than Murakami's) in one form or another about the commodification of the abstract and the intangible that emerges as a by-product of the postmodern era.[5]

This focus on information and its commodification is of course at the heart of the plot of *Hard-Boiled Wonderland and the End of the World* as well, and yet Murakami is careful not to allow this mild excoriation of

5. We might note, for instance, the emphasis on information contained in floppy disks in Shimada's novel *Rokoko-chō* (Rococo-ville, 1990), or on the commodification of personal relationships in his *Yumetsukai* (1989; translated as Dream Messenger, 1992), which will be discussed later in this book. See also Murakami Ryū's somewhat harsher views of Japan's consumerist frenzy in works like *In za miso sūpu* (In the Miso Soup, 1997), also to be discussed below.

postmodern commodification to obscure his more important critique, which draws his readers into the implicit debate on what happens to the individual identity in a society that has the potential not only to commodify information as an object, but to construct reality and identity arbitrarily to suit its own convenience. As in *A Wild Sheep Chase*, the real subtext that drives *Hard-Boiled Wonderland and the End of the World* is the extent to which the state controls one's identity, supplanting his or her original, experientially grounded identity with the so-called "white utopia" of consumer goods and commodity fetishism.[6]

In the context of this novel, such control amounts to making it appear that the protagonist enjoys the freedom of choice in his personal destiny, at least to a point, while all the while masking the fact that he is trapped always into moving down one of several predetermined paths open to him. We should recall in this regard that the protagonist at the "end of the world" appears to have the option of escape since his shadow has discovered what he believes to be the portal to the conscious mind. However, his decision to remain in the woods between the Town and the outer world—a proverbial "no-man's land" between the modes of consciousness—amounts only to the appearance of freedom. Finally, we cannot escape the fact that for the protagonist to remain in this constructed unconscious at all is to succumb to the power of the state, by whose authority his mechanized brain was created in the first place. In this way, so long as he is cut off from his own individual core consciousness, represented by the shadow, he is doomed to remain in an artificial and managed existence. The only two choices that remain to the protagonist are precisely mirrored by the reality of the blank utopia of contemporary consumerist society: easy participation in the economy of empty consumerism, tightly managed by a system of political, industrial, and media enterprises; or peripheralization and isolation. Like Rat in *A Wild Sheep Chase*, the hard-boiled protagonist struggles in this novel to maintain control over his identity, his ability to make choices, to think, and to interpret. This is clearly discernible in the peculiar fact that although the protagonist at the end of the world is given the special job of "reading" old dreams from the skulls of unicorns at the Town library (the unconscious manifestation of his job as a "calcutec"), he is forbidden to interpret them, even to think about them. His dream-reading is in a larger sense a metaphor for reading the cultural signs of the Symbolic Order—a

6. The term "white utopia" is used by Kawamoto (1986, 50) to indicate the mindless vacuousness of the world offered to Rat in *A Wild Sheep Chase*, and by allegory, the consumerist world in which Japanese live today.

Lacanian term encompassing the various mechanisms, particularly those grounded in collective morality, by which control is exercised over individual members of society. His task is to consume, but never to ponder or consider the nature of what he consumes. The real function of his work is to eliminate the last vestiges of identity that remain in the skulls of the dead beasts that, prior to death, had inherited the minds of those who enter the Town, for to read with neither interpretation, nor retention, nor even comprehension, ultimately voids the unconscious (in this case, the collective unconscious) of all thought and volition. It could, then, be argued that the protagonist's entrapment in such a world would be a form of death, and by extension that his decision to remain, thus to capitulate to state power, is a form of suicide.

Is this the realization of the moral fantasy attached to the formulaic novel? Is it the reaffirmation of life over death, of clarity and truth over mystery and doubt? Does it reaffirm the protagonist's identity in some way? By no means. At best the protagonist preserves his ability to peripheralize himself, but the end of the novel finally tells us only that there is no true escape, even temporarily, from the power of state ideology. This only reinforces our understanding (or at any rate Murakami's understanding) of contemporary reality: that the postmodern state is impregnable, irresistible, and that we ourselves participate in our own corruption by it. This peculiar juxtaposition of the formulaic and the mimetic can lead to a variety of speculations concerning Murakami's place as a writer, but the overwhelming conclusion must be that this, too, is a text of resistance—albeit futile resistance—which, like *A Wild Sheep Chase*, parodies the popular formula in order to lead the reader down a more dire path.

FROM ADVENTURE TO ROMANCE

Murakami's next book, *Norwegian Wood*, has been his one and only "million-seller" thus far. Significantly, the book also ranks as his first major attempt at the romance genre. Nevertheless, the reader notes a familiar duality in *Norwegian Wood*, as with the other texts, in the conspicuous opposition of the rural and the urban, the present and the past, and the political right and left. What we do not find—and perhaps this is one reason for the work's tremendous popularity—is the intrusion of the paranormal, the alternative realities that have come to be Murakami's trademark. Instead, the text is marked by a mimetic cynicism that is once again peculiarly juxtaposed to the structural formula of the romance novel.

My classification of *Norwegian Wood* as romance is based on the understanding of formulaic romance as an exploration of love as a prime factor in the human condition. However, this classification is admittedly tenuous, as were the classifications of the previous two novels for, as we have seen, neither of those texts upheld the moral fantasies normally attached to them. Of equal concern are a variety of academic studies (Modleski 1982; Radway 1984; Mulhern 1989) that have concluded that the romance is a specifically *female*-centered genre of literature. Tania Modleski (1982) has argued for an understanding of the formulaic romance as a marginalized form of fiction chiefly because it *is* a female form of literature. Similarly, Janice Radway's "Smithton Readers" insist that "[t]o qualify as a romance, the story must chronicle not merely the events of the courtship, but *what it feels like* to be the *object* of one" (Radway 1984, 64).[7] The dominant assumption in the romance formula is that it centers on the experiences of a female protagonist, and that while a central male character must exist, he is actually secondary. Early, prototypical examples of such novels have existed in the West, arguably, since Defoe's *Moll Flanders* and Richardson's *Pamela* in the eighteenth century, and flourished in the days of Jane Austen and Charlotte Bronte. Radway's study, however, focuses primarily on the Harlequin and Silhouette romance, the most recent and standardized trend in the romance novel, arguing—correctly, I think—that the majority of readers of such works are females within definable social and economic subcategories, primarily middle-class housewives.

For the purpose of examining Murakami's *Norwegian Wood*, however, a rather more general, less gender-specific definition of the term romance will be of greater applicability. While Cawelti's text lacks a specific chapter on the romance, he does provide a brief, useful sketch of the romance, based on the moral fantasy such texts typically uphold. His definition is also useful in its implicit bridging of the perceived gap between the popularized, formulaic romance novel—the so-called "supermarket romance"—and the more universalized definition offered by Frye (1957) of the archetypal "quest-romance." According to Cawelti, that bridge is grounded in notions of fertility, fidelity, and constancy.

> The crucial defining characteristic of romance is not that it stars a female but that its organizing action is the development of a

7. The "Smithton Readers" were members of a regular reading society who formed a controlled research group for Radway's examination of the various reasons that women read romance fiction.

> love relationship, usually between a man and a woman. . . . The
> moral fantasy of the romance is that of love triumphant and per-
> manent, overcoming all obstacles and difficulties. Though the
> usual outcome is a permanently happy marriage, more sophisti-
> cated types of love story sometimes end in the death of one or
> both of the lovers, but always in such a way as to suggest that the
> love relation has been of lasting and permanent impact. (Cawelti
> 1976, 42)

This statement, then, merely elaborates on Frye's contention nearly twenty
years earlier regarding the classical, archetypal romance, that "[t]ranslated
into ritual terms, the quest-romance is the victory of fertility over the waste-
land" (Frye 1957, 193). Translated into the terms of the popular romance,
this means the basic conflict between sustained sexual relations on the one
hand, with the potential to turn *recreational* sex into *procreational*, and
the proverbial "one-night stand" on the other, is as vital to the moral fantasy of romance as which character stands out as the focus of attention.
Whether *Norwegian Wood* is concerned more with its hero (the protagonist
of the work), or its heroine, Naoko, is not always easy to determine, but it
is accurate to say that the narrative examines the trials of Naoko through
the eyes of the hero/protagonist. Yet, despite this ambiguity of focus, that
is, the fact that one never sees Naoko except through the filter of another's
gaze, the reader's expectation of the exaltation of love in this work over less
meaningful (even mechanical) sexuality may be sufficient grounds to term
it a romance. Furthermore, the presence of certain structural elements that
are common to the formulaic romance, for example, the rivalry established
between Naoko and the vivacious "other woman," and the physical and
emotional mutilation of the heroine, suggest that Murakami is aware of the
recognized format of the formulaic romance. At the same time, his use of
that formula is once again subverted by a darker, more nihilistic subtext
that ultimately overshadows and disrupts the moral fantasy of fertility, constancy, and love conquering all.

    Norwegian Wood traces the protagonist's life and loves in Tokyo
during his college years but is told in distant retrospect, some eighteen
years after the fact. The setting of this retrospective narrative covers the
period from autumn, 1969, until autumn of 1970, during which, as I have
noted above, some of the most turbulent conflicts between the political
right and left took place. Yet, the book pokes fun at these political struggles,
mocking the seriousness of political activists both on the right and left as
the political confrontation reached its climax. The absurd ways in which
the factions are portrayed, from a rigidly structured flag-raising ceremony
outside the protagonist's dormitory, to the left-wing activists who bore stu-

dents even more than their drama professor after taking over a class one day, make it abundantly clear that the surface text of *Norwegian Wood*, at any rate, is not about the political specificities of counterculture in the 1960s.

In contrast to all the political activism going on around him, the protagonist spends his time with Naoko, forming the basis for activity in this text. Their relationship is a complex one, for Naoko suffers from an unexplained malady—some dense psychological barrier between her inner and outer selves—that prevents her from engaging in sexual intercourse. This condition remits only once, on her twentieth birthday, on which she suddenly becomes sexually capable, and she and the protagonist consummate their relationship for the first and last time. Following this real and symbolic wounding of Naoko—which also, of course, represents symbolically a brief moment of fertility—she begins a gradual physical, mental, and emotional decline that culminates in her entry into a rural sanitarium. The protagonist is naturally concerned about her, and feels not a little responsible for Naoko's mental scars. Yet his sense of guilt, and his resulting solicitousness toward Naoko, are also a necessary structural element in the Japanese formulaic romance, according to Chieko Mulhern, for the protagonist's guilt substitutes for a lack of grounding in Western-style chivalry.

> There is no denying . . . that dancing attendance on women is definitely beyond the average Japanese male's instinct or expertise. Hence, the heroine must be made unconscious, hurt, or otherwise physically incapacitated in the presence of the hero, preferably in a manner to cause him to feel responsible for her condition. (Mulhern 1989, 64)

Whether one chooses to accept entirely Mulhern's rather dim view of the Japanese male, she has indeed identified one of the most important and definitive motifs in the Japanese formulaic romance, one which marks *Norwegian Wood*, as well. The physical "injury" Naoko suffers is, of course, the loss of her virginity, but apart from the physical rending of the female commonly associated with coitus, Naoko suffers from very real emotional and psychological pains as well, and whether they are the direct result of her relationship with the protagonist, he cannot help blaming himself for her condition.

LOVE, RIVALRY, AND SEXUALITY

Following Naoko's hospitalization, the protagonist encounters a young coed named Midori, who perfectly fits the role of the "other woman" in the novel. Significantly, Midori is everything that Naoko is not: she is talkative, outgoing, cheerful, and most importantly, she presents herself as sexually available. Almost from the outset Midori maneuvers closer to the protagonist, placing him into situations in which he must choose between yielding to his sexual desire or remaining faithful to Naoko. As important as this conflict between desire and duty may be for the protagonist, the rivalry it implicitly creates between Naoko and Midori is at least as important.

The effect of the Midori/Naoko rivalry is intensified by the fact that it remains largely unresolved to the end of the story. In violation of convention in the romance formula, in which "other women" are neutralized by being "either married, in love with someone else, or else related by blood to the hero so that they pose no threat to the heroine" (Mulhern 1989, 60), Midori actually grows *more* inviting, *more* available, as the narrative progresses, testing to the limit the protagonist's fidelity. Strictly speaking, the result of this should be the greater vindication of the protagonist's honor and love for Naoko at the end of the novel, affirming the primacy of his feelings for Naoko over his desire for carnal pleasure with Midori. This, however, is not how the novel ends, for near the end, at the very point of seeming recovery from her mental illness, Naoko suddenly hangs herself in the forest near the sanitarium, leaving the protagonist to flee Tokyo in confusion. Once again, Murakami cannot bring his protagonist to the point of a decision, nor can he resist throwing one final surprise at the reader. The ultimate message contained in *Norwegian Wood*, far from reaffirming the reader's belief in love everlasting, seems to be rather that even true love and constancy cannot save anyone.

As with the previous two novels, Murakami's view in *Norwegian Wood* remains essentially a dualistic one, which uses contrast as a central mechanism to relay his subliminal message of despair. Some of these contrasts, such as his distinction between the absurd reality of the university/city, and the pastoral—yet unexpectedly lethal—country sanitarium where Naoko commits suicide, appear in previous books as well; we have observed the phenomenon in both *A Wild Sheep Chase* and *Hard-Boiled Wonderland and the End of the World*. But other contrasts, specific to the romance genre, are present in *Norwegian Wood*. The most important of these is the contrast between sexuality and love seen in the behavior of the protagonist toward Naoko and Midori. The matter is even more clearly represented in two peripheral characters: Reiko, who is Naoko's roommate at the sanitarium; and Nagasawa, who befriends the protagonist while both are living in the university dormitory.

Both Reiko and Nagasawa are given a detailed sexual exposition, but in their responses toward sex they are polar opposites. Reiko, for instance, reveals to the protagonist that she entered the sanitarium after being molested by a thirteen year-old lesbian, who then claimed that *Reiko* had attacked *her*. From this moment Reiko, never mentally stable to begin with, had been tormented by insecurities about her own sexuality and had thus withdrawn from the pointless sexual abandon of the urban world into this mountain hideaway. In terms of the romance, it is of mechanical importance that she should be thus guarded about her sexual needs, for it precludes her becoming a rival in the relationship between the protagonist and Naoko when he visits the sanitarium. The point is made even more unequivocal by the fact that Reiko is considerably older than the two lovers, with a wizened countenance. Murakami thus makes it clear that, for the time being, at least, the protagonist's attraction to her will not be physical, but fraternal and emotional in nature. In short, Reiko represents mature, controlled (perhaps over-controlled) sexuality.

Nagasawa, in clear opposition to this, suggests unbridled, pointless sexual activity. The first thing the reader learns about Nagasawa is that "people said he had a huge penis, and that he had already slept with a hundred girls" (*MHZ* 6:50).[8] While the actual number turns out to be somewhat more modest—around seventy—it is clear that for Nagasawa sex is something that can be measured only in terms of quantity. For a time he even persuades the protagonist to engage in this lifestyle for himself, but predictably, his reaction to meaningless sex is boredom and self-disgust, proving, according to Nagasawa, that he is "an ordinary, decent guy" (*MHZ* 6:53-54).

Nagasawa's determination in the pursuit of sex carries over into other aspects of his life as well. He sets goals—career and otherwise—and works toward them with a single-minded obsession that the protagonist both admires and fears. Moreover, while Nagasawa may be debauched, he is unswervingly honest about himself, as suggested by his assurance to his present girlfriend, Hatsumi, that one day he will leave her behind to pursue his career goals. This actually happens, and Hatsumi, after a brief marriage to someone else, commits suicide in despair. True to his character, when Nagasawa is told of the event, he remarks only that her death is too bad, but that she was warned.

8. While a translation of *Norwegian Wood* has been published by Alfred Birnbaum through Kodansha International, like those of *Hear the Wind Sing* and *Pinball, 1973*, it has not been readily available outside of Japan, and thus I have elected not to cite page numbers from it. However, a new translation by Jay Rubin has recently been released by Vintage Books, and readers are encouraged to take advantage of it.

In the larger scheme of the urban versus the rural, Nagasawa comes to epitomize the "real" world of Tokyo, and with an irony similar to that in the previous novel, one that is typical not only of Murakami, but of other postmodern writers as well, Tokyo is presented with a facade of sanity that only disguises the turmoil and despair of the postmodern age lurking beneath the surface.[9] Nagasawa himself, in his excessive consistency and openness, strikes one as a character of immense rationality, and yet his logical predictability is not, in this case, an attractive feature. Rather, the rural setting of the sanitarium, with its surreal atmosphere and host of bewildered and schizophrenic inmates, is presented as the "sane" world. Here is where Reiko becomes important as the other side of the sexual coin, for her own absolute honesty, which she tells the protagonist is the first rule for everyone at the sanitarium, marks her as a parallel character to Nagasawa. Whereas Nagasawa's honesty is designed to protect himself, however, Reiko's is therapeutic, intended to heal wounds, rather than to justify inflicting them. Unfortunately, this honesty, and Reiko's genuine, sororal love for Naoko, proves ineffectual, and Naoko commits suicide near the end of the novel, before the hero can see her again.

As noted above by Cawelti, however, the death of the heroine in a romance does not necessarily preclude its fulfillment of the moral fantasy of love's primacy (one recalls that at the end of *Romeo and Juliet* both lovers lay dead; their love is vindicated by the remorse that remains). Rather, it is the protagonist's response to this event that commands the reader's attention. The real subversion of the romance formula comes at the end of the novel, when the protagonist, after wandering around Japan for a month, cleansing himself symbolically of Naoko's death, returns to Tokyo and, for the first time since Naoko's death, calls Midori. She asks him where he is, and he realizes his dilemma, quite the same as in the previous two novels: he has no idea where he is. "All around me were hordes of people walking past, all bound for nowhere. I called out again and again for Midori from the middle of nowhere" (*MHZ* 6:419).

These final lines of *Norwegian Wood*, filled with anxiety and doubt, turn the moral fantasy of love triumphant into a farce, leaving the reader as confused as the protagonist about where things finally stand. Far from finding perfect happiness, or at least inner peace and vindication, in ex-

9. Hino Keizō, whose novel *Yume no shima* (Isle of Dreams, 1985) vied for the Tanizaki Prize against Murakami's *Hard-Boiled Wonderland and the End of the World*, deals almost exclusively with the theme of the beautiful, empty shell of Tokyo in the 1980s. One thinks also of the persistent theme of Tokyo as a vibrant city masking boredom and despair in Shimada Masahiko's *Dream Messenger*.

change for his fidelity to Naoko, the protagonist ends the book crying out for the most overtly sexual of the three main female characters in the novel, only to realize that he himself is completely lost. His love has neither rescued Naoko nor himself, leaving the reader somewhat at a loss.

FORMULA AND POSTMODERNITY

In all three of these novels, one finds the unlikely—indeed, the oxymoronic—juxtaposition of the predictability of the literary formula and the unpredictability of the actual world. But what is Murakami's point in creating novels along such clearly recognizable formulaic lines, only to render those formulas false by subverting their predictable conclusions? Why, in other words, does Murakami inject the mimetic into what is, by definition, *non*mimetic literature?

There are a variety of ways we may answer this. On a superficial level, we might simply place Murakami among the many writers in Japan (and around the world) who, though serious about their work, are unconcerned with producing "art." Authors like Richard Brautigan, Tim O'Brien, and Ian Watson seem to represent this recent trend in the English-speaking world; in Japan, one thinks of the above-noted Shimada Masahiko, Yoshimoto Banana, Shimizu Yoshinori, Murakami Ryū, or Hino Keizō. These are all authors who work in areas that are often demarcated as "popular," from science fiction to fantasy. Yet their work, while often playing with the kinds of formulas above—mystery, adventure, and so forth—could by no means be described as highly formulaic. Instead, they lead us on a vain quest that ends, as often as not, with more questions than answers. Such gestures are the hallmark of postmodern literature from the 1970s onward, and whether politically charged or not, these literary efforts are unsettling.

I wish again, however, to touch briefly on the point that the fictional output of authors such as those noted above, like Murakami's, is never innocent of political expression. This is an argument that will re-emerge in the chapter below on historiography, but if the analyses I have performed above show anything, it is that this kind of "serious popular" fiction today is a mode of writing that is deliberate, its selection purposeful. Whether Murakami is aware of it or not, in organizing the plot of *A Wild Sheep Chase* in such a way as to create a structure of conflict between an elusive state and the autonomous individual, he, too, makes an overt interpretation of the world in which he sets the work, a world that resembles the real one closely enough to suggest not parody, but real representation.

I also wish to historicize the production of literature such as this, to understand when and why such fiction has become especially relevant and popular in recent years. In this regard we can, following Huyssen, suggest 1970 as the watershed after which what might be called "dialectical literature"—literature whose artistic approach critically engaged, and sometimes synthesized with literary forms of the past—began to wane, replaced by a mode of written expression that is, as noted earlier, nontransgressive, noncritical, at least where methodology is concerned. I would go so far as to suggest that a paradigm shift of sorts occurred around 1970, at which point the "text/subtext" model of literature I have described above came into common use. That is to say, the method of (partially) concealing serious subtexts —political, ideological, historical or ontological critiques—within the language of "pop" fiction (adventure, fantasy, romance) is a fairly recent phenomenon.

As I noted briefly in my introduction above, Huyssen argues in a very similar vein that the "postmodernism" of the 1960s is, in fact, better characterized as an extension of avantgardism, the very cutting edge of modernist experimental form. Drawing the distinction between expression that cuts against the grain of previous expression, and that which elects not to critique its predecessors, Huyssen's descriptions of pre-1970 and post-1970 models of postmodernism are historically applicable to the general political climate of these times as well.

There is certainly merit to this argument. Judging from the fiction produced during the past twenty-five years or so, it seems clear enough that a group of younger writers who began their writing careers after 1970 did indeed emerge to spearhead production of fiction that is the result of some sort of major shift in basic principles of expression. I am thinking here both of style and of an author's stance toward the function of fiction as "art." A look at the writing style of an earlier novelist such as Pynchon, for instance, who débuted in 1963 with his Faulkner Foundation Award-winning *V.*, quickly reveals the author's urge to forge a new mode of literary expression, to create a new mode of literary art through language that both entertains and challenges the educated reader. Reading Ōe produces a very similar sensation, though Ōe rarely demonstrates Pynchon's playful humor in his own experiments with language. This is inevitable, however, when one considers that both writers—but most explicitly Ōe—write in conscious response to previous literature. That is to say, if Pynchon is the literary heir to stylistic experimentalists such as Joyce, then Ōe is the descendant of Sakaguchi Ango, of Tamura Taijirō, even (in his resistance to neo-romanticism) of Mishima himself. Both Pynchon and Ōe share as part of their *raison d'être* a desire to reconstitute the literary language in which they work, chiefly through densely woven prose that reflects the complexity of the historical moment in which they live.

Younger writers who emerged after the worldwide political upheavals of the 1960s, on the other hand, clearly do not share this enthusiasm for reinventing literature as an art form, for original stylistic experimentalism, or indeed for the notion of "literature" at all. As I noted earlier, one does not need to look far to see a significant disparity both in style *and in intended audience* between the writing of Pynchon and that of Ian Watson or Richard Brautigan. The gaps between Ōe, or Nakagami Kenji, on the one hand, and Murakami, Shimada Masahiko, or Yoshimoto Banana, on the other, are equally noticeable. The last three—the full list is really quite long—intentionally avoid the kind of linguistic density, the intellectual and thematic complexity that mark the writing of Ōe and Nakagami. Instead, their work is deliberately simple in its expression, unabashedly lacking in artistic or aesthetic sensitivity.

Like his peers, Murakami Haruki is uninterested in creating new literary styles for their own sake, or in resisting past styles; he *is* interested in presenting a political and social critique through a literary style that is transparent, always familiar to readers. What makes Murakami's work genuinely postmodern in this regard, however, is the *absence* of challenge to the stylistic density of Ōe; rather, like other writers of today, he studiously, self-consciously resists the limitations of any one style or genre, the adoption of which might force him to avoid some other, opposing mode of expression. It is this rejection of dialectical thinking that so disturbs Ōe, leading him to lament in 1989 that young intellectuals of the time were incapable of more than superficial absorption of each successively imported cultural theory, followed by its "discharge" in favor of the next. Writes Ōe, "Despite this remarkable trend for absorbing new cultural theories, almost no effort was made to interpret them meticulously in view of specific situations in which Japan found itself" (1989, 204).

Yet the model sought by Ōe is more complex than this. Inasmuch as he believes "pure literature" to have been replaced by a fetishism for cultural theory (which is basically true), Ōe does not hope simply for young Japanese intellectuals to understand more fully the cultural theories of their times—structuralism, poststructuralism, and so forth. Rather, he seeks an intellectual body of youth capable of thinking synchronically, by which he signifies a form of dialectic that allows for opposing theories, leading eventually to a series of syntheses that continually move the evolution of Japanese intellectualism forward. But in doing so we note two interesting implications: first, that the theoretical development sought by Ōe is very similar to that seen in postwar literary expression, indicating that Ōe (perhaps a little nostalgically) seeks a replacement for the loss of "pure literature" that has already occurred; and second, we note the presence of a teleological awareness in Ōe, reflecting his evident faith in an ultimate "end" to the project of modernity, as Habermas has it. In short, Ōe reveals that, for him, postmodernism might be only a temporary irritant, a brief hiatus in the steady intellectual evolution of mankind, resulting, if we are optimistic, in our improvement, if not perfection.

The idea, however, is at best anachronistic. Ōe is right when he assumes the gradual decay of Japanese "literature"; in fact, he may well be the last of his kind. But in place of "pure literature," or of "literature" at all, he seems peculiarly unwilling to look beyond the "cultural theories" (most of which have literary manifestations) and to recognize that "literature" (a term that has come to signify the presence of artistic intent) is replaced by "fiction," by "writing." And yet, while the aesthetic sensibilities that mark "literature" may be in decline, the kind of writing that Ōe seeks most to preserve—that which creates cultural models—may actually be in a better position today than it was thirty years ago. The trend toward de-emphasizing the aesthetic by writers like Murakami and Shimizu (or Watson, Brautigan, or Ben Bova) does not negate their role as spokesmen, guides, even consciences, for the societies that produced them.

In other words, while stylistically Murakami Haruki and his contemporaries may well have rejected the stylistic debates about how to carry artistic writing to its "next" level of sophistication (they reject, in fact, the deterministic linearity of the "next"), they have by no means rejected their responsibilities as writers as Ōe seems to believe. Their work is not for an intellectual readership, neither for a wholly popular audience; instead, they seek to reach out to all readers, intellectual and casual alike. Their real achievement, if we seek one, is to create a mode of writing that is simultaneously entertaining, accessible to a majority of readers, yet also grounded in an awareness of contemporary realities, appealing to social critics and literary scholars alike.

The arguments made by Ōe above are mirrored in much of the debate in the West concerning postmodernism itself. Where I, following Huyssen and Hutcheon, have defined aesthetic aspects of the postmodern as a stylistically eclectic, multiple mode of expression, and emphasized the politicization of the content of such writing, more conservative theorists such as Charles Newman and Masao Miyoshi take issue with precisely those stylistic elements that, in my opinion, make the works of contemporary writers postmodern. Newman, for instance, takes for his postmodern models the experimental writings of Pynchon and John Barth, which "possess a complexity of surface, a kind of verbal hermetic seal which holds them together, irrespective of linear pattern or narrative momentum" (1985, 91). As Miyoshi does in the case of Ōe, Newman responds positively to the intentional complexity of the language itself, a very modernist gesture, for it implies the artistic content in the work.

Against such writers as Pynchon and Barth, Newman opposes Ann Beattie and Raymond Carver, whose work is marked by "an obdurate unsurprised and unsurprising plainstyle which takes that famous 'meaning between the lines' to its absurd conclusion, and makes the middle ground mimesis of an Updike or Cheever seem rococo by comparison" (1985, 93). Newman's rejection of such "ordinary" language clarifies in a most useful way the lines of debate that have grown up over the nature of the postmodern, for whereas I would characterize the experimental works of Pynchon and Barth as an early strain of the postmodern—what Huyssen terms avantgarde, in fact—these are precisely the authors Newman holds up as exemplary of the postmodern. Precisely what Newman would call the writings of post-1970 authors such as Beattie and Carver is unclear; what is clear is that he reacts negatively to their seemingly simplistic celebration of the ordinary.

My purpose in raising this issue here is not to deny the postmodern strain that underlies the work of Pynchon—indeed, his playful scenarios might lead some to conclude that he has more in common with Murakami than with Ōe!—but rather to defend the inclusion of writers like Murakami and Carver in a category that, while obviously separated from the postmodern/avantgarde writers of the pre-1970 era, nevertheless represents a legitimate strain of postmodern writing. I wish, in other words, to argue, as Huyssen does, for two distinct phases of postmodernism, one attached to the aftermath of the Second World War, and another more relevant to the end of the turbulent 1960s. The first, in the wake of the atomic bombings and the mechanistic slaughter of the Jews by the Third Reich, rebelled against the teleology of "modernism," which included the assumption that modern was better, that humans were advancing away from their barbaric past. In artistic terms, this strain also rejected the paradigms of earlier "polite" literature in favor of new modes of expression that were angry, complex, and earthy, reflecting, I think, the ambiguities and contradictions of life in the 1950s and 1960s, an acute consciousness of the gap between perceptions of modernity as convenient, and the reality that the "modern" had not liberated humans from their bestial side.

The latter strain of the postmodern, on the other hand, while grounded similarly in a rejection of the teleology of the "modern," also rejects the notion of the "new" as its primary function, something the earlier postmoderns were never quite able to do. That is to say, in reinventing modern literary language to reflect the complexities and ambiguities of modern life in the 1960s, Pynchon and Ōe nevertheless strike out against their predecessors, engage their stylistic and intellectual foundations, and in so doing create a new and unique mode of writing—one that, whether they accept it or not, eventually takes on the trappings of "art." Writers like Murakami and Carver, on the other hand, intentionally borrow eclectically from previous styles, mixing and matching, trying different combinations of genre and style. The result, as most scholars of the postmodern have noted, is a sense of nostalgia, yet also of contemporaneity. Perhaps the best point to be drawn from these two strains of the postmodern is that, while both are obviously political, both acutely focused on the societies that produced them, the former expresses considerably greater hostility toward previous artistic forms; the functional methodology of the latter is simply to go "beyond the modern."

The above clarification is relevant and useful here, for it provides a salient comparison with the response to Murakami Haruki by Masao Miyoshi, one of the foremost scholars of Japanese literature in the United States. Miyoshi, who has followed the trends of Japanese postmodernism for more than a decade, nevertheless finds little to appreciate in the manifestation of postmodernism presented by Murakami. In his epilogue to *Off Center*, Miyoshi associates Murakami with Yoshimoto Banana, describing the work of the former as "trivia," "story-less stories," whereas Yoshimoto's are "entirely couched in baby talk" (1991, 234-36). This may well be true, just as Newman may be correct in contending that Carver's and Beattie's works are characterized by "elisions of inadvertency and circumspection" (1985, 93). Yet at some level we must recognize that both Newman and Miyoshi determinedly maintain a hierarchy, a binary by which the sophisticated, the obscure, the abstruse, is always privileged over the simple and transparent. The arguments of both make it clear that the complaint is linked more to language, to expression, to the *aesthetic* aspects of the writers in question. In other words, both Newman and Miyoshi, according to my analysis, tell us little more than what is already known and acknowledged: that the writers both in Japan and the West who are in the process of taking over the reins, so to speak, are not artists, but merely novelists. I do not mean to suggest here that aesthetics have been banned from postmodern expression after 1970; I would, however, argue that postmodern aesthetics are more about pastiche, about the various "retro-booms" in style and language, than about the creation of something novel for its own sake. This last is, in my opinion, a remnant of the modernist drive.

I see the gap between my position and Miyoshi's, then, as both emotional and intellectual: his dim view of Murakami is at least partially grounded, I suspect, in a nostalgic desire to reclaim the aesthetic function of literature as art, even (or perhaps especially) *politicized* art. Yet this, like Ōe's aspiration of recuperating "pure literature," is probably anachronistic in an era of political fragmentation, a time when hierarchies placing Art over Kitsch (or serious over popular) cannot survive the hyper-multiplicity of contemporary thinking.

As is readily evident from even brief exposure to Murakami's writing, there is a minimalist element in the text that cannot be denied. We should be wary, however, particularly in cases like Murakami's or Yoshimoto's, of too readily applying labels that suggest an artistic impulse. Inasmuch as the term "minimalism" in itself, when applied to literature, suggests the use of a simplified, purified language in order to express an aesthetic ideal, I am reluctant to term Murakami a "minimalist" out of respect for his consistent efforts—and those of many other contemporary writers—to avoid the characterization of their work as "art." Furthermore, while to argue for the minimalism of Murakami as an artistic impulse would no doubt prove a convenience in opposing him to Ōe, as indeed I wish to do, it would in itself merely uphold a binary that I have sought to weaken, that is, the suggestion that Murakami's style is nothing more than a reaction against the "complexity of the surface" described by Newman above. It may indeed be read as such, but it is critical to see in Murakami's style not a drive toward creating a new mode of art, but rather an attempt to collapse the distinction between "intellectual" and "common" writing.

Moreover, in terms of identity, and in keeping with the general theme of this book, we should bear in mind that Murakami's experiments with minimalist expression, like his experiments with the literary formula, are a form of resistance against the firm identification of "serious" and "popular" literature. In other words, in the course of writing fiction that seems both to affirm and also deny the underlying parameters of both serious and popular fiction all at once, Murakami methodically constructs an identity "crisis" for both.

It would be easy, following Jameson, to apply the logic of pastiche to the experiments we have seen above, a mode of borrowing and mixing uncritically various (often opposing) modes of expression, the "random cannibalization of all the styles of the past" (Jameson 1991, 18). And to a point such a critique might hold its own, except that Murakami's use of pastiche here is neither random nor uncritical. Rather, we see here a move to deconstruct the opposition not only of "serious" and "popular," but indeed of "mimetic" and "formulaic" fiction as well, calling into question the very identity of these forms.

Is this not what really bothers Ōe, Newman, and Miyoshi, among others, so much about contemporary fiction? They are threatened by the very suggestion that the minimalist style of Murakami or Yoshimoto could compare—even coexist meaningfully—with the complexity of Ōe or Pynchon. Certainly their anxiety is consistent with Jameson's own concerning the mixture of genres and styles, particularly those centering on history and fiction writing, that emerges from his assault on the predilection toward pastiche on the part of recent writers. The reasoning behind this is not difficult to discern: pastiche inherently destabilizes identity by denying or negating incompatibilities, and it is precisely this stable identity—of a permanent, unchanging "reality" to serve as referent for the writing of history, for instance— for which Jameson feels nostalgic.

In this sense, somewhat ironically, the positions of Jameson and Murakami are not so far apart as they might seem. Murakami's own use of pastiche, as I have noted previously, is not so much a celebration of the liberation of style, as Hutcheon might have it, but a means of highlighting the replacement of individual identity in contemporary Japan with "something else." At the same time, Murakami is wary of identity that is *too* stable, for in his own model of identity construction, as we will see in later chapters, the self emerges through a discursive process of constant interaction that is always fluid and flexible. Rather, Murakami would argue that the "something else" that has replaced this flexible, organic identity is altogether too stable, too fixed, a ready-made, yet artificial substitute identity (as consumer, as worker bee) in Japan's rapid capitalist state.

To return to my initial statement, then, Murakami's utilization, and subsequent subversion, of the literary formula is a gesture intended to raise the issue of identity, both literary and individual. It is, I think, extremely important that we distinguish in cases such as these the method from its intended purpose as far as possible, because in the end Murakami's purpose in creating formulaic literature is precisely the opposite of what Cawelti (correctly) identifies as conventional. Murakami's agenda, as the above analyses clearly demonstrate, is not to reaffirm the dominant ideology, but to expose it as an intrusive force imposed on the individual.

It is also crucial that we go a step beyond the inherent scope and limitation of Cawelti's structuralist model above, for his purpose finally is only marginally separated from the modernist gesture of separating "high" and "low" forms of culture. That is to say, while Cawelti employs terminology that does effectively eliminate loaded binaries such as "high v. low," and the even more charged "serious v. popular," his own reliance on "mimetic v. formulaic" reveals his reluctance to part with the binary in the end. The term "mimetic" for Cawelti is virtually synonymous with "inventive," and despite his efforts to eliminate implicit value judgment from his new system of classifying fiction, in the end the modernist tendency to privilege the inventive ("art") over the formulaic ("pop") is never quite eliminated from his argument.

The present analysis suggests, on the other hand, that Murakami himself has no particular interest in the subversion of the high-low binary for its own sake, for his approach to literature is not aesthetic but political. In this regard, the element of the formula that most interests Murakami is that of the fantasy, for therein he is able to reveal one of the more striking features of contemporary Japan: that "reality" and "fantasy" are *no longer distinct*.

What, after all, is the literary formula all about? It is about predictability, unproblematic realities, and homogeneity within genres and subgenres. And, to state the obvious, the formulaic novel is popular with mass audiences because it is easy to handle.

Having said this, let me comment briefly on the "real" world that Murakami (only partially) invents in the three novels above. Aside from their reliance on formula, what links them together? The answer is that all portray a dominant social ideology of control, of materialism, of desire and easy gratification. All portray societies of extraordinary wealth and easy—yet meaningless—pleasures, operated by obscure organs of state power. And yet, all give the impression of the state's innate hostility to the heterogeneous subject, the cognizant, rational individual. It is against the temptation to participate in, or collaborate with, this social ideology of state control, materialism, and pleasure-seeking that the protagonists in these novels struggle. At every step, it seems, they are encouraged to give in to their various temptations. In this sense the state seems to acquire an almost demonic quality, the evil tempting the pure.

What, for instance, does the world of the sheep offer to Rat? It offers a life of perfect comfort, somnambulant ease, a mindless, utopian dream world with neither pain nor memory. It also offers Rat a first-hand look—passively, of course—at the world of power politics. It offers things "too wonderful for someone like me" (*MHZ* 2:355; *WSC* 283), as the apparition of Rat phrases it at the end of *A Wild Sheep Chase*. And in return?

The sheep demanded nothing less than Rat's memories, his experiential self, his subjectivity, his mind, and his soul.

The same is offered to the protagonist of the end of the world, whose initiation into this world of mindless bliss is symbolically carried out in the removal of his shadow, representing his inner self. In exchange he is offered a life of eternal peace—but also eternal obedience!—a life without thought, will, or pain.

Even the protagonist of *Norwegian Wood* is offered a choice of this type, though one presented not in the metaphysical terms of mind or soul, but of pure physical pleasure—sex. What, we may ask, do characters like Midori and Nagasawa really represent, except easy physical gratification without consequences, a virtual relationship in which commitment is superseded by pure desire? On the other side of this equation stand Naoko and Reiko, both of whom, in their attendant emotional and physical impairments, represent severe challenges to the protagonist but, spiritually and emotionally, potentially commensurate rewards as well. Unfortunately, as is usually the case in Murakami fiction, the protagonist comes to understand this too late, and at novel's end he stands alone in a phone booth, uncertain of where or who he is. The tragedy of this novel is not merely Naoko's death, but also the eradication of the protagonist's identity. The loss of Naoko represents his last hope of meaningful understanding with another person. It is an apocalyptic message that becomes central in other, later works as well—most notably, *South of the Border, West of the Sun*, and *The Wind-Up Bird Chronicle*.

I began this book with the assertion that Murakami's popularity and importance as a writer are grounded in the same feature of his work: a constant, acute awareness of the precarious place of the individual in contemporary Japan. This much is borne out in the analysis above, a reading of three of Murakami's novels that suggests the systematic eradication of the individual identity in Japan in favor of a collective, state-controlled identity. However, I do not, nor does Murakami, suggest that the state appropriates the identities of its individual members without compensation. Its intervention, rather, is more subtle—what Hidaka Rokurō (1984) has termed "induced integration"—the gradual absorption of the individual into the system of consumerism. As he goes on to note, however, this "integration"—what Murakami presents as the offer of participation in the system—is rarely presented in dictatorial terms. "Mass control is accomplished not by hard but by soft methods; it is not one-dimensional but many-sided and many-shaped" (Hidaka 1984, 90). He goes on to note that "[t]he mass of people are cocooned by a ready-made livelihood, a ready-made culture, and ready-made education. This ready-made quality is not felt to be disagreeable. There is no sense of compulsion in it" (91). At the same time, however, even Hidaka describes a sinister element at work in the removal of opposition to the system, one extraordinarily consonant with Murakami's depiction of the Japanese state above: "Anyone who voices an objection to the system of control," writes Hidaka, "either of the society or of the workplace, is shunted off the rails of profit enjoyment, either openly or by covert means. Such people are always a minority. The harsh expulsion of a minority acts as a warning to others" (Hidaka 1984, 92). This is eerily reminiscent of the "Man in Black's" warning that "'If I chose to, I could put you out of business for good. Then what kind of a 'journalist' would you end up?'" (*MHZ* 2:144; *WSC* 109). This, according to the protagonist's partner, is what actually happened to one hapless journalist, whose professional life ended. "'We're a pretty small community in the mass media, and he was a good example. It was like a skull at the entrance to an African village'" (*MHZ* 2:83; WSC 57).

Such cases would be, of course, extreme; as Hidaka's comments suggest, participation in the Japanese system is generally seen as agreeable, even desirable. But my readings above suggest an increasingly rigid social codification that encourages members of Japanese society to identify themselves with desires that are manipulated in such a way as to drive the economy. In an era of intense third-world competition in the area of manufactured goods abroad and near-saturation of goods at home, this economy is increasingly dependent on images, manufactured fetish items, for its continued survival.

It may be worthwhile to ask, extreme examples aside, whether this is necessarily a bad thing? Is it so terrible to provide society with what it seems to desire? Do people, on the whole, truly know what they want? And finally, one might ask whether this economy of desire and gratification is the result of a collusive effort in Japanese political, industrial, and media circles, as Karel van Wolferen has claimed (Althusser says the same of all industrialized states), or is it simply the inevitable result of a postindustrial society that has nothing left to manufacture?

I will return to this theme in the chapters below on desire, identity, and mass culture, which will offer an opportunity to look not only at the structure of desire itself, but also at the relationship between desire, subjectivity, the unconscious, and mass culture. For the present it will suffice to reiterate that while a close analysis of Murakami's methodology as a writer of fiction proves essential in understanding the underlying subtext he conceals, it should not be permitted to overshadow the significance of the subliminal political gestures present throughout his work. This will become particularly clear in the final chapter of this book, in which I will discuss the author's approach to the historical past, and to the politics of representing that past.

Chapter Two

Metonymy, Magic Realism, and the Opening of the "Other"

Psychology thus became a science lacking its main subject matter, the soul.

—Erich Fromm, *Psychoanalysis and Religion*

In the previous chapter I discussed some of the structural idiosyncrasies of Murakami's fiction and how they related to politically charged issues of identity, subjectivity, and ideology. In this chapter I would like to turn to a more ontological concern, that of the "real" and the "unreal," and the author's use of the paranormal, the intrusion of the supernatural on otherwise normal worlds. I shall also discuss the relationship between self/identity and the state, particularly in terms of subject formation via nationalism and national goals. The link between this and the other chapters is thus identity, but as with the structural use of formula, the author's focus in the interrogation of identity remains deeply subjective and individual.

As noted above, since the beginning of his career Murakami's role in the Japanese literary world has been simultaneously that of a widely read national and international writer of popular fiction, and as a spokesman for a generation that lost (or surrendered) its identity in the aftermath of the political activity of the 1950s and 1960s. With a style that was, particularly in his first works, cool and detached, yet also confused, melancholy, and nostalgic, his was the right voice for a generation grown disillusioned with political struggles that turned to naught. There was little in his first book, *Hear the Wind Sing*, that reached out and grabbed the reader in the way that, say, Murakami Ryū had reached out and grabbed readers three years earlier with his own Gunzō Prize-winning debut, *Kagirinaku tōmei ni chikai burū* (1976; translated as Almost Transparent Blue). In sharp contrast with that work, filled with the rage of an impotent counter-culture determined to persist in its experiments with sex, drugs, and violence, *Hear the Wind Sing* was almost poetic in its understatement. Yet its quiet melancholy and abstract references to the failure of Zenkyōtō, chiefly through the movements of "Rat," seem to have suited audiences and critics alike in 1979. One is struck not so much by the underlying anger of Rat as by the sheer impotence of the protagonist to quell his disillusionment with the end of the 1960s. This seems to have captured the mood of Murakami's contemporaries better than the raw, livid anger of Ryū.

Few readers in 1979 needed reminding that, less than ten years before, Japan's long-standing political struggle in the postwar era between students/labor and government/management ceased. The reason for this cessation is not difficult to see: by 1970 the unifying causes of this struggle began to be eliminated one by one: the U.S.-Japan Security Treaty (Anzen Hoshō Yoyaku, known as AMPO for short), probably the most fiercely contested of the issues, was settled (unilaterally) in 1970; Richard Nixon's peace initiative with the People's Republic of China in 1971 began to thaw the dangerously confrontational situation on both sides, between which Japan had been precariously positioned; Okinawa was returned to Japanese sovereignty in 1972; U.S. troop withdrawals from Vietnam began around the same time, and the war ended in 1975. At home, the Japanese economy was in recession but would shortly embark on its now famous "bubble" growth period, ushering in a level of affluence unseen even in the era of "rapid growth" (1955–73). In short, during the period from 1970 to 1979, in which Murakami sets his early works, ordinary Japanese grew decidedly less concerned with politics and more determined to share in the wealth and affluence of their country. As John W. Dower (1992) writes,

> By 1972 the Left thus had lost hold of many of its most evocative peace issues: U.S. bases in Japan, the Security Treaty, nuclear weapons, arms production, Okinawa, and China. A year later, with the armistice in Vietnam, the last great cause that had provided a modicum of common purpose among the opposition was removed. The average citizen turned inward, to bask in Japan's new international affluence as an economic power and become consumed by material pursuits, exemplified in such mass-media slogans as "My Home-ism" and "My Car-ism." (Dower 1992, 27)

Ironically, this very affluence, combined with a marked decline in political tensions both internal and external, may have posed (indeed, may still pose) the most serious threat to the development of a sense of self or individuality in contemporary Japan. At least, this is the impression one has from reading the literature of Murakami Haruki, who is concerned less with the specific issues of the counterculture movements than with the sense of identity and subjectivity they provided to their participants. The implicit question throughout Murakami's literature has always been: how are Japanese of Murakami's generation and beyond to define themselves as individuals in the post-counterculture era?

It is important to understand this as a generation-specific problem. Murakami belongs to the leading edge of the first generation to be born in the postwar period, without memories of hardship in the Second World War or participation in the reconstruction of Japan following it. Unlike the previous generation, which understood hunger and deprivation and could define itself in terms of affluence via its own participation in the efforts of the rapid growth era, Murakami's generation, not unlike the generation in the United States that reached maturity in the 1950s, did not understand affluence as a goal in itself, and thus could not identify itself in those terms.

One significant reason, then, that the student movements—the concept of counterculture in general—found such favor with young people in postwar Japan and the United States was that it provided a means of self-identification, a connection with something positive and dynamic. Writing of the discontent of his own generation in the United States, Todd Gitlin points out that affluence in postwar America amounted to crawling out from the shadow of the Depression and the deprivations of the Second World War. But this is also precisely what engendered the famous "generation gap" of the 1950s and 1960s:

> Where the parental generation was scourged by memories of the Depression, the children of this middle class in the late Forties and Fifties were raised to take affluence for granted. The breadwinners were acutely aware of how hard they had worked to afford the picture window, the lawn, the car, the Lionel trains; and since they could, most of them, remember a time when the sweat of their brow availed them little, they were flooded with relief and gratitude, and expected their children to feel the same. (Gitlin 1987, 17)

Could one not say the same of the generation—Murakami's generation—that grew up in the relative affluence of rapid growth, without having known the hardships of the Second World War and the immediate postwar years? Murakami was three years old when the occupation ended and seven when the postwar period was declared "over" in a 1956 white paper published by the Economic Planning Agency, a declaration that coincided roughly with the beginning of rapid growth; he was raised in Ashiya, a notoriously affluent part of the Kobe area (he himself refers to it as a "yuppie" zone). By the time Murakami and his contemporaries were reaching their teens, affluence was less a distant dream than a customary way of life, and no doubt life has grown more comfortable for every succeeding generation in Japan since the end of the Second World War. And yet, an awareness remains, echoed also in Gitlin's comments above, that the sense of identity provided through an easy, affluent culture is a bestowed identity, not one created through the real challenges of survival.

THE STATE AND IDENTITY

Historically there is much truth in this. Even a superficial look at the history of the postwar, and more importantly, the post-postwar (after 1970) reveals that there has been an inexorable shift toward a social ideology devoted solely (or nearly so) to economic concerns, in which identity formation, such as it exists at all, is grounded mainly in the extent and nature of one's participation in contemporary Japanese consumerism.

Much of the literature on Japan's fate as an economic superpower supports this thesis. Andrew Barshay's (1988) analysis of the relationship between the intellectual and the state, for instance, argues that, beginning in the 1960s and continuing through the end of the "rapid growth" period, the Japanese public was gradually transformed, presumably through attractive and successful economic programs such as "rapid growth" and the "income doubling" plan of 1961–70, into an entity susceptible to a high level of control by the state. "Over this same time period—one of 'miraculous' economic growth at home and vast expansion of Japanese interests overseas—the 'public' in Japan came to represent an *object* to be administered rather than a self-conscious social entity" (Barshay 1988, 231). Similarly, Hidaka Rokurō (1984, 69) argues that whatever sense of political oppositionalism the Japanese may have felt in the 1950s and 1960s was gradually defused by "high economic growth and the concomitant change in life styles," leading to the absorption of oppositional energy into the mainstream of culture, resulting in the convergence of the right and left into a single line. Thus, the real political "crisis" in Japanese politics, Hidaka claims, "is the crisis of the continuing gradual self-destruction of both conservative and reformist forces as autonomous entities" (34). In other words, the dialectical model of political (or historical) progression is disrupted by the lack of real difference between mainstream and opposition. David Williams (1994, 29–35), on the other hand, characterizes Japanese society in terms of a "center" consisting of the bureaucracy, the Liberal Democratic Party, and the major industrial entities, and a "periphery" made up of various (chiefly left-wing) opposition groups, including both political parties and industrial forces not yet admitted to Japan's "elite." Nevertheless, his analysis suggests that this structure does not allow for particularly active political or social debate in Japan and that the "opposition" forces are largely ineffectual against the center.

In this context of at least apparently deepening political homogeneity, we also confront the impact of a heavily regulated Japanese school system on the formation of identity. Williams argues that the sheer continuity of a uniform system, generation to generation, has all but ensured a high degree of conformity in society. "Families and the mass media have come to reinforce the Japanese sense of nationalist identity because parents and opinion leaders have passed through the same school room" (1994, 8). Journalist Honda Katsuichi scornfully refers to this phenomenon as the "tadpole society," blaming the lack of original thought in Japan on the emphasis in the Japanese school system on memorization rather than on critical reasoning. "In order to create a tadpole society," writes Honda, "the Ministry of Education defines education as regurgitation. The Ministry of Education decides what is good to think, while denigrating individual opinion. Individuality is punished, and no one is encouraged to think on one's own" (Honda 1993, 129). Hidaka argues similarly, claiming that students of today are passive, uninterested, and politically apathetic (1984, 151). Political apathy is, of course, one of the most defining characteristics of contemporary postindustrial societies, and Japan is no exception. Takagi Masayuki blames this on the economic hardships of today's students, who face increasing pressures to succeed, and greater competition from their peers for smaller advantages. Thus, he argues, students no longer have the time or resources to expend on idealistic pursuits like political activism (1985, 205).

The issue returns again and again to the economic. Emphasis on economics is, of course, nothing new in Japan, certainly not a product of only the past thirty years. On the other hand, it could be stated that in no other period in the history of modern Japan has there been so single-minded an emphasis on economics than during the postwar, and especially the last thirty years. Hidaka argues that Japanese society today is devoted to a "philosophy of putting economic considerations before all else" (1984, 74), and he is deeply disturbed by the implications of a state devoted solely to the advancement of business interests.

> Just as support for a free market economic system without
> moral principles becomes an ideology justifying the unhindered
> pursuit of profit, so support for a democratic system in which the
> sense of the people as rulers is abandoned becomes a materialis-
> tically oriented ideology justifying only an increase in creature
> comforts and the material standard of living. Business has striven
> to provide a section of the people with democracy, but it has been
> a democracy "by and for business," not "by and for the people."
> And, to a certain extent, it has succeeded. (Hidaka 1984, 27)

But how is Japan of the past thirty years different from Japan of
the prewar/war years (1868–1945), or that of the postwar (1945–70)?
Without wishing to overgeneralize, I would argue that the main issue is that
of goal orientation—national goals prior to the Second World War, and a
mix of national and personal goals in the postwar era.

Modern Japan, until its defeat at the hands of the Allies in 1945,
could be called a society deeply devoted to national goals. And while these
goals obviously changed somewhat as the nation developed, it is reasonable
to say that at the center of prewar state ideology lay the perceived need to
form a unitary national polity of loyal, obedient imperial subjects whose
first priority would also be the preservation and improvement of the state,
embodied conveniently in the person of the emperor himself. The system
developed in the Meiji period to achieve this goal was, Williams argues,
necessarily authoritarian and antiliberal due to the historical tendency in
Japanese politics, clearly visible in the Tokugawa system, toward a "poly-
centric" power structure (1994, 24). "Only a strong state had any chance
of overcoming the fractured nature of Japanese politics," writes Williams.
"Liberalism was a virtue that nationalists believed Japan could not afford.
The propagandizing schoolroom, the episodes of police repression, and the
tireless pursuit of elite consensus are all part of this effort" (25). Naturally,
the notion of a "strong nation" rested on the support of the general popu-
lace—to be constructed out of a peasant class that traditionally had *not*
participated much in politics—and for this reason, "[t]he struggle to transform an apolitical peasantry into a modern nationalist-minded population
capable of sustaining state goals has stood at the heart of the Japanese
programme of national-building" (8).

This project of building a strong, modern state was largely sustained until the successful conclusion of the Russo-Japanese War (1904–
5), at which point, as Oka Yoshitake claims, much of the focus and unity of
national spirit that had marked the first three and a half decades of the
Meiji era dissipated (1982, 197–225). Insofar as the major goals of early

and mid-Meiji Japan were achieved with the end of the Russo-Japanese War,[1] clearly Japanese society needed something new with which to exhort its people to continue their support for the state.

> Also central to the period following the Russo-Japanese war was a debate among the so-called opinion leaders concerning national goals. The goal of national independence had been substantially achieved as a result of victory over Russia, so it was believed essential that a new national goal be placed before the people, particularly the young. (Oka 1982, 211)

Oka goes on to characterize the final years of Meiji through the early years of the Taishō period as one of transition, in which a variety of new national goals for Japan were debated. His argument is framed in terms of a generational disparity, the powerful sense of a gap between older Japanese of the time, particularly those old enough to remember the early years of Meiji, and younger Japanese who had grown up in the comparative comfort of the later years. This is particularly helpful to the present discussion, because shortly I will apply the same kind of analysis to the Japanese postwar period. Oka's analysis takes into account particularly the experiences of older Japanese, who understood themselves as Meiji subjects in a sense that was somewhat different from how their younger countrymen saw themselves. Castigating youth for its pursuit of what they saw as selfish goals, older Japanese claimed that their patriotism and selflessness had grown out of anxieties for the well-being of the state in its early years.

> Perhaps . . . anyone who had spent his or her youth sometime between the pre-Restoration era and the first decade of the Meiji period (1868–1877) had been dominated by a sense of nation (*kokkakan*) rather than a sense of self (*kojinkan*). The youths of the present, however, were by and large concerned only with pursuing their personal interests, and only a tiny minority aspired to relate themselves in any way to the fortunes of the state. It did not auger well for the country. (Oka 1982, 209)

Young Japanese of the early twentieth century, then, appear to have some of the sense of selfism and political disinterest that the youth of today

---

1. Oka lists the major goals of the early and mid-Meiji period as "treaty revision, solution to the Korean problem, establishment of constitutional government, and the induction of Western civilization" (1982, 214).

have, though Oka rightly notes that their pursuit of selfism was in itself a form of political expression, a new drive to develop genuine individualism, and "independence in 'the true sense of the word'" (Oka 1982, 212). This new kind of thinking unquestionably helped to pave the way for the era of so-called "Taishō democracy" that began with the end of the First World War in 1918, was weakened by radicalism that developed out of rural poverty (Williams 1994, 135), and ended with the invasion of Manchuria in 1931. This led, as is well known, to the beginning of what the Japanese term the "Fifteen Year War," during which the Japanese people were probably more intensely aware of their identity as Japanese than at any time since the Russo-Japanese War, though one can but wonder if it was worth the price paid.

My reason for presenting these brief observations on Japanese prewar identity is to make the point that Japan in the prewar period was defined by a strong sense of national goals, and that government policy stressed the inclusion, the maximal participation, of the population at large in achieving these goals. It stressed a program of "taking a largely apolitical peasant population and turning them into nationalist-minded soldiers, savings-minded housewives and patriotic schoolchildren, all willing in spirit to make sacrifices for the nation" (Williams 1994, 26). And to a very large degree these efforts were successful. As such, Japanese who lived through the Meiji, Taishō, and early Shōwa years could claim at the very least some sense of identity in terms of their participation in the national goals of the state—or their resistance to them, as the case may be.

Similar arguments can be made for the first two and a half decades that followed the end of the Second World War. In the wake of Japan's defeat the obstacles to be overcome in pursuit of reconstruction and economic recovery were awesome, both in the physical and the philosophical sense. Issues that stood at the forefront of Japanese intellectual discussions included questions of war responsibility (argued out particularly among writers), the redefinition of Japanese subjectivity (*shutaisei*), the merits and risks of the imperial system, and the elimination of militarism and totalitarianism. These issues also impacted the practical aspects of the recovery, of course, but Japan's survival in the postwar world depended initially on the swift repair of its economy, helped along by loans and other aid from the United States (Williams 1994, 136), and the establishment of a moderate, democratically oriented government to replace the militarist one.

As has been frequently noted by historians, the early policies of the U.S.-led Allied Occupation supported many of these reconstruction goals. A number of those who had led Japan's militarist government were executed or imprisoned for war crimes,[2] and a new Constitution, largely drafted by Douglas MacArthur and his staff, was announced in 1947. The Japan Communist Party (JCP) enjoyed a brief resurgence in the first two years of the postwar, and many assumed that the democratization of Japan would be led by the left, possibly even the extreme left.[3]

Yet the Occupation's "reverse course" toward the right, beginning with the issuance of arrest warrants by MacArthur's headquarters for twenty-four leading members of the JCP in 1948, led to rather different consequences for Japan, both politically and socially. While the shift in policy, responding to rising concerns about the spread of international Communism, was probably inevitable, the move shocked many Japanese intellectuals, particularly because it included the rehabilitation of former war criminals. Nevertheless, the "reverse course" of the Occupation is probably one of the more overstated events in modern Japanese historical discourse; in hindsight it seems clear that even in 1945 the Occupation authorities sought to create a democratic system in Japan similar to that of the United States, along with a free market economy to support it (see Koschmann 1996, 15). The more or less unilateral decision by MacArthur to preserve the imperial house, albeit as a symbolic entity, also ensured that Japan's postwar "transformation" would not be so great as some had come to expect.[4]

Indeed, a number of key commentators have argued in recent years that postwar Japan turned out not to be so different from prewar Japan after all (Hidaka 1984; Honda 1993; Williams 1994). Aside from discred-

2. A good many others were released only two days after the executions of Hideki Tōjō and six others. Among those released were Kishi Nobusuke, who later became Prime Minister, Kodama Yoshio, eventually implicated in the Lockheed scandal in 1976, and Abe Genki, once involved with the *tokkō*, or "thought police" of the war years. Hidaka's reading of the executions is that they were symbolic: "The execution of Tōjō and the other war criminals was simply a symbolic ritual to put the war behind us" (1984, 20). See Hidaka 1984, 19-22. See also Bailey 1996, 134.
3. For a detailed discussion of the movements of the left in the early postwar years, particularly their attempts to define Japanese subjectivity, see Koschmann 1996.
4. As Koschmann points out, the preservation of the emperor even as a symbolic part of the Japanese state precluded the possibility of a true democratic revolution in Japan. He refers to Claude Lefort's 1986 analysis of the structure of democratic movements, in which Lefort argues that the "body politic" (in Japanese, *kokutai*) must rid itself of its "head"—i.e., the monarch—before it can liberate itself and assume the control of a true democracy. However, as Koschmann points out, "In Japan . . . the 'king' (Emperor Hirohito) was not 'decapitated' symbolically or actually. . . . As a result, some Japanese philosophers such as Watsuji Tetsurō could argue in the early postwar that the 'democratic revolution' in the form of SCAP's reforms would not, in itself, change the 'national body' (*kokutai*) at all" (1996, 12).

iting and effectively outlawing militarism and transforming the imperial system into a symbol of national unity, much of Japan's prewar economic and political structure remained in place. The economic cartels of the prewar and war years, known as *zaibatsu*, were dismantled, at least partially, but within a decade powerful new industrial coalitions known as *keiretsu* had replaced them, and more importantly, had allied themselves closely to political and bureaucratic circles in order to assist in policy decision-making. This, too, in the context of Washington's persistent hostility to the left following the Communist victory in China and the onset of the Korean War, seems to have been acceptable to the U.S. policymakers. "By 1955, conservative politicians, the higher economic bureaucracy and the business elite of the country's principal industrial groupings (*keiretsu*) had coalesced into a power establishment capable of seeing off the left-wing opposition as well as the country's large but politically ineffective labour unions, while managing Japan's new strategic alliance with the United States" (Williams 1994, 28).

It is this "coalition" that emerges only a few years after the Occupation lifted to dominate Japanese political and social policy, maintain the economy, and ensure Japan's continued alliance with the Western bloc. This is the "establishment" that planned and executed the highly successful "income doubling plan" of 1961–70, while overseeing the period of "rapid growth." It was also responsible for pushing through the U.S.-Japan Security Treaty in 1960, and again in 1970. In general terms, there is no denying the formidable strength of such an entity to withstand the pressures of the many political parties and protest groups that formed to challenge its authority from the 1950s through the 1980s. Part of its success, of course, lies in the highly subtle nature of its power structure—one whose effectiveness, according to Williams (1994, 36–42), lies in its rare ability to make a complex bureaucracy operate smoothly while its elusiveness (hence its frequent unaccountability) stems from the fact that its power is spread among both government and nongovernment agencies (see Williams 1994; Wolferen 1985).

At the same time, the so-called establishment, this power system, survives because it provides something to the Japanese people that left-wing ideologues have consistently failed to offer: a comfortable life through participation in the great consumerist machine that is the Japanese domestic economy. Even Hidaka (rather grudgingly) admits that the commodities available in Japan today are not only nice to have, but even necessities. Furthermore, he concedes, Japanese are not coerced into purchasing these things, but willingly seek them out. "So it is not merely a matter of the lives of the masses being manipulated by politicians and their politics, since the lives of the masses actually regulate certain aspects of politics" (Hidaka 1984, 92). At the same time, he notes a gradual shift in the attitude of the Japanese masses toward a phenomenon he terms "economism," signifying here not the primacy of economics in state policy, but in the daily lives and mindsets of ordinary Japanese. "Economism" is a form of behavior, "a situation in which the tendency to give priority to economic values strikes deeply into the individual consciousness of each citizen and affects his daily lifestyle" (71). Moreover, he concludes, "economist" behavior is not merely encouraged; it is required as a prerequisite for true acceptance as a member of society.

> In some rural areas it has become the common practice to shower the bride with all the latest household electrical appliances and a lavish wardrobe costing millions of yen. This behavior cannot be understood simply in terms of the rising standard of living. It constitutes a ritual incorporation of the individual into the society rules by these conventions. It is a ritual of passage by which one allows oneself to be controlled. (Hidaka 1984, 28–29)

The average Japanese, then, is drawn into the system of consumerism, becomes used to a certain level of participation, and strives to increase his or her level of participation as a means of evaluating his or her "growth" within that system. This is the nature of the "controlled society" (*kanri shakai*) as Hidaka conceives of it. It is also an apt description of the basic workings of the "symbolic" in contemporary Japan, the mechanism by which individuals are drawn in as participants in the rules of the dominant social ideology. As will be described at greater length in chapter three, control over individual desire is relinquished to the symbolic in return for validation— positive valuation—by the symbolic on *its* terms, in this case, the terms of consumption. Given this willingness to be controlled, contemporary Japan's social and political system cannot be called totalitarian, nor even authoritarian; rather, it is a case of control over passivized subjects, what Hidaka terms "induced integration" (participation); "it is characterized by induced integration rather than oppressive control. But the path that people are induced to follow is surprisingly narrow, and the sense of loss of purpose is spreading, especially among young people, as they are deprived of opportunities for self-expression and self-fulfillment" (Hidaka 1984, 9).

As Oka does in his discussion of late Meiji/early Taishō politics, I wish to look briefly at the implications of Hidaka's special concern for the young here. Why should the young be an object of greater concern than their elders? I would argue, as Oka does, that the answer is at least partly generational. In short, there is a significant gap in experience between those old enough to remember the hardships of the Second World War and its immediate aftermath, and those who grew up in the comparatively affluent "rapid growth" era. Intellectuals such as Maruyama Masao and Ōe Kenzaburō were formed by their experiences in the war, and by their direct engagement with the major issues that emerged in the postwar. In dialectical terms one might say the intellectual confrontations of the 1950s and 1960s forced them to contemplate and establish a clear sense of where they stood in the face of those issues. And if they did not identify with the goals of the postwar state or the methods employed to meet those goals, then they identified with their resistance. Briefly put, their own subjectivity was constructed via the opportunities for intellectual and ideological engagement in the postwar, while those opportunities were in turn born out of the need and opportunity to reform and reconstruct Japan from the ground up.

These opportunities did not exist in quite the same way for younger Japanese who grew up in affluence and were presented with few or no major national goals by which they might develop their own sense of identity. Indeed, that this kind of introspection was missing from those born after the war is evident in the emergence in 1967–68 of the violent Zenkyōtō (Unified Student Struggles) movement. By the time Murakami entered Waseda University in 1968, the unity of purpose and clarity of ideology that had marked previous student movements such as the longstanding Zengakuren (Zen Nippon Gakusei Jichikai Sōrengō, or "National Federation of Students' Self-Government Associations") were all but lost. Whereas Zengakuren—which dated all the way back to May 1946, and had even deeper roots in the aftermath of the First World War and the Russian revolution of 1917—maintained a clear resistance to international problems like the Vietnam war, continued U.S. occupation of Okinawa and the proliferation of nuclear weapons, Zenkyōtō by contrast seemed to exist in opposition to organization itself. Rejecting the notion of "student self-governments" that stood at the heart of Zengakuren ideology, Zenkyōtō "completely lacked any guiding ideology; built upon emotional energy, it lacked from the very beginning the kind of systematized thinking that might have extended its life" (Takagi 1985, 126). Zenkyōtō's disenchantment with the more ideological (and more peacefully conducted) Zengakuren is also evident in the violence of its tactics, which took the form of riots, building takeovers, hostage taking, and mass university shutdowns. As Takagi writes, "Rather than terms like 'struggle' (*tōsō*) it is more fitting to apply words like 'rebellion' (*hangyaku*) to the Zenkyōtō movement" (1985, 110).

The emotional intensity of Zenkyōtō, along with the undisciplined nature of its tactics, bespeaks the youth—and commensurate lack of experience—of its participants, and goes far to explain the movement's short life. Yet I think it is important to understand the Zenkyōtō period as a reaction against a movement that had lost its connectivity with younger Japanese. If Zengakuren was born out of a complex mixture of the idealism, the hardship, and the goal orientation of the early postwar, then Zenkyōtō was an expression of the frustration of younger people who no longer had faith in the potential of movements like Zengakuren to succeed. In short, while it is possible to read Zenkyōtō as an immature offshoot—even a sequel—to Zengakuren, it is probably more accurate to view it as the *assassination* of Zengakuren, a rebellion directed toward the right, but equally targeted on the left. A kind of mass tantrum, Zenkyōtō despised the right for having created the system, and the left for failing to bring it down.

It is equally important, however, to understand the Zenkyōtō activists' internal motivation, subliminally, at least, in terms of identity formation. Whereas their elders had participated in a positive movement with concrete social and political goals, responding to their own memories and experiences, Zenkyōtō activists sought to do something that was strictly their own, even if it did, in a sense, amount to the collective suicide of political activism among young people in Japan.

The failure of Zengakuren—the aftermath of Zenkyōtō—led finally to the quiet restoration of order through the same inexorable economic machine that had been operating throughout the "rapid growth" period, unhindered by student radicalism. Japanese society of this post-Zenkyōtō period, if not unitary, was certainly one in which economics took almost complete precedence, while political opposition on the left, though never disappearing altogether, turned considerably more moderate and, according to Honda (1993), began a gradual shift toward the political center that culminated in the 1980s. The result of this loss of tension, the lack of political opposition, as noted above, has been a "controlled" society in which consumerism has replaced opposing political ideologies. As noted above, it is a society that affords its members a high standard of living but maintains control of mass desire through control of education, the mass media, and industrial production. As such, contemporary Japanese have the opportunity to "choose" their lifestyle, but their selections—expressions of their desire—are always driven down predetermined channels.

Murakami writes, then, from the perspective of a generation gap, arguing that the social grounding of his generation's identity—and that of generations to come—was reduced after the 1960s to mindless consumerism, a system lacking the benefits of political opposition, or even national goals extending beyond the scope of greater economic profits. For young Japanese of the late 1960s and early 1970s, the Zenkyōtō movement provided a means of self-expression not necessarily offered by the easy comfort of home life and possessions. It is little wonder, then, that the end of the movement should have generated so severe an identity crisis among Japanese of Murakami's age and younger, particularly when the highly charged political movement was simply replaced with a more intensive consumer capitalism. Consumers had been "induced," to use Hidaka's term, into purchasing washing machines in the 1950s, color televisions in the 1960s, and larger automobiles in the 1970s. In the 1980s it was computers, video games, VCRs, and home entertainment systems. The products changed with the technology, but the game was always the same. Tanaka Yasuo's 1980 novel *Somehow, Crystal* (Nantonaku, kurisutaru), which celebrated—and at the same time poked fun at—the plethora of consumer goods available in contemporary Tokyo, also made clear the fact that consumerism was now the symbol of culture in Japan. A decade later, in a film intended to show various layers of Japanese cultural ideology, Donald Richie described Tokyo in the 1980s as "consumerism gone wild" (see Kolker and Alvarez 1991).

It is, then, perhaps only natural that Murakami Haruki, with his quiet, detached assertion that Japanese are losing their capacity to know or understand themselves, should have struck so resonant a note with his readers in 1979. As I noted earlier, he spoke initially to his own generation in *Hear the Wind Sing*, which focuses on an eighteen-day period, from August 8 to August 26, 1970, hinting at the depressing prospect of returning to the universities in the autumn of that year, *after* the conclusion of AMPO 1970.

And yet, as the intervening years have demonstrated, Murakami's fiction also speaks to a younger generation of readers, one that must have sensed that even as Murakami described his own struggle to understand who he was in the fall of 1970, he also described their own similar struggles at the end of the decade. From the start Murakami has shown contemporary readers their own anonymous faces in the mirror.

THE NAMELESS, FACELESS NARRATOR

To an extent, Murakami achieves this in the nondescript, detached, nameless narrator through whom he normally tells his story. Indeed, it was not until more than ten years into his career that Murakami gave his narrator a definite name at all, and most supporting characters, when named, were

called something unconventional, often something derived from their function. The characters in *Hear the Wind Sing*, for instance, are "Rat," "the
Woman Missing a Finger," a Chinese bartender called "J," and "Boku." All
of the characters have something to offer the narrative, but none of them
shows much character development. In *Pinball, 1973* (1973-nen no pinbōru,
1980), the sequel to *Hear the Wind Sing*, one meets twin sisters who have
no names, and a pinball machine that talks. *A Wild Sheep Chase*, as we
have seen, contains even more bizarre types: the hero's clairvoyant girlfriend, known as "the Girl," sometimes "the Girl with the Ears," "the Boss,"
"the Man in Black," "the Sheep Professor," "the Sheepman" and so forth.
In *Dance Dance Dance* (1988) Murakami plays with his own name, and
calls one of his characters "Makimura Hiraku;" another is named Gotanda,
whose name is recognizable to Japanese readers, at least, as one of the more
affluent areas of Tokyo. Excepting "Naoko," a girlfriend who turns up early
in Murakami's literature and will be discussed at length below, it was not
until *Norwegian Wood* that the author gave his characters names that might
be considered conventional.

Why should this be? Again, the answer is related to identity. Who
is the narrator of *Hear the Wind Sing*, or of *Pinball, 1973*, now that the
fervor of the 1960s is over? Where is his unique individuality? What does it
look like? How can it be seen, touched, used to express the self? Murakami's
implicit question is, always, how can the first-person protagonist forge connections with another (conscious or unconscious) and thereby identify himself, prove to himself that he exists? This is the question that is explored
from the author's earliest works to the most recent.

MAGICAL REALISM AND THE UNCONSCIOUS

To speak of seeing or touching the "core identity" of the individual, of
course, is to suggest a metaphysical process by which the inner mind can be
accessed, and this forms one of the most recognizable trademarks in Murakami literature. In virtually all of his fiction, with the one notable exception of *Norwegian Wood*, a realistic narrative setting is created, then disrupted, sometimes mildly, sometimes violently, by the bizarre or the magical. As Yokoo Kazuhiro puts it, "[Murakami explores] how the world might
or might not change after introducing one tiny vibration into our insignifi-
cant daily lives" (Yokoo 1994, 31–32). It is for this reason that Murakami's
work seems to fall into the general category of "magical realism," though
one must exercise great care in distinguishing Murakami's strain of magical
realism from other more politicized forms of the genre.

In a very simple nutshell, magical realism is what happens when a highly detailed, realistic setting is invaded by something "too strange to believe." It is the underlying assumption that permits Tita to pour her emotions into her cooking in Laura Esquivel's *Like Water for Chocolate* and have her diners experience those emotions as they eat; it is the slight aberration of historical fact that allows Salman Rushdie's Saleem Sinai to claim in *Midnight's Children* that the history of postwar India turns on major events in *his* life; it is the mechanism by which Mikage Sakurai and Tanabe Yūichi eat together in a shared dream in Yoshimoto Banana's *Kitchin* (Kitchen, 1988). It is the mechanism by which Shimada Masahiko brings to life "guardian spirits" who help children connect with one another in *Yumetsukai* (1992; translated as Dream Messenger, 1996), by which the world begins to turn backwards and time goes in reverse in Shimizu Yoshinori's *Guroingu daun* (Growing Down, 1989), and by which a video game world comes to life and begins to claim casualties among Tokyo's children in Itō Seikō's *Nō raifu kingu* (No Life King, 1984). And, more to the point, it is the means by which Murakami Haruki shows his readers two "worlds"— one conscious, the other unconscious—and that permits seamless crossover between them by characters who have become only memories, memories that reemerge from the mind to become new characters again.

As noted above, however, the concept of magical realism bears certain political and cultural specificities that should be addressed before applying the term to Murakami's work. For instance, Alejo Carpentier claims that magical realism is a specifically Latin American idea, one that expresses the natural wonder felt by the people of Latin America toward their land as a "marvelous"—yet real—place (Carpentier 1995). Angel Flores, on the other hand, argues for a more politicized, but equally region-specific definition of magical realism as a postcolonial discourse that rejects traditional Euro-American emphasis on realism and positivism in favor of a worldview that permits the "magical" to coexist with the "real. But Flores wishes to see similarities between magical realism and the surrealism of Kafka, an idea that is useful to us here, because surrealism, especially in its earlier forms, is very much connected with the workings of the unconscious, interventions of the inner mind on the perceptions of the external conscious, the external world. In this sense Murakami's fictional world certainly bears close resemblance to those depicted by the surrealists.[5] Such a notion also

---

5. It is inevitable that some crossover occur between magical realism and surrealism. Faris (1995) argues that the chief distinction between the two is one of interpretive potential and authorial intention: "[I]n contrast to the magical images constructed by Surrealism

helps us to reconnect magical realism via surrealism to its even deeper, anarchistic root, Dadaism, whose nihilistic stance toward Western positivism unquestionably lives on in Latin American magical realist texts. Carpentier's description of the "marvelous" in his term *lo real maravilloso* ("the marvelous real"), on the other hand, is more reminiscent of Russian Formalism, specifically of Viktor Sklovsky's *ostranenie*, or "defamiliarization," in which the author, poet, or dramatist is urged to make the ordinary *extra*ordinary, different, unfamiliar to the reader or audience member (Sklovsky 1991). Carpentier, similarly using terms reminiscent of avantgardism, describes the marvelous as something "amazing because it is strange. Everything strange, everything amazing, everything that eludes established norms is marvelous" (1995, 101).

Others suggest a more fluid definition of magical realism, denying its firm affiliation with any other political or aesthetic theory or system, much the way some have approached postmodernism itself.[6] Luis Leal, for instance, suggests that we view magical realism as a worldview that may appear under numerous circumstances, using numerous methodologies or literary styles. He is suspicious of any attempt to identify the methodology of magical realism exclusively with particular political or artistic purposes.

> Magical realism cannot be identified either with fantastic literature or with psychological literature, or with the surrealist or hermetic literature that [Julio] Ortega describes. . . . Magical realism is, more than anything else, an attitude toward reality that can be expressed in popular or cultured forms, in elaborate or rustic styles, in closed or open structures. . . . In magical realism the writer confronts reality and tries to untangle it. (Leal 1995, 121)

---

out of ordinary objects, which aim to appear virtually unmotivated and thus programmatically resist interpretation, magical realist images, while projecting a similar initial aura of surprising craziness, tend to reveal their motivations—psychological, social, emotional, political—after some scrutiny" ("Scheherezade's Children," 171). We should not neglect the fact, however, that surrealism is, first and foremost, about the unconscious, while many magical realist texts have little or nothing to do with the unconscious, but are rather meant to be read as literal juxtapositionings of the real and magical worlds.

6. Brenda Marshall, for one, strongly denies the determinability of a fixed definition for postmodernism, insisting instead that the postmodern is merely a way of viewing the world. "We begin our definition with 'Postmodernism is . . .' and are already in trouble. We cannot get very far without 'is.' Language lays a trap: it says something must be, always be. Thus, by attempting to define postmodernism, it is given primary ontological status . . ." (1992, 3-4).

Leal's willingness to open up the field, to admit that virtually any form of literature or art may express itself as magical realist, is of some use to this discussion, for one may propose, using Leal's description of magical realism as technique or worldview, that the literature of Murakami Haruki merely borrows the techniques of magical realism without necessarily connecting itself in the regional attachments that Carpentier and Flores would insist upon. In short, Murakami's use of magical realism, while closely linked with the *quest* for identity, is not necessarily involved with the *assertion* of an identity. Put another way, magical realism in Murakami is used as a tool to seek a highly individualized, personal sense of identity in each person, rather than as a rejection of the thinking of one-time colonial powers, or the assertion of a national (cultural) identity based on indigenous beliefs and ideologies.[7]

A similar view comes from Wendy Faris, who argues that magical realism, now identified with postmodernism, particularly in its "juxtaposition of seeming opposites" (Hutcheon 1989, 6), that is, the magical and the real, expands its sphere of influence from the political and cultural into the realm of entertainment. "Magic realist fictions do seem more youthful and popular than their modernist predecessors, in that they often (though not always) cater with unidirectional story lines to our basic desire to hear what happens next. Thus they may be more clearly designed for the entertainment of readers" (Faris 1995, 163).

To be sure, this will help us to understand better Murakami's place not only in Japan, where he stands at the apex of Japanese postmodern literature, but in world literature, where he is part of the same postmodern movement that has begun to erase the barriers between art and entertainment, popular fiction and popular film (Faris cites the popularity in recent years of magical realist films such as *Field of Dreams, Ironweed, The Witches of Eastwick,* and *Ghost* in addition to writers such as Rushdie and Gabriel Garcia Márquez). It also highlights the fact that Murakami, like Rushdie or Toni Morrison (in, for instance, *Beloved*), uses magical realist technique in order to advance his own agenda, political, cultural, or otherwise. As noted above, it supports most of all his desire to depict the nature of the inner

---

7. This is, however, by no means to suggest that such an agenda would be out of place in modern Japan, where an identity crisis has been noted since the early Meiji period. Susan Napier (1995, 1996) points to the works of Izumi Kyōka, and even some by Natsume Sōseki, as early examples of "fantastic" literature in Japan that are concerned with expressing Japanese identity. In more recent times, the same concern can be seen in Ōe Kenzaburō's revival of rural Japanese mythologies in such works as *The Silent Cry* (Man'en gannen no futtobōru, 1967).

mind, or the unconscious Other, to use the Lacanian term, and how this informs the construction of the self, the individual subject.[8]

Murakami's Construction of "Inner Space"

Murakami's model of the internal consciousness has remained fairly uniform throughout his career; his motifs and terminology have not changed significantly in the past 20 years. In general it is presented as a uniformly coded division between the world of the light and that of the dark, the latter corresponding to the unconscious realm. Murakami envisions the inner world of the mind as dark, cold, and sterile. At times the unconscious is only symbolized, other times it is real. In *Pinball, 1973* the protagonist enters an ice-cold, pitch-black warehouse, formerly a cold-storage facility for chickens, to locate Naoko, a girlfriend who died at the end of the 1960s. In *A Wild Sheep Chase* the same protagonist reencounters his dead friend Rat, this time in a mountain villa, but again in total, freezing darkness. *Hard-Boiled Wonderland and the End of the World*, as we have seen, alternates its chapters between the conscious protagonist, who lives in daylight, and the unconscious one, who fears light, works at night, and must wear protective dark glasses when he goes out during the daytime. The protagonist of *Dance Dance Dance* discovers a musty, dust-filled room in a deep corner of his mind, dark, gloomy, and filled with dusty skeletons—quite literally the skeletons of his past. And in *The Wind-up Bird Chronicle* his unconscious is presented as a maze-like hotel, in which "Room 208" is the core, the center of his whole being. It is this center, the location of the core identity, that concerns us here.

Murakami himself uses the expression "black box" to describe this portion of his protagonist's unconscious. The expression first comes up in *Hard-Boiled Wonderland and the End of the World*, when the protagonist is told by a scientist who has been tinkering with electrical circuits in his brain that the core consciousness is like the "black box" used to record flight data on aircraft: it contains all the information necessary to form the individual identity, but it is impervious to attempts to open it and observe its contents. This is identity.

> "In other words," I said, "the 'black box' is the unconscious mind of the individual?"

---

8. Lacan's theories concerning identity and self-formation will be discussed at length in the chapter that follows.

"That's right. All people act according to certain principles. No one is exactly like anyone else. In short it's a matter of identity. What is identity? A unique system of thought based on the collected memories of our experiences from the past. A simpler term for it is the mind. No two people have the same mind. Of course, most people have no real grasp of their own cognitive systems." (*MHZ* 4:373; *HBW&EW* 255)

Nevertheless, the fact remains that most of Murakami's literature is concerned with opening up that "impregnable" box of memories and experiences and holding it up to the light for analysis. Nor, one might add, is this strictly a fictional concern for the author, who uses the same "black box" metaphor in discussing the AUM Shinrikyō cult members in *The Place That Was Promised: Underground 2* (Yakusoku sareta basho de: Underground 2, 1998): "In *Underground*, I dealt with the AUM Shinrikyō . . . as a menacing but unknown quantity—a 'black box,' of sorts. In *Underground 2* I have attempted to open up that 'black box' a bit" (Murakami 1998, 12). What Murakami seeks finally is some means of looking at the core identity of the individual and discerning what leads it either to become part of the "system" of Japanese society, or, alternatively, to face the risk of falling through the cracks, taking its chances outside the rigidly structured Japanese social system.

THE EARLY WORKS: METONYMICAL LINKS

In his early works, however, Murakami is clearly less certain of what he is dealing with in the mind. The compactly conceptualized metaphor of the "black box" has not yet come into being. Instead, he focuses initially on what *emerges from* the mind and how it impacts the protagonist. And yet even in these early works one finds a sophisticated understanding on the part of the author of the unconscious as the source for the assertion of the conscious self, or subjectivity. In its simplest form the model resembles the Lacanian one, which envisions the "unconscious Other" as a sounding board against which the self, the speaking subject, or *je*, constitutes and understands itself. Murakami is also in agreement with Lacan that the relationship between the conscious self and the unconscious Other is essentially a *linguistic* one, for he himself conceives of the images that lurk within and emerge from the inner mind as *language*. And finally, just as Lacan grounds much of our psychological interaction with the unconscious Other in the desire to gain knowledge of that Other, Murakami's protagonists unconsciously create metonymical links with the contents of their inner minds in order to draw them out, engage them in discourse, and then send them back to where they came from. This is not to say that the conscious self is capable of manipulating the unconscious Other at will, however; rather, as Lacanian theorists have frequently pointed out, these connections are wholly unconscious, nonvolitional. Furthermore, because the unconscious—again, the "black box"—is inaccessible, the Other is finally unattainable, and these connections, even when successfully made, as they are in Murakami's fiction, are unsatisfying. "Lacanian Desire is both representational," writes Ellie Ragland-Sullivan (1986, 77), "—a referential content of images and meanings inscribed in the place of the Other(A)—and an indestructible force that shows up in the order of chronological time as an insatiable mechanism of yearning."

In other words, the mechanism is "insatiable" because the real object of desire, the unconscious Other, the inner part of our selves, is inaccessible to the conscious self, and therefore various substitutes, grounded in linguistic connections (one might think of them as "psychological metaphors"), must be created. In Murakami's magical realist universe this is taken a step further, however, and the linguistic connections, which in real life are unknown, unconscious, or even unintelligible, magically become visible and tangible. In short, they become *magically real*.

Murakami begins to reveal his model of the mind to readers in earnest in 1980 with the novel *Pinball, 1973*, and the short story, "The Story of the Poor Aunt" (Bimbō na obasan no hanashi, 1980). In both works he presents the notion of memory—the object of desire—in a textualized form, that is, one constituted of language, specifically, of words.

Textualization of the Inner Mind

As noted above, Murakami Haruki's early literature pivots on the intersection of the nostalgic, the linguistic, and the magical. In order to conceptualize for himself and readers how the conscious self is informed by the unconscious Other, he posits a specific nostalgic object of desire in his protagonist's mind. He then "textualizes" it in the sense of creating a chain of linguistic connections between the object itself, usually the memory of a missing or deceased friend, and how it will appear to the conscious protagonist. Finally, he causes the protagonist's obsessive desire for the object to bring it magically from inside the mind out into the external world. The result is something just a little more than a mere image—for these objects are tangible, they are real—but less than realistic, as I have suggested above, in the sense that their presence is incongruous with the detailed realistic setting created by the author.

"The Story of the Poor Aunt" illustrates the textual nature of these "nostalgic images." In this work, the protagonist lounges by a fountain in a park, when suddenly the idea of a poor, middle-aged woman flashes through his mind. In that instant the idea of the "poor aunt" is imprinted on his consciousness, and soon after he discovers the vaguely defined image of a "poor aunt" on his back. He can see her clearly, and she, perched on his back, peers back at him over his shoulder. Moreover, as if deliberately to head off the easy dismissal of the "poor aunt" as a mere hallucination, Murakami makes certain that other characters in the story can see her as well. The protagonist attempts in a variety of ways to explain to us what she is. She is like the member of the family who always turns up at weddings, but to whom no one speaks; she embarrasses herself by using the wrong fork; she brings an unwanted gift. Everyone knows who she is, and she inspires a vague sense of pity, but no one really wants to have anything to do with her.

Yet because she *is* a "text," those who see the "poor aunt" visualize her in different ways. To one she appears as a dog that died in pitiful agony of esophageal cancer; to another, she looks like a schoolteacher he once had, who lost her husband during the war and was herself burned in an air raid. The metonymical link here is simply a vague kind of pity, an emotion familiar to all, but one to which each individual responds differently. Finally, appearing on a talk show to explain his oddity, the protagonist declares that the poor aunt on his back is *tada no kotoba*, "just words" (*MHZ* 3:55). In describing his image thus Murakami renders the emotion of pity into a text that he then invites the reader to rewrite and reinterpret *ad infinitum*, bringing the text to life anew each time it is read.

Such play with linguistic connections is also parodied in early Murakami fiction. In "Kangarū tsūshin" (*MHZ* 3:90–109; 1981; translated as The Kangaroo Communique, 1988),[9] the protagonist is a department store manager who must write a letter of apology to a dissatisfied customer. His impulse to write her a fairly long and intimate personal letter, however, comes from seeing kangaroos at the zoo. How is this connection formed? We are not told. Murakami merely teases his readers by claiming that there are thirty-six specific steps, each of which must be followed in precisely the right order, to get from kangaroos to the letter in question. Similarly, in

9. "Kangarū tsūshin" was published as "The Kangaroo Communique" by both Alfred Birnbaum (*Kyoto Journal*, August 1988) and Philip Gabriel (*Zyzzyva*, April 1988). It has been reprinted in *The Elephant Vanishes* (New York: Knopf, 1993).

"1963/1982 Ipanema no musume" (*MHZ* 5:81–88; 1963/1982 Girl from Ipanema, 1982), the protagonist contends that there is a mysterious connection between the famous song and a hallway in his high school. The textual weaving leads from the hallway to combination salads, and finally to a long-lost girlfriend who loved vegetables.

These are, of course, little more than games, exercises in word association. One is sympathetic to Masao Miyoshi's somewhat irritable declaration that Murakami's writing amounts to little more than "a symbol-deciphering game" (Miyoshi 1991, 234). In these cases it is barely even that; stories like the two just noted may at best be described as "play" in nostalgic connection-building, but in which the symbols themselves are never really present.

But more serious and sophisticated examples may be found, particularly in the longer works. *Pinball, 1973* provides two interesting examples of metonymical linking that may be analyzed with a fairly high degree of certainty. These center, as noted previously, on two distinct narratives, each involving missing friends: "Rat," who has gone missing at the end of *Hear the Wind Sing*; and "Naoko," the narrator's girlfriend in 1969, who is dead. The setting of the novel, as the title suggests, is 1973, but the narrator's nostalgic focus is on the transitional period from 1969 to 1970.

Pinball, 1973 is organized much as *Hard-Boiled Wonderland and the End of the World* later would be, into chapters that alternate between the worlds of light and darkness. In the former the reader sees the first-person protagonist, "Boku"; in the latter, "Rat" appears in a lyrical, third-person narrative. The interest in this part of the novel lies not merely in watching the movements of Rat, who (we eventually realize) lives in the unconscious mind of the protagonist as a memory, but in seeing how he emerges into the external, conscious world to interact with the protagonist. As with the "poor aunt," however, appearances are always unstable, and when Rat emerges "into the light," he bears no resemblance to his original form. This, incidentally, is foreshadowed in the final lines of *Hear the Wind Sing*, which ostensibly quote Friedrich Nietzsche: "Can one understand the depths of the gloom of night in the light of day?" (*MHZ* 1:120)

This essential metamorphosis of the object of desire into something else mirrors the process of signification and metonymy—the substitution, as it were, of one word or image for another, related one—but it also signals the mystery of the unconscious and the insatiable nature of that desire. The nostalgic image is one of a symbolic nature, strictly a surrogate, and for this very reason it can never be satisfactory. As a critique of representation this strikes a resonant chord with postmodernism as well: neither history nor the past can ever be anything more than text; thus one can never apprehend the past as anything but language or words.

In similar terms, one may understand why the "past" in Murakami's texts—in this case specific memories—may not appear in the present (conscious world) as it did in the past (unconscious world). As language, it must be represented metonymically; images with (in Murakami's case) complex, obscure connections to the original object or concept must be used to "represent" it symbolically, similar to the way the historical document or text stands in for the reality of history itself. It should, then, come as no great surprise that the memory of Rat in *Pinball, 1973*, when it emerges, bears no visual or physical resemblance to the man himself. In fact, it appears as twin sisters, roughly twenty years old, whom the protagonist discovers sleeping on either side of himself one morning after a night of heavy drinking.

ENTRANCES, EXITS, AND RODENT TRAPS

The metonymical connection between Rat and the Twins (as they come to be known, for they have no names) seems obscure at first but in fact is decipherable. Once again, the reader must play a game of signification. The process is as follows: the Twins, realizing that their lack of names is becoming problematic for the protagonist, invite him to name them, and provide some suggestions: "Right and Left," "Vertical and Horizontal," "Up and Down," and so forth. This kind of naming is a source of controversy in Murakami's literature and has led Karatani Kōjin, among others, to argue that Murakami seeks to deconstruct meanings and realities in the world. "To dissolve proper names into fixed signifiers is to dissolve them into bundles of predicative terms, or to put it another way, into bundles of generalized concepts," he claims. "What Murakami Haruki tries so persistently to do is to eliminate proper names, and thus make the world more random."[10]

But the names the Twins offer, while unconventional, are neither random nor general; rather, they suggest very clearly a symbiotic relationship in which one half of the pair is meaningless without the other. The relationship between the Twins suggests a structuralist model, yet as with

10. Quoted in Nakamura 1998, 105. The original is Karatani 1990b. Hatanaka Yoshiki (1989, 138-39) argues similarly that Murakami seeks to create immense distance between us and the world he shows us in his use of peculiar proper names on the one hand, but recognizable ones for popularly known places and objects such as "Dunkin' Donuts" or "Maserati," on the other.

his model of the internal and external minds, interchange is possible. When the protagonist objects that the Twins can be easily identified by their sweatshirts—one says "208," the other "209"—they wordlessly peel off the shirts and exchange them. Clearly there is to be no permanent, visible means of identifying the Twins.

At the same time, the Twins seem to represent the opposite, yet symbiotic relationship between the protagonist and Rat, as well: the protagonist is a settled, fairly conventional man, whereas Rat is a rebellious, angry retro-hippie who has been out of place since the end of the Zenkyōtō period. Finally, however, the metonymical relationship between Rat and the Twins is cemented through the linguistic connections that Murakami weaves. In response to the "names" offered by the Twins above, the protagonist suggests "Entrance and Exit," which leads him to philosophize on the nature of entrances and exits. "Wherever there is an entrance there is also an exit. Most things are built that way: mailboxes, electric vacuum cleaners, zoos, turkey basters. Of course, there are also things that are not built that way. Mousetraps, for instance" (*MHZ* 1:129). Invoking the mousetrap, and the memory of once having caught a mouse (*nezumi*), brings the protagonist back to the more important rodent in his life, Rat himself. The protagonist's nostalgic desire for his missing friend thus pivots on the word *nezumi*, brought via obsessive nostalgic desire and magical realism into the external world in the form of the Twins.

LOST LOVERS AND PINBALL

A similar analysis can be performed on the image of "pinball," which appears in the title but whose importance is not evident until well into the text. One may, of course, make the obvious parodic connection between *Pinball, 1973* and Ōe Kenzaburō's brilliant novel, *Man'en gannen no futtobōru* (1967; translated as The Silent Cry), but parody, while certainly visible in the relationship between Ōe's brother characters, Mitsusaburō and Takashi, and their depiction as passive and active heroes, respectively, is secondary to the use of pinball as a metonymical image of nostalgic desire. In fact, while one could hardly imagine the title of Murakami's book to be accidentally similar to that of Ōe's, the parodic element strikes one more as a diversion from the real issue at hand.[11] The actual focus of this work is

---

11. During a conversation with the writer on October 22, 1994, in Cambridge, Massachusetts, Murakami acknowledged the similarity between the books' titles, but denied that he had intended to parody the content of Ōe's work.

nostalgia and memory, and the importance of pinball lies in its relationship to Naoko, the protagonist's deceased girlfriend.

Pinball, 1973 begins with Naoko. The opening lines contain the protagonist's confession to being obsessively fond of hearing stories from strange lands. This leads him to relate some of the stories he has heard over the years, including some supposedly told to him by visitors from other planets. Finally he comes to his favorite stories of all, those related by Naoko herself. In one instance, he recalls, Naoko told him the story of a man whose job was to locate good spots for digging wells, and how he was struck and killed by a train; in another, we learn of a lonely train platform on which a dog paces endlessly back and forth. Are these stories supposed to be true, or are they merely fabrications for the protagonist's amusement? One suspects the latter, for none contains a coherent plot; rather, all the stories give the sense that they are intended as descriptive sketches of mental images rather than real narratives.

Our confidence, however, is shaken when, in the "real time" of *Pinball, 1973*, the protagonist suddenly decides to visit the train platform in Naoko's story of four years earlier and to look for the dog. He waits for about an hour, measured in the number of cigarettes he is able to chain-smoke (replacing conventional time measurement as he replaces conventional use of naming), but sees no dog, only a group of old men fishing in a nearby pond. Finally, however, he notices a dog sitting next to one of the men. Coaxing the animal through the fence separating the pond from the train platform, he pats it on the head several times, then leaves satisfied.

But he cannot be wholly satisfied. As he returns home, he realizes that the closure he seeks for his relationship with Naoko is not so easily obtained. This is hardly surprising when one reflects that the best he can hope for is to encounter a textualized image of Naoko, something which, as noted above, can never satisfy his desire. This thought torments him on the way home:

> On the train going home the same thing kept repeating itself over and over in my mind: everything is finished, forget about it. Isn't that why you came all this way? But there was no way I could forget that I had loved Naoko, or that she was dead. Because nothing was really finished. (*MHZ* 1:136)

Not long after this, the image of the dog reemerges, this time in the form of a telephone switch panel that has gone dead in the protagonist's apartment. When the Twins ask the repairman from the telephone company what the switch panel is for, he replies that it is like a mother dog who looks after her puppies. "But if the mother dog should die, then the puppies also die, right? So we bring in a new mother dog to replace the old one" (*MHZ* 1:156). The pivotal word is "dog," which links Naoko's story (and thus Naoko herself) to the switch panel which, as a mechanical device, leads shortly thereafter to a pinball machine.

As if to make certain that no one misses the connection between Naoko and the switch panel, the Twins insist on holding an impromptu funeral for it at a local reservoir. There the protagonist makes a stirring speech that draws somewhat incongruously on Kant and hurls the switch panel out into the deep, charging it to rest in peace. Only a few pages later the protagonist raises the image of pinball and, in particular, a machine he was fond of during his college years known as "the Spaceship," once again forming a link to the extraterrestrial stories told to him early in the work. Soon he is obsessed with finding this machine, and this forms the title quest of *Pinball, 1973.*[12]

When the machine is finally located, through the cooperation of a college professor with an encyclopedic knowledge of pinball and a philanthropist who collects old pinball machines, the protagonist must enter a pitch-black, ice-cold warehouse (quite literally his "black box") to complete the journey. Entering the inky blackness, he flips the electricity on, bathing the place in blinding light, revealing row upon row of pinball machines coming to life, their flashing lights giving the reader the impression of seeing rows of electric tombstones. It is an eerie, magical, intensely spiritual journey into the "other world" of his inner mind, a world of death and memory, but it grows even more bizarre when, locating "the Spaceship," he does not play it, but instead holds a conversation with it in the tones of lovers meeting again after a long separation. As with the dog, however, nothing is solved in this encounter with the unconscious Other, for the meeting is temporary and mitigated by the layers of symbolism through which Naoko must be expressed.

The strong contrast between light and darkness in this scene, a regular motif in Murakami literature, as noted previously, remains still in its early stages in *Pinball, 1973.* One notes that the protagonist is not permitted to see Naoko in her "true" (or at least more familiar) form for the

---

12. The presence of a "quest" here might suggest the possibility of a formulaic reading such as those performed in the previous chapter, but neither the style of writing nor the presentation of the quests (in terms of establishing reader expectations) support this. In fact, I have long been of the opinion that *Pinball, 1973* was an experimental, transitional work for Murakami, and that he discovered in the course of writing it the potential for formulaic quest fiction, culminating in the writing of *A Wild Sheep Chase.*

blanket of darkness placed over the scene. Readers can only imagine what he would have found had he left the lights out. But this, again adhering to the final lines of *Hear the Wind Sing*, is the one unbreakable rule in Murakami's literature: no protagonist is ever permitted to illuminate fully the interior of his mind and see his memories as they once appeared.

This becomes clearer in later works. In *A Wild Sheep Chase*, as we recall, the same protagonist actually does meet Rat as Rat, in the confines of his inner consciousness. The location, Rat's secluded villa in the mountains of Hokkaido, remains cloaked in darkness, because Rat insists that it be dark. A similar admonition is given Okada Tōru not to turn on his flashlight in *The Wind-Up Bird Chronicle* by the woman who inhabits the hotel room at the center of his consciousness. What will Murakami's hero find should he ever break this injunction? There can be no way of knowing, for the unconscious mind is as much defined by its darkness as the darkness is required by the unconscious. To illuminate the unconscious in the Murakami universe, then, would be merely to transform it into consciousness, the realm of the light, and so the exercise would be pointless.

TARGETING THE POLITICAL CENTER

Murakami's efforts at locating a sense of individual identity in his first two works might be regarded as largely apolitical. In both *Hear the Wind Sing* and *Pinball, 1973* the protagonist deals with his sense of loss in the aftermath of the Zenkyōtō period but never really focuses the source of this loss on any particular entity, political or otherwise. With *A Wild Sheep Chase*, however, Murakami begins to portray the Japanese state as a sinister presence that seeks to promulgate a sense of collective, constructed identity among members of contemporary Japanese society. As noted earlier, the implicit assumption here—probably a historically correct one—is that the disappearance of the student radicals after 1970 was due either to their mass assimilation into the "system" of Japanese society or, alternatively, their destruction by that system, which is intolerant of individualism. This has become the theme in virtually all of Murakami's writing, fiction and nonfiction, since 1982. In every novel he writes, a world of perfect contentment is offered to the protagonist (or, in *A Wild Sheep Chase* to Rat) in exchange for his individuality.

In *A Wild Sheep Chase*, for instance, as we have seen, the narrative is centered on the image of an all-empowering sheep that inhabits its host like a parasite, then uses the host to carry out its plans of domination. In the same gesture, however, it must gradually eliminate the contents of the host's mind in order to replace them with itself. Here, too, we find that Murakami portrays this elimination of the mind as a breakdown in linguistic connections. Cognition or perception (*ninshiki*) is a product of language, and therefore its elimination is equivalent to the elimination of language, and vice versa. As the Man in Black tells the protagonist,

> "When the two pillars of Western humanism, individual perception and evolutionary continuity, lose their meaning, then language will also lose its meaning. Existence will cease to be individual and will turn into chaos. Your individual existence will cease to be unique, only chaotic. My chaos will be your chaos, and vice versa. Existence is communication, communication existence." (*MHZ* 2:156; *WSC* 120)

The nature of this "chaos" is that of an infinite abyss, lacking a knowable structure, and thus communication becomes impossible because no known referent exists there. Communication is rendered impossible because the sheep eradicates its host's linguistic relationship with his internal self. This frees the host from the tediousness of thinking, but it also strips him of any semblance (or remembrance) of individual identity. The sheep's use of the host, then, is by no means benevolent, though it may appear so at first. Neither "the Sheep Professor" nor "the Boss" survives his encounter with the sheep with his mind intact, nor, indeed, does Rat, whose suicide at the end of the novel is his final conscious act. Ultimately the utopian dream offered to each successive character is revealed to be a thinly disguised sentence of death. At the end of *A Wild Sheep Chase*, Rat (now a memory/ image) explains to the protagonist why he chose death over the utopian dream of the sheep. "'It's because I like my weaknesses. I like my pains and hardships. I like summer sunlight, the smell of the breeze, the songs of the cicadas. I can't help liking them'" (*MHZ* 2:356; *WSC* 284). It is, however, uncertain how the destruction of the sheep will impact the fate of the individual in Japanese society, for the power structure created by the sheep remains in place at the end of the novel, while the protagonist is left with nothing.

A similar fate awaits the protagonist of *Hard-Boiled Wonderland and the End of the World*. Because of electronic switches implanted in his brain—again, by an organ of the state—he faces perpetual imprisonment in an artificially constructed fragment of his core consciousness known as "the Town." Like the empty utopia offered to Rat, the Town is perfectly peaceful but rigidly intolerant of even fragments of mind or volition. We recall the eradication of the protagonist's shadow as he enters the Town's only gate. What is this shadow, if not his individual soul, his inner self? We do not need to analyze deeply to realize that the shadow, the most ancient marker of time, is symbolic of the protagonist's memories and identity, his past, and thus his mind. Not unnaturally, the longer the protagonist is without his shadow, the less inclined he is to give up the easy peace of this mindless utopia. Nevertheless, at the end of the novel he compromises, refusing either to reunite with his shadow or to let it die altogether. Instead he helps his shadow to escape (to where, we cannot know) and accepts life in the no man's land outside of the Town.

Finally, in *Dance Dance Dance*, the protagonist is simply wooed by those who have exchanged their identities for participation in the orgiastic economy of pointless consumption in contemporary Tokyo. The prominent appearance of high-priced prostitutes in this work is a constant reminder that all of the affluent characters in the novel have prostituted themselves to the system. As the protagonist learns, however, sex is not the only part of our humanity that can be purchased; indeed, one is uncertain whether to be amused or alarmed by the persistent attempts of other characters to "buy" the protagonist's friendship. In exchange simply for being a friend he is offered a Maserati, an expensive apartment, high-priced prostitutes, and even an all-expenses-paid vacation to Hawaii. It is a situation the protagonist finally cannot resolve with his determination not to be corrupted; at the end of the book he flees to Hokkaido to sort things out in the quiet countryside, away from the fetish-consumerism of Tokyo.

Murakami's central theme for most of his career has thus been that the concept of individual identity runs counter to the dominant social structure of post-1970 Japan, what he refers to as the "system." In fact, this is even the subject of Murakami's recent nonfiction works, *Underground* and *Underground 2*, both of which will be dealt with in a later chapter. The notion of counteridentity as a mode of resistance is especially central in *A Wild Sheep Chase*, in which the protagonist is intimidated by "the Man in Black," who tells him that he can either play along with the system, ensuring the success of his business, or he can resist and simply disappear without a trace. Examples of those who do not "play along" are to be found along the wayside. These include "the Sheep Professor," who lives out his life in miserable solitude in a crumbling Hokkaido hotel, and "Rat," who resists more fiercely and faces a choice between submission or suicide. He chooses the latter.

Identity in Murakami is therefore a matter of will. The question in Murakami, as for many writers before him, is often one of action versus passivity. At the same time, while most Murakami characters are passive, they are not devoid of identity; rather, their passivity, almost a total paralysis, stems from their inability to decide how to act without participating in the consumerism that surrounds them, thus maintaining their sense of individuality. Ultimately, they all seek to preserve, and in some cases, to restore their identities by rooting about in their internal minds, recognizing that the inner mind is the ultimate source of self.

SOUTH OF THE BORDER, WEST OF THE SUN: MAGICAL REALISM, OR GHOST STORY?

Most Japanese critics have noted the paranormal in Murakami's literature, but few seem to have grasped the essential structure of the internal and external minds that are supported by Murakami's use of magical realism, or the critique of the society versus the self that it presents. Expressions such as "the other world" persist, and even Yokoo Kazuhiro, who accurately describes a literary landscape that is primarily realistic, finally resorts to the conventional descriptive terminology of the "ghost story" to understand the author's literature. The various "ghosts" he points to are the Twins in *Pinball, 1973*, "the Girl with the Ears" in *A Wild Sheep Chase*, and "the Girl in Pink," who is the granddaughter of the scientist responsible for the protagonist's predicament in *Hard-Boiled Wonderland and the End of the World*. The primary object of Yokoo's inquiry, however, is *South of the Border, West of the Sun*.

South of the Border, West of the Sun, regarded by a number of critics as a failure for its lack of truly new ideas (see, e.g., Mukai 1993, 300–3; Saitō 1993, 258–61), was evidently written in the same spirit as *Norwegian Wood*, using the general structure of the popular romance. Unlike in previous Murakami literature, however, the protagonist of this work, named "Hajime," is happily married with two children and, more important, he is no longer a peripheral, isolated type, but a successful bar owner (reflecting, no doubt, Murakami's own experience running a jazz cafe in the 1970s). As if deliberately avoiding the financial pressure under which the protagonists of his previous novels operate, Murakami takes pains to show that the hero of *South of the Border, West of the Sun* is well-to-do and even enjoys a stable home life with his family.

But beneath this veneer of stability lurks a familiar emptiness: Hajime soon reveals a lingering attachment to a girl named "Shimamoto" whom he knew as a child and who, he is convinced, is his "soul mate." As the novel progresses it becomes clear that the easy comfort of Hajime's home is actually a thin disguise for the sense of emptiness in his marriage.

While hardly a loveless relationship, there is no real inner connection between the protagonist and his wife.

In this novel, for the first time in Murakami fiction, three distinct types of knowledge are outlined that combine to form a true "connection" between two people: the first is emotional, a kind of innate understanding that apparently emerged between Hajime and Shimamoto during their childhood; the second is sexual, represented in the relationship between himself and his girlfriend Izumi's cousin in high school. The third is knowledge of the historical past, "the mind," which comes only through complete trust and thorough disclosure. The conflict in this story stems from the fact that Hajime can never combine all three types of knowledge in any single person. His desire, then, is to combine the emotional bond he once had with Shimamoto, the sexual desire that engulfed him with Izumi's cousin, and knowledge of the historical past he has with his wife now. The latter two aspects seem easily within reach, but the internal emotional bond Hajime shared with Shimamoto is missing.

It should come as no surprise, then, that "Shimamoto" turns up suddenly in the novel to help Hajime to satisfy (partially) his desire. But like "the Twins" or "the Spaceship," one is aware that she can only be a nostalgic image emerging to stand in for the original Shimamoto of his childhood. No major transformations from darkness to light are necessary in this case, since Murakami need only have her grow up into a woman. However, perhaps feeling the need for some differentiation between the original and the image, Murakami portrays the childhood Shimamoto as having suffered from a crippled leg that has since been cured in the grown character.

When Shimamoto turns up in Hajime's bar one night, he becomes instantly attracted to her, even before he knows who she is. After she has revealed her identity and given a plausible story about finding him by reading about his bar in a magazine, they begin an affair that goes on for about a year before they finally consummate their relationship. Spending a weekend at the Hajime's villa at Hakone, "Shimamoto" makes love to him, promising to reveal everything about her past to him the following morning.

Predictably, however, "Shimamoto" disappears following their one night of intense physical passion without having revealed her story at all. So complete is her disappearance that Hajime cannot even find her footprints in the gravel outside the villa. This is what leads Yokoo to conclude that Shimamoto is "without question an apparition from another world, rather than from the real world" (Yokoo 1994, 23), and to schematize the novel into two very distinct worlds: the "real" and the "other," right down to the title: "south of the border" refers, he believes, to the "real" world, whereas "west of the sun" is the land of the dead.

To this point Yokoo's argument is consistent with my analyses above; the unconscious Other *is* a place in which "the dead"—or at least memories of them—continue to exist. In this sense we might even choose to think of the memories of lost friends as the "ghosts" of Hajime's past, who live in the "other world" of his internal mind. But Yokoo assumes that these images are separate from him, that the impeccable timing of their convenient appearances and disappearances is attributable to their knowledge as spirits of both past and future. "The fact that 'Shimamoto' disappears immediately after the protagonist resolves to leave everything behind and go away with her can only be attributed to the fact that she has forecast his distant future" (Yokoo 1994, 37).

Such a schematization is not altogether insupportable, but in the end Yokoo's reluctance to recognize the psychological underpinnings that go along with a magical realist setting, and his failure to see that the source of these "ghosts" is Hajime himself, leaves him with more mysteries than he can possibly solve. When, for instance, did the real Shimamoto actually die, he wonders, or was she perhaps a spirit even when Hajime knew her as a child? He concludes, with little textual support, that Shimamoto must have met with an unhappy death in her early twenties and has now come back to haunt her old friend. "It is quite possible, in fact," he argues, "that many of Murakami's characters come into being after having previously met their own ends" (Yokoo 1994, 23); this is an idea that, to a point, does not necessarily conflict with my theory of the nostalgic image.

Doubtless one may read *South of the Border, West of the Sun* as a kind of romantic ghost story (see Saitō 1993). To externalize Shimamoto as a ghost does at least acknowledge the presence of the paranormal in Murakami literature. But such a reading by itself does little to shed light on Murakami's *raison d'être* as a writer and fails completely to address the real identities of the other "ghosts" in his earlier works. Why would Murakami create "the Twins," for instance, as the ghost or ghosts of people who are never to be mentioned otherwise?

Instead, it strikes me that to view these kinds of characters as nostalgic images originating as part of the unconscious Other, drawn out from within *the protagonist's* mind, in a concentrated attempt to recover *his* past and thereby reconnect with the constitutive parts of *his* personal identity, provides a more effective and plausible reading of the author's work. Such a reading would account for the remarkable sense of timing noted by Yokoo above. Moreover, this scheme is demonstrably applicable to all but a few of

Murakami's major works. And, of course, it would go a considerable distance in providing answers to Yokoo's most pressing questions about Shimamoto, specifically, *who* she is, *why* she has come, and to *where* she returns.

There is, in fact, very little in *South of the Border, West of the Sun* that should strike us as mysterious when viewed in the context of previous Murakami literature. If anything, we might say that the work is *too* overtly structured around the predictable appearance and disappearance of Shimamoto. We see it coming from the beginning. The novel's weaknesses stem not, as Yokoo suggests, from its leaving too many questions unanswered, but rather from its inability to strike out further into new territory. Mukai Satoshi suggests that the work was written solely in order for Hajime to express his sense of emptiness and his need for Shimamoto to fill that void. The work is, in his opinion, too fixated on its central theme of loss (Mukai 1993, 303).

This is certainly true, but it would be an overstatement to suggest that Murakami breaks no ground in *South of the Border, West of the Sun*. Rather, several important developments in Murakami's exploration of identity occur here. First, the notion of the "black box," the objectified core identity of the individual, reemerges prominently for the first time since *Hard-Boiled Wonderland and the End of the World*. In this case, however, the "black box" is not a matter of science fiction, but a real, organic thing that represents the inner self. This is not to suggest that readers are given any new insights about the interior of that box, however; indeed, Murakami has discarded even the poetic descriptions of his "end of the world" in that previous novel, with its golden unicorns and medieval walls, in favor of the far less revealing expression *nani ka*, "something." Hajime tells Shimamoto that he has long been aware that "something" has been missing from inside of him, and that only she can restore this. He seeks a similar "something" from Izumi in high school, and is likewise frustrated until he meets her cousin and finds himself inexplicably and powerfully drawn to that "something" at her core, an attraction so strong that his sexual penetration seems like an attempt to reach inside of her and touch it.

> The only important thing was that we were violently engulfed by *something*, and that inside of that *something* there had to lurk some hidden thing that was important to me. I wanted to know what that thing was. I *had* to know. Had it been possible I would have plunged my hand into the core of her flesh to touch that *something* directly. (*KMTN* 60; *SBWS* 45)

In the context of previous Murakami literature, there can be no doubt but that this "something" is the same missing "core identity" that leads the protagonists on their various quests in previous books. Throughout *South of the Border, West of the Sun*, and later in *The Wind-Up Bird Chronicle*, we encounter this term, one that, despite its abstract nature, seems to stir in the Murakami hero a greater passion than ever before.

The second major development seen in *South of the Border, West of the Sun*, more important than the first, is Hajime's newly developed determination to reach out and come into contact with the core identities of those around him. This is an extraordinary thing for Murakami, whose characters, as I have repeatedly stated, have always been so absorbed in themselves and their own problems that critics are virtually united in dubbing them *jiheiteki*, a medical term meaning "autistic" but in this case perhaps better expressed with the idiom "self-centered" or "self-absorbed." Even apologists for Murakami's work, such as Katō Norihiro, Aoki Tamotsu, and Kawamoto Saburō agree that Murakami's characters are too out of touch with their society, though this is generally understood to be a symptom of the times (see esp. Katō Norihiro 1986; cf. Aoki 1985; Kawamoto 1985, 1986). Kuroko similarly uses the term *jiheiteki*, lamenting that "contemporary man is now capable only of relationships with passive objects" (Kuroko 1990, 14). Murakami is not unaware of this characteristic in his hero, of course, as is clear in *Hard-Boiled Wonderland and the End of the World* when his unconscious protagonist is told by a fellow character, "I wonder if there isn't something else you need? . . . I feel that if you had that something, it would help you to open up, just a little, the hardened shell of winter that surrounds you" (*MHZ* 4:321; *HBW&EW* 268). The conscious protagonist is told essentially the same thing, that he has surrounded himself with a protective barrier, one that finds concrete representation in the impenetrable walls that surround the town as well (*MHZ* 4:389-390; *HBW&EW* 268).

It is, then, a sign of change that in *South of the Border, West of the Sun* Hajime is passionately concerned with making contact with another. Kuroko sees evidence of this impending change even earlier, in the 1989 short story "TV piipuru" (TV People), in which the protagonist learns, too late, that the secret of existence, of life itself, is to communicate with others (Kuroko 1993, 206–8). In this story, as later in *The Wind-Up Bird Chronicle*, his wife is an enigma to be solved, but by the time he understands this it is too late, and she is gone forever. It is with *South of the Border, West of the Sun*, however, that the Murakami protagonist becomes truly militant in his desire to make contact with others.

And yet, while one is tempted to see something altruistic in this shift of attention, from the self to an external other, the fact remains that seeking connectivity with the identities of others is, finally, an expedient for the protagonist to discover himself, for in seeking out "Shimamoto" or, in *The Wind-Up Bird Chronicle*, his wife Kumiko, the hero still seeks an other who will reaffirm *his* existence as well. This is clear from the very first chapters of *The Wind-Up Bird Chronicle*, a work that, despite its considerable length (more than 1,200 pages) and complexity (at least three major narratives are given), is still simply about recognizing and acknowledging another (or an other) person.

THE WIND-UP BIRD CHRONICLE: THE OTHER STRIKES BACK

One might say that Murakami spent the first fifteen years of his career preparing to write *The Wind-Up Bird Chronicle*, in which every major motif and theme from his previous work is present. The inner mind is presented as a gloomy, maze-like structure, a hotel, as it turns out, at the center of which is a dark, vaguely sinister room in which a woman awaits the protagonist, Okada Tōru, and repeatedly demands that he learn her name. This is the object of his desire, Kumiko herself, the key to the main conflict in the novel, for Kumiko emerges early in the text as an enigma that Tōru feels compelled to solve lest his relationship with her disintegrate.

But what makes the work exceptional among Murakami literature is the complexly interwoven threads of textuality that mark a new departure for the author. I have noted above that Murakami showed a tendency toward textualization (of image, memory, history) from his earliest literature; in *The Wind-Up Bird Chronicle* he reaches a new level of intertextuality, weaving a tapestry of narrative that encompasses two distinct historical periods (present-day Tokyo and Manchuria during the Second World War), and three disparate stories connected by shared magical experiences, violence, and a persistent struggle for control over the core identities of the characters involved.

Brevity precludes a detailed synopsis of *The Wind-Up Bird Chronicle*, but the principal plots may be broadly sketched. In the main story line, Okada Tōru expresses concern that he does not understand his wife, Kumiko, and fears he will lose her. This is what actually happens in the second volume of the novel, where it is revealed that her brother, Wataya Noboru, a sinister politician of some note, has spirited her away. The quest of the novel is thus the retrieval of Kumiko and the restoration of Tōru's relationship with her; the conflict, obviously, is between himself and Noboru, who goes from merely sinister in the early parts of the novel to purely evil by the end of the third and final volume, where we learn that he makes a practice of doing precisely what the protagonist of *South of the Border, West of the Sun* wanted to do to Izumi's cousin: he reaches into the bodies of women and physically removes their "core identities," leaving them bereft of an individual self. To counter this, Tōru's occupation in the third volume is to restore the "internal balance," or core identity, in women who have lost it. All the while he continues his search for Kumiko.

The second narrative, told to Tōru for purposes not clear until the third volume, concerns a veteran of the Japanese campaign in Manchuria named "Lieutenant Mamiya" who, while on reconnaissance with an intelligence unit in Outer Mongolia, is captured by a troop of Mongolian cavalry led by a Soviet officer we come to know as "Boris the Skinner." The nickname comes from his penchant for torturing prisoners by skinning them alive. Readers are given a graphic description of this as the leader of Mamiya's unit is interrogated. Finally, Mamiya is flung into a deep well in the Mongolian desert and left to die. He is eventually rescued, however, and reencounters "Boris the Skinner" at a gulag in Soviet Asia, where he tries to kill his enemy but fails. The significance of the narrative is to foreshadow a similar antagonism between Noboru and Tōru, with the expectation that Tōru will also be called upon to destroy his enemy. The reader must wait in suspense to know whether he will succeed where Mamiya failed.

Finally, the third narrative concerns a woman calling herself "Akasaka Nutmeg" and her son, "Akasaka Cinnamon." This mother/son team operates an exclusive clinic specializing in restoring equilibrium to internally unbalanced women and eventually employs Tōru to do the actual work of healing. Mingled with this text is the story of Nutmeg's father, a cavalry veterinarian who witnessed several massacres in Manchuria during the war, and her husband, murdered in 1975, whose body was found lacking all of its internal organs. These subnarratives are told to Tōru by Cinnamon, who encodes them as computer files he titles "Wind-Up Bird Chronicles," each with its own episode number. This is the only way he can communicate such stories to Tōru, for Cinnamon has been mute since childhood.

What permeates the entire novel is the sense of magical connections between various distinct "worlds": the internal and external "worlds" of Tōru, the historical "worlds" of 1930s Manchuria and 1980s Tokyo, the physical and spiritual "worlds" of the inner body, assaulted by Wataya Noboru and restored by Okada Tōru. And, of course, there is the "wind-up bird" of the novel's title, a creature never seen, but whose call is said to be the sound of the bird winding the springs that keep the earth turning—and thus keep time/history moving forward. The significance of the bird is, of course, this movement of time, and its appearance signifies a temporary stoppage in time, a moment when characters with special mystical abilities have visions of past, present, and future, all at once. This sense of unhinged chronology is neatly symbolized in the fact that the numbered episodes of Cinnamon's "Wind-Up Bird Chronicles" are offered to Tōru out of order, seemingly at random.

Yet the novel begins and ends with Tōru, Kumiko, and Noboru. We do not meet Noboru initially; he is represented in the couple's cat, currently missing, which they call by the same name. Even so, the cat becomes a source of tension between Tōru and Kumiko (who accuses her husband of indifference toward their pet), just as the real Wataya Noboru eventually becomes a source of almost lethal antipathy between them. He is, we finally realize, the cause of Kumiko's loss of "internal balance," rendering her incomprehensible, even unrecognizable, to Tōru. Her pleas for help come from the very first chapter of the book, when she telephones Tōru from the unconscious hotel noted earlier and insists that if he can give her just ten minutes, "we can understand each other" (*NK* 1:7-8; *WUBC* 5). Her talk then turns seductive, finally overtly sexual, and Tōru hangs up on her without giving her the ten minutes she so earnestly desires.

Yokoo, writing even as this novel was being serialized in *Shinchō*, wonders who this woman can be and suggests that her use of the telephone symbolizes an age in which direct human communication is no longer possible (Yokoo 1994, 52). This is true, of course, but there is more to the image of the telephone than merely the fact that Tōru cannot see who he is talking to; rather, it is merely one more version of the "tunnel" that always separates the internal and external minds of the Murakami protagonist. As to the identity of the "telephone woman," as she is called in the novel, few regular readers of Murakami will fail to have grasped that she is Kumiko by the end of the novel's second chapter, in which we are given ample clues about the severe gap that exists between Tōru and his wife.

For instance, in a perfectly everyday scene, Kumiko comes home from work, exhausted, to find that Tōru has cooked her a meal of stir-fried beef and green peppers, having forgotten that she cannot tolerate this combination. Kumiko also berates him for having purchased blue tissues and flowered toilet paper, which she also cannot abide. Not unnaturally, while recognizing that these are "completely trivial things, hardly the sort to cause so much commotion" (*NK* 1:56; *WUBC* 30), Tōru begins to question how much he really knows about his wife. He wonders—rightly!—if this might not be the start of something much more serious, if he is not perhaps merely standing poised at the entrance of something much more deadly.

> This could just be the entrance. Inside there might be a world
> stretching out that was just Kumiko's. It made me think of an
> enormous room, pitch dark. I was in that room with nothing but
> a tiny cigarette lighter. By the light of that flame I could see only
> the barest fraction of the room. (*NK* 1:57; *WUBC* 30)

In the context of previous Murakami novels, Tōru's inability to recognize the
voice of the "telephone woman," despite the fact that she knows everything
about him, fits a regular pattern; his admission in the passage above cements
our suspicions that the quest in this novel will be for Tōru to bring himself into
direct contact with her hidden, unrecognizable "core consciousness."

It will not be easy, however, for shortly following this incident
Kumiko goes to work, never to return. She is, we eventually learn, imprisoned by her brother, who eliminates her ability to act on her own volition
by disrupting her core identity. We do not actually see this operation performed on her, but we learn something of its nature from the narrative of
another character, Kanō Crete, a former prostitute whose last customer was
Wataya Noboru. She describes how Noboru literally reached into her body
and pulled out something utterly unknown to her, again reminiscent of the
"black box" metaphor from previous Murakami literature. The operation,
however, is unquestionably erotic.

> "Then he plunged something into me from behind. . . . It was as
> though I had been split in two, right down the middle. But the
> pain wasn't normal, because even though I was in agony, I was
> tormented by pleasure. Pain and pleasure became one."
>
> *   *   *
>
> "Then, from within my opened flesh, I felt *something* pulled
> out of me that I had neither seen nor touched before. I couldn't
> tell how large it was, but it was dripping wet, like a newborn
> baby. I had no idea what it was. It had been inside me only a
> moment earlier, but I had no knowledge of it. Yet this man had
> taken it from inside of me.
>
> "I wanted to know what it was. I wanted to see it with my
> own eyes. It was, after all, a part of me. I had a right to see it. But
> I couldn't. I was too caught up in the torrent of pain and plea-
> sure." (*NK* 2:234–35; *WUBC* 302–3; italics mine)

In the third volume Tōru learns that something similar has happened to Kumiko, when a seedy character named "Ushikawa" tells him
that "*something* has been missing from inside of Kumiko all this time. *Something* that had been supporting her like a pillar until it finally collapsed"

(*WUBC* 3:358;[13] italics mine). The reader can well imagine that Kumiko has suffered the same fate as Kanō Crete.

Various other narratives in the work suggest that Kumiko and Kanō Crete are not the only victims of this form of assault. Kumiko suspects something peculiar in the relationship between Noboru and her elder sister, who died of food poisoning as a child, a suspicion Tōru later comes to share. One thinks back also to the death of Akasaka Nutmeg's husband, whose body was discovered with its internal organs removed; did this foreshadow a similar operation on the bodies of the three women mentioned above? Akasaka Cinnamon's narrative about his grandfather in Manchuria also includes a scene in which Chinese prisoners are bayoneted to death, special care being taken to destroy the internal organs in the process. Even the skinning of Lt. Mamiya's commander in Mongolia might be seen as a process of penetrating the outer body in an attempt to gain whatever may lurk inside—in this case, information.

As the examples above suggest, there is a clear link between the "core identity," sexuality, and violence, one that is perhaps inevitable given the fact that coitus itself involves a penetration and is thus innately a violation, a literal invasion of the body. Murakami's use of images related to bladed weapons—the knife used to skin Lt. Mamiya's commander, the bayonet used to kill the Chinese prisoners, or the knife Wataya Noboru wields in the final confrontation with Tōru—suggests no more or less of a penetration than Noboru's invasion of Kanō Crete's body.[14]

Perhaps it is inevitable, then, that the means to restoring the core identities that have been lost is also sexual, and that Tōru, an essentially passive being up until the end of the novel when he bludgeons Noboru to death with a baseball bat, is the key to this. Much of his function as a mystical healer is foreshadowed in his relationship with Kanō Crete, the former prostitute who, through magical means, now visits Tōru in his dreams. Significantly, her character overlaps with that of the "telephone woman," Kumiko, for when they meet it is in the unconscious hotel room, and Kanō Crete writhes atop him wearing a blue dress he recognizes as his wife's.

Most important, however, is that unlike the encounter between Kanō Crete and Wataya Noboru, in which Noboru clearly occupied the position of dominance while Kanō Crete was helpless, the sexual roles between her-

---

13. This section has been cut from the translated version.
14. The similarity is worth noting between this assault and the removal of the protagonist's shadow, and the hard-boiled protagonist's slashed belly, in *Hard-Boiled Wonderland and the End of the World*. The state always represents some form of intrusion—usually violent—in Murakami's world.

self and Tōru are reversed in his dreamscape, where in the first instance she performs fellatio on him, and in the second he lies on his back and she sits astride him, and he ejaculates into her. This reassertion of control, of a dominant role, not only helps Kanō Crete to reestablish a sense of self, severely disrupted by Noboru, but also suggests through the superimposition of her character on Kumiko's that the secret to reversing the effects of Noboru's mutilation is for the victim to take an active role.

The opposition of action/passivity represented in the behavior of Noboru and Tōru, respectively, is cemented in the third volume of the novel, in which Tōru works as a healer for Akasaka Nutmeg, who is drawn to him by a purple mark on his face, a mark that appeared after a narrow escape from his unconscious hotel room just as Noboru entered, bent on killing him. The mark is a sign of his mystical power, but also a living presence, an external emblem of the "black box" that lurks inside his mind. Like that "something" that was drawn out of Kanō Crete, it is warm and alive, pulsating with energy. Like a sacred relic, it contains the secret to the magic healing powers Tōru possesses: his "patients" are healed through direct contact with the mark. Here, too, total passivity and sexuality combine to recreate the earlier scenes with Kanō Crete/Kumiko in his dreamscape. As he sits alone on a sofa, his eyes covered with dark goggles (the darkness, as usual, signaling the approach of an "unconscious" experience), a woman enters the room (he can tell from the scent of perfume that it is a woman) and begins to stroke the mark on his face with her fingers, "as if she were trying to discern in it some secret buried there in ancient times" (*NK* 3:64; *WUBC* 372). What follows is purely sexual:

> Then she stopped stroking me, got up from the sofa and, coming from behind me, used her tongue. . . . Her tongue was cunning in the way it nuzzled my skin. Varying the pressure, the angles, the movements, it tasted the mark, sucked at it, stimulated it. I began to feel a warm, wet ache down below. I didn't want to get hard. It would have been too meaningless. But I couldn't stop it. (*NK* 3:64; *WUBC* 372)

After the woman leaves, Tōru discovers, just as he does after his dreams involving Kanō Crete, that he has ejaculated.

Thus the sexuality related to identity helps us to place into greater relief the true import of the suggestive telephone calls Tōru receives, but flees from, at the start of the novel. Kumiko's attempts to reach out to Tōru are, long before he can possibly realize it, aimed both at revealing herself completely (as she does in describing her body over the telephone) and at receiving the same kind of healing that Tōru offers to his anonymous clients. Tōru's inability to recognize her voice merely perpetuates the injunction against any image from the darkness of the unconscious appearing (or, apparently, even sounding) the same in the light of the conscious world. At the same time, Noboru's removal of Kumiko's core identity, literally erasing herself, makes it inevitable, perhaps, that she will not be recognizable as the same person to Tōru in any case.

THE ACT OF NAMING

As noted above, names are a point of some interest in Murakami literature. In the early works they are used as a means of identifying the images that emerge from the protagonists' minds, sometimes for creating metonymical links between those images and the original object of desire. In other cases the names, usually absurd ones, are offered simply as a source of humor in the work.

The above discussion of *The Wind-Up Bird Chronicle* offers ample evidence that Murakami has not given up on the use of unusual names for his characters. But in this work he also adds a new facet, one more closely related to the critique of identity I have been describing, for part of Tōru's quest, as I noted above, is to discover the name of the woman in the hotel room, to identify her, and thus to free her from her unconscious prison.[15] This is, of course, merely a recreation of the principal theme seen in Murakami fiction from the beginning: the need for acknowledgment of the self by an other in order to establish identity. The only difference is that in this case the task is performed by an external other.

It is also the central theme of *The Wind-Up Bird Chronicle*. When Okada Tōru meets the woman in the unconscious hotel room in the second volume of this work, she tells him sadly, "You want to know who I am. Unfortunately, I can't help you with that. I know all about you, and you know everything about me. Unfortunately, I know nothing about myself" (*NK* 2:138; *WUBC* 247). Immediately after this, the woman announces Tōru's quest in the novel:

> "Seek out my name, Okada Tōru. No, you needn't even look for
> it; *you already know it!* You need only remember it. If you could

15. Murakami reinvigorates a theme made popular by Takahashi Gen'ichirō's novel *Sayōnara, Gyangutachi* (1982), in which bestowed names (hence bestowed identity) are rejected in favor of names selected by the principals themselves, but eventually bestowed names come back into fashion as a sign of affection between lovers, a means of showing one's love. However, the narrator notes, names are useless in the normal sense, because they are used exclusively between the lovers, who do not disclose one another's names to others.

just find my name, I could get out of here. Then I think I can help you find your wife—Okada Kumiko, right? If you want to find your wife, then you must find my name first. That will be your leverage. You have no time to lose. Every day that you delay finding my name, Okada Kumiko recedes a little farther from you." (*NK* 2:138-139; *WUBC* 248; Murakami's emphasis)

The woman is, of course, Kumiko herself, but without her core identity, now stolen by Wataya Noboru, she cannot find her way back to herself. However, the mere name, "Okada Kumiko," as the above passage suggests, has no power to connect with her in the absence of that identity. Near the end of the final volume, in fact, when Tōru has finally understood the truth, he tells her that she is Kumiko, but this has little effect on her, so long has she been drifting, anonymous, in this unconscious world. Like the unconscious protagonist of *Hard-Boiled Wonderland and the End of the World*, the longer she is separated from her "black box," the less likely she is to understand the means to reconnect with it or, for that matter, to care about doing so.

At the moment that Okada Tōru "names" Kumiko, thereby attempting to restore her identity, Wataya Noboru enters the room, wielding his knife. The two men struggle, and Tōru beats Noboru to death with his baseball bat. At the same moment, the "real" Noboru in the conscious world collapses of a brain hemorrhage and teeters on the point of death. Later, hearing that he remains on life support, Kumiko goes to his hospital room and pulls the plug, and then gives herself up to the police.

One might imagine, now that Tōru has solved the mystery of Kumiko's whereabouts and dispatched his enemy, that the novel will conclude with the return of Kumiko *as* Kumiko and that *The Wind-Up Bird Chronicle* might be the first novel in which the hero gains his heart's desire. Indeed, this might actually be the end result, but the reader never witnesses it. Instead, Tōru must content himself with corresponding with Kumiko while she recovers, restoring her life energy, rebuilding her identity. We might well imagine that Tōru's power as a mystical healer would save her, but, predictably, with the destruction of Wataya Noboru, Tōru's connection with the "other world" of the unconscious disappears, and with it his ability to heal. He can only wait for his wife to rediscover her individual identity, now that he has helped her to rediscover her name.

CONCLUSIONS

What the analyses of the works above suggest is that identity formation, for Murakami, is grounded both in a crucial relationship between the con-

scious and unconscious selves, and also in the relationship between the self
and others in society. Murakami suggests through his tangible construction
of the inner self and his dealing with memories that something always intervenes, disrupts communication, between those individual selves, and also
between the self and "external" others. In the stories above this is expressed
as a powerful nostalgic desire for something hiding inside the protagonists'
minds, something that can only be brought out through the intervention of
magic. In this way Murakami borrows a theoretical approach to art that
has been used in other regional literatures to express an alternative *cultural* identity, typically one aimed at resisting the hegemonic power of Euro-
American positivism—expressed mainly as the assumption that the "real"
and the "magical" cannot mingle. Murakami, also, resists the groundings
of positivism, both in his approach to reality and to history, as we shall
shortly see, but his agenda in challenging concepts like reality and truth
operates both at the cultural *and* the individual level, the latter of which
takes precedence for him. He denies historical absolutism in order to present
his alternative history, one that is not general nor grand in scale, but intensely personal; he denies the absolutism of reality, not merely to challenge a philosophical concept, but more practically in order to gain access,
fictionally, to something normally too abstract to permit concrete narrativization or representation. He denies the absolutism of the current ideological system at work in Japanese society in order to define more clearly those
who slip through the cracks of that system.

In the next chapter I will follow up on the issues of identity formation with a more detailed discussion of how the self is constructed in Murakami's fictional world, and what kinds of theoretical concepts may be
brought to bear on the subject. As we have seen, Murakami approaches
identity formation through the discourses of self and other, the relationship
between subject, object, and desire. Moreover, as the discussion above makes
abundantly clear, these relationships are almost always linguistic in nature—for Murakami the nostalgic image is "just words." It is only in the
past several decades that theorists of the mind have come to understand
the relationship of the inner and outer minds as a linguistic one, or the
workings of desire, repression, and displacement as related to metonymy—
usually understood to be a peculiarly literary notion—and so it is to those
theories that I would now turn.

Chapter Three

Desire, the Symbolic Order, and Mass Society

> The relation of the self to the Other is entirely produced in a process of gap.
>
> —Jacques Lacan, *The Four Fundamental Concepts of Psychoanalysis*

Those who have spent even a little time pondering Murakami Haruki's fiction will recognize the pressing need for some psychological grounding to his work. As I have pointed out in some detail in the previous chapter on magical realism, Murakami's use of that technique represents a drive toward the unconscious, and an attempt to locate the identity, the self, of his protagonist.

The psychological underpinnings of Murakami's literature are complex, but even an untrained observer will note the ready correlation between Murakami's vision of the unconscious and prevalent theories in twentieth-century psychological inquiry. Specifically, his division of the psyche into distinct yet symbiotically and linguistically connected realms is closely evocative of the conceptualizations of Jacques Lacan, whose vision of the relationship between self and Other, and whose hypothesis regarding the Symbolic Order, is organized around the relationship between desire, the object of that desire (the repressed unconscious Other), and the intervention of the Symbolic Order (a linguistically grounded version of Freud's "superego"). Moreover, in terms of his mass cultural approach to psychoanalysis, Lacan's interests appear to have something in common with Murakami's, for both men are interested in the notion of social resistance, where it emerges and, more importantly, where and why it fails to do so. But an additional reason lies behind my interest in exploring Murakami via Lacan: unlike so many of his contemporaries in the field of psychological

109

inquiry, Lacan approaches the unconscious with a certain wariness, even fear. He understands, as Freud did, that the unconscious is an alien world, the perfect analogy for which is Pandora's Box, whose opening entails definite risks, both for subject and analyst. "It is always dangerous to disturb anything in that zone of shades," writes Lacan (1978, 22, 30), who is troubled by the fact that "what was thought to be an infernal opening should later have been so remarkably asepticized."

Some further exploration of the relationship between Lacan's intertwining of the Self/Other/Symbolic and Murakami's model of Self/Other/State may also provide useful theoretical insights for some of the portrayals of contemporary Japanese subjectivity we have already observed in Murakami's work. Obviously, the breadth and depth of Lacan's thinking and influence on modern psychological theory being what it is, there is no possibility of summing up the totality of his work in the scope of this chapter. I do not intend to attempt this. What I do intend, briefly, at least, is to examine the role of the symbolic in the foundation of the self.

Of considerable interest in this regard is Lacan's characterization of the unconscious as being "like a language" (1978, 20). What does this mean? Lacan suggests that the unconscious is a system—a closed system of signifiers. In so describing the unconscious, he means in part to demystify it: "it is this linguistic structure that gives its status to the unconscious. It is this structure, in any case, that assures us that there is, beneath the term unconscious, something definable, accessible, and objectifiable" (1978, 21). Here Lacan acknowledges both the work of Lévi-Strauss in structuring social systems, and Saussure's structuralist theories about language at the turn of the twentieth century. Essentially, his intention is to demonstrate that the unconscious is neither metaphysical nor mystical, nor even entirely abstract theorization. As nuclear physicists have clearly demonstrated the effects of atomic manipulation, even if we have yet to see the atom itself, Lacan hopes to show us how the unconscious can be studied and charted, if not yet seen.

But Lacan's real interest is not in properly functioning systems of signification. Rather, he is concerned with rupture, with splits and gaps that appear in the fabric of that structure, for this is both where we discern the unconscious and also where we encounter what Lacan terms the "real," something akin, I believe, to what I termed the "precultural," or the "prelinguistic" in my introduction. It is an elusive term, one that Lacan likens to Freud's *Trieb*, "drive" or "pulsion," taking us to the deepest levels of cause in human behavior. Alan Sheridan writes of the real as "what is prior to the assumption of the symbolic . . . in the case of the subject, for instance, the organism and its biological needs" ("Translator's Note" in Lacan 1978, 280). The two descriptions are interrelated, but not in agreement, for Lacan's reading of Freud's *Trieb* is strictly that of psychical drive, rather than pure, base physical instinct (Freud's *Instinkt*), observable in prelinguistic humans (infants). For our purposes, however, it is important to see this in a more abstract sense, not merely as a stage in human development but as an ideal toward which we strive, an attempt to reverse the effects of Babel and speak again in the "pure" language of divinity. For Murakami the prelinguistic refers to a place in the mind where the self may meet its unconscious "Other" without the intervention of symbolic systems, of rules and social custom, and become whole. Thus, I believe it is this obscure area of the "real"—the realm of the precultural—that forms the locus of desire for Murakami's protagonists. As we have seen, however, this "real" realm is never accessible, because it is, finally, impossible to return to that state.

This gap, or rupture, is also where certain psychical transformations are conducted, as the result of the mind's attempt to create a harmony between the unconscious and the real. "In this gap," writes Lacan, "something happens. Once this gap has been filled, is the neurosis cured? . . . the neurosis becomes something else, sometimes a mere illness, a scar, as Freud said—the scar, not of the neurosis, but of the unconscious" (1978, 22). Where is this gap to be found? Lacan argues that it occurs in the so-called "law of the signifier," that is, the symbolic. Its creation is the result, he suggests, of some trauma, though I wonder if we could not also understand that split as occurring as the result of excessive longing, as massive desire for the reconnection with the inner self, disrupted by the intervention of the symbolic early in our development?

This, I would argue, is where Lacan and Murakami finally meet, in this moment—truly the briefest of moments—at which the unconscious reveals to us some portion of itself. One might metaphorize this, in Murakami's case especially, as being something like the shutter of a camera opening and closing, creating only a split-second of exposure, the briefest of gaps. Through this gap, the darkness of the unconscious—Lacan refers to it as a "world of shade"—is momentarily illuminated. Like the recording of an image on a strip of film, the flash illuminates, only momentarily, a vision of the hidden contents within, leaving only the ghostly remnant in the conscious mind. This is the function of the gap.

> What is ontic in the function of the unconscious is the split through which that something, whose adventure in our field seems so short,

is for a moment brought into the light of day—a moment because the second stage, which is one of closing up, gives this apprehension a vanishing aspect. (Lacan 1978, 31)

We have certainly encountered such a vision in Murakami's fiction. As the protagonist of *Pinball, 1973* says, "At any given moment something may take hold of our minds . . . for two or three days it might wander around in our minds, then return to its place of origin. . . . Darkness" (*MHZ* 1:201). Murakami's vision of the concept, memory, or idea that "grabs" the conscious mind, releasing the chain of signification to produce a correspondent image or symbol, only then to return to its *moto no tokoro*—its "place of origin"—is very much like Lacan's model, appearing in a "gap" that develops between the inner and outer selves. Yet that concept, though it appears to be knowable, is in fact a mystery, an enigma, as I have said before. Who are the Twins, who is the Sheepman, what is the "wind-up bird"? We have some sense—the sense, perhaps, of the analyst—of what these images may signify, but the Murakami protagonist is always at a loss on such points. Lacan, on the other hand, points to such encounters in the gap as "discoveries," though only such as lead, as we have seen again and again, to a sense of loss. "Now, as soon as it is presented, this discovery becomes a rediscovery and, furthermore, it is always ready to steal away again, thus establishing the dimension of loss" (Lacan 1978, 25).

Out of this loss, Lacan argues, neurosis grows. In Murakami's fictional world, as we have seen, this neurosis takes the form of an obsession, followed by the magical conjuring of an image of the object of desire. Thus, the object revealed in the "flash" takes on a tangible form. However, Lacan's use in the above citation of the term "rediscovery" is important, related to the notion of "repetition," a term he recovers from Freud's original *wiederholen*, as opposed to "reproduction" (*reproduzieren*). The difference is both crucial and relevant to our readings in Murakami as well: in the latter, like a photograph or a painting, something is reproduced *as it appears to us;* in repetition, however, that object is represented symbolically, metonymically, thus producing the aberrations, representational gaps, and chains of signification that we have seen so often in Murakami's novels and stories.

The grounding of this image, this flash in the unconscious gap, is desire. The ultimate purpose of that desire, however, is not always clear. Even if we may say that one's desire is to reconnect with some inner part of the self, as is the case with the Murakami character, what, precisely, does one expect to gain from the connection? Indeed, even whether this is to be termed a reconnection is in some doubt; are we truly restoring something that was once possessed, then lost?

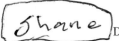

In one important sense, the answer is yes. We seek, in our encounter with the gap, a reconnection with the real, the prelinguistic. As Lacan also found, we can only speculate about the nature of this realm. Yet his probing is revealing, particularly in its revelation of a subject *beneath* the subject. In his response to Descartes' famous dictum *cogito, ergo sum*, for instance, Lacan insists that what enables Descartes to declare his subjectivity in this way at all is the act of speaking, *language*. There must be, he reasons, something behind (or prior to) that linguistic act that drives it outward. This is, presumably, the precultural, primordial "self," and it is one of instinct rather than cognition.[1]

Obviously, the prelinguistic subject is not the same as the unconscious subject, which is, like its conscious counterpart, always constituted by culture—by language and experience. As the previous chapter showed, this inner subject remains close to the surface and operates always through a system of signifiers. This is the normal, and at the same time the most superficial object of the conscious subject's desire, what Lacan terms *objet petit a*, the simple "other" related to other people and our own internal self.[2] Yet even this comparatively common desire, Lacan and Murakami would agree, is doomed to failure. The symbolic—Lacan's Other (*grand Autre*, an internal power to which we grant external, autonomous status and our own submission)—intervenes between the conscious subject and *objet petit a*, suppressing our desire and supplanting it with that of the Symbolic Order. Thus, the symbolic is related to the idea of gaze, Lacan's *regard*, which emerges out of the subject's awareness of being observed. That is to say, at the moment we see another person we recognize simultaneously our subjectivity, and our own objectivity, for we become aware that we are also watched. Following this, we begin to imagine that we are watched all the time by a third gaze, one that is omniscient and empowered over us. This, says Lacan, is the symbolic process—an inevitable process—by which

---

1. I use the term "self" here with certain reservations, for a "primordial" or "prelinguistic" *self* seems about as likely as Baudrillard's "prelinguistic" apprehension of reality. We are speaking here, as Lacan was, more of the vestiges of a most basic kind of memory, irrecoverable and incomprehensible to cultural (linguistic) man.
2. Throughout this chapter I shall be relying on Lacan's own differentiation between the "other" (*autre, objet petit a*), using the lowercase "o," and the "Other" (*grand Autre*). The former refers to our desire for other subjects, whether within ourselves or external to us, including the unconscious other; the latter refers to the Other that forms part of the Symbolic Order. It is critical to bear in mind at all times that the Other, while given a quasi-external status by the self as an autonomous entity that freely intervenes between us and others, is nevertheless an internal projection, a production of the (imaginary) gaze.

we have created God, morality, state power, ideology, structure, and meaning. Writes Juliet MacCannell,

> In Lacan there is no escape from the process of symbolisation, which is essentially the process of alienation, in the relationship of self to other, and self to self. In the glance, he writes, we see the other. But because we can see him or her, we also know the other can see us: we can take the point of view of the other, in a transitive relationship. This is the moment, in Hegelian terms, of 'recognition'. And it is this moment that falls to the power of the Other, who enters the scene immediately to disrupt this transivity: a *third* point of view, that which is constitutive of the Lacanian *regard*, arises. We see ourselves being seen and seeing. It is this third dimension which creates the specifically human (alienated) condition. (1986, 136)

According to Lacan, then, the Symbolic Order (though constituted by ourselves) always intervenes, steps between ourselves and the Other, the object of our desire. This process is always grounded in language, in the intervention via language of symbols between us and the object of our desire.

As the previous chapter suggested, the conscious self in Murakami's landscape is always cut off, except indirectly (dreams, slips of the tongue, *déjà vu*, etc.) from his unconscious mind, thereby creating the most definitive aspect of the author's model of the conscious/unconscious dichotomy. Lacan similarly describes the human subject as *à la dérive*, "afloat," separate from the comfortable grounding of the inner mind. As Ellie Ragland-Sullivan writes, "*à la dérive* refers to a boat cut loose from its moorings. Detached from any direct access to its own unconscious knowledge, the human subject is also adrift" (1986, 75).

Lacan conceives of this separation as the result of linguistic intervention in the as yet unformed subject's infancy. Language, he suggests, simultaneously creates a realm of repression, and a metonymical hierarchy by which objects of desire are placed at a distance, out of reach. One cannot help noting something Platonic in this mistrust of language, which Lacan considers as separating us, as it were, from the true essence of what we desire. Language, like poetry in the Republic, comes between us and the thing itself. This is, of course, Lacan's version of the Oedipal separation of mother and son, and the origin of the desire for the phallus as well. But Lacan's model indicates that the intervention of the symbolic, as the term inherently suggests, is a linguistic one—that our initiation into the world of words, of signification, marks the beginning of repression. As Ragland-Sullivan notes,

. . . the phallic injunction to separation or differentiation creates repression by pushing an infant into the world of language. Just as the child has been manipulating objects for many months, it now learns to manipulate words in the same manner: both to situate itself in the world and as an aid to mastering the experience of division from the mother. (1986, 75)

But the world of language, for Lacan as for Murakami, is the world of death by repression, because it separates us from our most basic desires. MacCannell (1986) suggests that for Lacan the body is life, but that life is a phenomenon of prelinguistic Man; language, on the other hand, is death, and represents a fundamental illogicality of human development. That is, we willingly drive ourselves forward toward our own demise.

Language delivers us not to life but to death, at least symbolically, it replaces the body. "'Life' for language is other than what one calls life. Drives which elevate this life to language make as much of a place for that which, in terms of somatic support, signifies death. . . ." Shakespeare knew that the discourse of a Fool is, in confusing times, wiser than that of the Sage. Should we not prefer life to death? In short, why subject ourselves to language, or to language as symbolic? (MacCannell 1986, xiii)

It is not difficult to see the similarities in thinking between Murakami's fictional landscape and Lacan's model of the mind, in which the object of desire in linguistic man is always already once removed from its source, and wherein that source is entirely unattainable, being a part of the repressed unconscious Other. Inasmuch as the linguistic subject is incapable of conceiving any object or idea without the intervening barrier of language and cultural experience, the development of language in the human subject becomes an impregnable barrier between us and the object of our desire. It is that barrier or intervention, ultimately bound up into a system of cultural and social meanings, that has come to be known in Lacanian theory as the "Symbolic Order."

Lacan's Symbolic Order is, I think, the most important facet of his contribution to modern psychoanalysis and forms the focal point of most major studies on his thought. Unlike Freud's superego, an internal device providing us with moral standards and self-critique, something like the conscience, the Symbolic Order is a social contract grounded in the commonality of language (on which is grounded Law), the expression of a "higher truth" that governs the behavior of human beings, disrupting their pursuit of the object of desire, the unconscious Other. Its most common manifestations were once found in expressions of religion and morality, later in promises of "civilization."

At the same time, by grounding his concept of "order" in the *symbolic*, Lacan uncompromisingly places us into the realm of language: metonymy and metaphor. The matter of self and the Symbolic Order is, as a result, cast into a discursive mode, which by definition requires interaction, for the use of symbol itself implies a common understanding of the language being used. "*I* is a verbal term," Lacan argues, "whose use is learned through a specific reference to the other, which is a spoken reference. The *I* is born through the reference to the you" (1988, 166). In other words, the Symbolic Order cannot exist for the isolated individual and more than language can develop for the singular, isolated subject, and since the Symbolic Order is required, according to Lacan, to define selfhood, the isolated individual cannot exist as subject or self.[3]

EXISTENCE AND CIVILIZATION IN MURAKAMI HARUKI

This becomes a fundamental issue in the literature of Murakami, whose protagonists, especially in the first ten years of his career, are so self-absorbed and socially isolated that we cannot help wondering if they exist at all, or at least to what extent they possess a sense of self. Responses differ as to the relative merits of this isolation—read alternatively as a form of transcendent egoism by Karatani Kōjin, as a kind of superhuman self-control by Aoki Tamotsu (see previous chapter). Most arguments seem to conform, however, to the apocalyptic declaration by Kuroko Kazuo, that we live today in a "Walkman society" (Kuroko 1990, 14).

Perhaps no writer has been more consistent in presenting such characters in his fiction than Murakami. I have noted above Kawamoto Saburō's contention that the Murakami narrator is a man "cut off from society, who has not the slightest scent of life about him," and that while normally employed, "in the course of his work the Murakami narrator interacts as little as possible with society" (1986, 46, 48). But while Murakami's protagonists indulge in the freedom of this isolation, they do not revel in it, nor does the author necessarily approve of such a stance toward society. This is not an alternative lifestyle we are encouraged to try out; it is the reality of contemporary Japanese society. The consequence, according to the argument above, is a society of nonpeople, or at best, a society of people who

3. This idea, which is fundamental to existentialism as well, also arises in Jean-Paul Sartre's *Being and Nothingness* (1943).

have developed new strategies for self-identification. This is what Murakami's literature shows the reader in each successive novel and short story.

Murakami is, of course, by no means the only Japanese author of the past several decades to show an interest in the notion of the gaze. One of the more interesting in terms of its assertion of the malleability of identity through alterations in both external appearance and shifts in gaze is Abe Kōbō's 1964 novel *Tanin no kao* (translated as The Face of Another, 1966), in which a scientist's face is horribly disfigured in an explosion of liquid nitrogen. As he considers the possibility of constructing a new, artificial face for himself, a plastic surgeon warns him of the importance of external expression in creating identity through others: "[T]he expression is something like an equation by which we show our relationship with others. It's a roadway between oneself and others" (Abe 1966, 27). When that path is blocked, he goes on to say, one becomes cut off from the world, and begins to lose one's sense of existence: "It's an established theory in infant psychology that the human animal can validate his ego only through the eyes of others" (Abe 1966, 28).

The scientist then goes on to create a new face for himself in the form of an incredibly lifelike mask. In its creation he goes to considerable lengths to consider each detail: complexion, angularity, blemishes, and so forth, and their effects on the identity of the wearer. When the mask is finally complete, the plastic surgeon's use of the infant psychology analogy seem particularly appropriate: he has created a new life, one whose experiences—even those that would have been mundane to the scientist himself, such as a streetcar ride—become new and exciting. More importantly, however, is that the mask, as the portion of the scientist most outwardly and directly exposed to the public's gaze, becomes an autonomous being of its own, and he finds himself increasingly under its control.

> It was a strange feeling. My real face tried to murmur quietly in a small voice, slipping deep into inconspicuous belly folds. . . . This shouldn't be. . . . I only asked the mask to help me recover . . . I never once asked it to do things its own way. (Abe 1966, 125)

Gradually the mask becomes emboldened, and as the scientist gets drunk one evening, "the mask" makes indiscreet remarks about his superiors at work. His previous identity is by this time virtually lost—"as if I had become someone other than my real face. . . . The real face definitely could not get drunk the way the mask did" (Abe 1966, 151–52). Finally, "the mask" goes so far as to seduce the scientist's own wife, and he expresses his astonishment at how easily she gave in. Only later does he learn that she had long since guessed his true identity.

The importance of this work lies in the way in which Abe depicts severe contrasts between the scientist before his accident, as a distracted academic, in his bandages as a frustrated, timid, self-proclaimed "faceless monster" (Abe 1966, 134), and finally as "the mask," self-assertive and bold, even leaning toward the sinister.[4] The fact that his personality, his very identity, changes with the outer shell that encloses it makes clear the importance of the outer, external gaze of others, and how they view him as an object, or other.

Though by no means as ambitious a work as *The Face of Another*, Furui Yoshikichi's 1976 story, "Ningyō" (translated as The Doll, 1997) is considerably more explicit in its exploration of the external gaze. In this story the protagonist, a young woman named Ikuko, travels to Tokyo to establish her own family register. She bears as a gift a large doll given to her by her uncle. Presumably because she has come to Tokyo in order to start a family register of her own, thereby separating herself from her uncle's family (her parents are dead), Ikuko experiences the peculiar sensation of being a "nonperson," an empty vessel without intrinsic identity of her own; instead, she only discovers her "self" through the responses of others, who seem intent, however, on mistaking her for someone else. "'I have been mistaken for other people four times in a week,'" she complains to her doll, "'and the people who mistook me looked so incredibly shocked when I told them they were wrong. So, who am I anyway? Am I not just me, myself, not just a single person anymore? Lots of different me's must be walking around out there" (Furui 1997, 121).

After establishing her new "identity" via the family register at Tokyo's City Hall, Ikuko has the sensation of displacement, of detachment. She has difficulty remembering her own address, and begins to sense in the gaze of others that a gap has opened between herself and the world around her. She can no longer maintain her unique, unchanging identity as "Ikuko." At the same time, she finds in this situation an odd sense of liberation, as if she were reconnecting with a lost past, as she finds herself "defined" by others.

> In the midst of these days spent in a state of detachment from her own self and the world around her, it was only those moments

---

4. In one rather interesting scene, "the mask" purchases an illegal air pistol, while the scientist wonders what on earth he will ever do with such a thing (124–25).

when she was mistaken for someone else that this barrier fell away. She felt as if she had suddenly come to her senses and was looking around. However, she was not returning to her own self. Rather, it was the sensation of returning to a realm where distant memories dwelled. She didn't know her own face. She seemed to have a face that could belong to anybody. She felt she was looking in the mirror when she looked at the people around her. (Furui 1997, 126)

Two relevant points emerge from Ikuko's experience: first, her identity, though fluid, is linked always and inexorably to the others around her; and second, these links are themselves bound to memory, experience, the past.

Development of the self, of identity, cannot happen in a vacuum; it requires the presence and participation of an other, some entity external to or separate from the subject. "What determines me," argues Lacan, ". . . is the gaze that is outside" (1978, 106). This is also an argument that enters Murakami's literature quite early as a matter of pure discourse: the protagonist of *Hear the Wind Sing* admits that as a child he was extremely "quiet" (*mukuchi*). Fearing some psychological problem, his parents took him to see a doctor, who told him that communication is the very essence of civilization.

> Civilization is communication, he told me. If you can't express something, it is the same thing as not existing. Understand? Zero. Suppose for a moment that you are hungry. All you have to do is say "I'm hungry." I would give you a cookie. Go ahead and eat it. (I munched on a cookie.) But if you don't say anything, there is no cookie. (The doctor cruelly hid the plate of cookies beneath the table.) Zero. Got it?
>
> *   *   *
>
> The doctor was right. Civilization was communication. Once you lost something you needed to express or communicate, that was the end of civilization. (*MHZ* 1:25–26)

One could hardly ask for a more appropriate example either of Lacan's insistence that we are products of interaction, of discourse, or of the mechanism of social control by which the subject is drawn into the world of rules, grammar, language, the commonality of the symbolic. Failure to communicate is a failure to exist, a realization that clearly unnerves the protagonist. The above example is almost *too* appropriate in its expression of temptation, literally dangling an object of desire before the protagonist's eyes and calling it "culture."

Communication, by its very nature, suggests order, structure, and therefore rules and control. It implies cooperation, agreement between participants in the discourse. Such cooperation is also essential in establishing a healthy relationship between the self and its unconscious other. This has been articulated within the psychological community at least since the 1930s, when George Herbert Mead wrote, presaging Lacan, that "[t]he importance of what we term 'communication' lies in the fact that it provides a form of behavior in which the organism or the individual may become an object to himself" (1956, 201). Mead was among the early theorists of the mind who argued that the development of the self (what I have been terming "identity") is achieved through a discursive relationship between oneself as subject, and a perception of oneself as object. Only through language, Mead argues, do we have the capacity to see ourselves as object as well as subject, and in the process of normal discourse—as we converse with others—we are also in continual and meaningful discourse with ourselves as object, or other. But, he cautions, the self does not develop this capacity for self-reflexive discourse on its own; it must be created through meaningful interaction with external others.

> The self, as that which can be an object to itself, is essentially a social structure, and it arises in social experience. After a self has arisen, it in a certain sense provides for itself its social experiences, and so we can conceive of an absolutely solitary self. *But it is impossible to conceive of a self arising outside of social experience.* (Mead 1956, 204; italics mine)

This capacity for self-reflexive discourse is, in Mead's opinion, unique to humans because it is uniquely grounded in symbolic language, a specifically human characteristic. "I know of no other form of behavior than the linguistic," writes Mead, "in which the individual is an object to himself, and, so far as I can see, the individual is not a self in the reflective sense unless he is an object to himself" (1956, 206). Mead's reliance on language is a proper precursor to Lacan's linkage of the conscious and unconscious by metaphor and metonymy, and the two are in general agreement about the commonality of language—that the symbolic is meaningless unless it is shared throughout the society that uses it, thereby ensuring its effectiveness not only in identity formation, but (in Lacan) as a mechanism of social control in the form of the Symbolic Order.

But how is the symbolic defined and organized in contemporary postindustrial societies, and what hold does it have over its individual members? Why do we, as free individuals, submit ourselves willingly to strict social controls that are merely constructions of our own making? What does the Symbolic Order offer to us that is sufficiently attractive to persuade us give up our individual autonomy for it? Lacan himself noted that the motivations offered to the individual in past societies are no longer relevant today: religion, morality, civilization, order (MacCannell 1986, 125).

I think that to a point this question was answered in the previous chapter, in which a sense of belonging, of participation, coupled with an idea of goal orientation, were paramount in producing the kind of "induced integration" into the national ethic of consumerism (or, as Hidaka terms it, "economism") necessary to drive the economy. Indeed, it is worth noting that, like Hidaka, Lacan argues that the intervention of the Symbolic Order is rarely perceived as particularly sinister by those intervened upon; rather, like any organic being, such intervention naturally moves in directions best suited to ensure the Symbolic Order's continuity, which is to say the continuity and stability of society, of culture itself. MacCannell writes that "the drive of culture is neither benevolent nor malevolent; it is a mindless, inexorable drive toward division, splitting. It is aimed, but only at producing, through this fission, the energy and the power to perpetuate itself" (1986, 151).

MacCannell's reading of Lacan in this regard is interestingly similar to prevalent readings of Japanese culture in general, particularly in terms of how it "homogenizes" its members. She argues that the trade-off for one's conscious desires is a "place in the Order," but a place in which interaction with others is strictly controlled, thereby allowing the individual a sense of high achievement, yet simultaneously rendering the "achievement" meaningless, for it exists entirely as a construct, meaningful only within the context of the Symbolic Order, which is itself a construct, given external, autonomous status, as noted above, yet paradoxically drawing its authority—indeed, its very existence—from the individuals it controls. Thus, its evaluation is empty and meaningless.

> What the Symbolic promises to the human in exchange for his gift of conscious desire to it is its positive evaluation of him. Lacan writes that, in reality, the Symbolic is no-thing; the 'primary signifier is pure non-sense' (4FC, 252); but it is that nothing which doubly splits the human from not simply his so-called 'own' desires, but, more importantly, from the other humans without whom desire literally makes no sense. Giving him a place in the Order promises to 'evaluate' him. And so it does; it gives him infinite value, rather cheaply bought, since he, like it, is nothing. The trick is that nothing divided by nothing yields not nothing, but infinity. . . . (MacCannell 1986, 125)

The previous chapter demonstrated this to be basically true in the case of Japan, as well. If we transpose the term "ideology" into "Symbolic Order" we come away with something resembling the actual structure of Japanese desire. As we saw, the history of the postwar in Japan has been marked by the systematic absorption of the individual into a system of consumerism—the newest manifestation of the Symbolic Order. Thus, cast into Lacan's terminology, one can say that the Japanese today live within a symbolic that channels and controls their desires, affirming participation in the consumerist society while minimizing individualist (unique) expression. This is not merely a matter of discouraging individual opinion, as Honda argues above; it is, rather, a cyclical system of education that forces children into competition with one another at an early age for admission to better schools, which in turn will lead to a better position in society, and a greater level of participation in the consumerist structure.

ALIENATION OF DESIRE: THE SELF DIVIDED

As I noted above, Murakami Haruki's literature is grounded in the crisis of self-identity that results when the subject is irrevocably separated from the object, the self from the Other, the object of desire. In this we have perhaps the clearest expression of the real social consequences of late-model capitalism in contemporary Japanese literature, for at stake is nothing less than the constitution of the individual, autonomous Japanese subject. In short, the Japanese are caught in the precarious balance between giving up their autonomy for the good of the social group (the very basis for civilization in classic Freudian thought), and the gradual realization that social order in Japan no longer offers any meaningful sense of self in exchange for this sacrifice. In fact, what the Japanese symbolic offers to its contemporary subject is a culture of consumerism, of artificial gratification, rather than of meaning and substance. Japanese society has been built on a construct in which meaning, social standing, and identity are inextricably connected with the goods we consume—cast into a framework of "friendly" competition with one's neighbors, who in turn define themselves in relation to us. Built upon such a weak and artificial foundation, Murakami warns, it is only a matter of time before the Japanese realize—too late—that they are not "real," for they have no inner resources by which to define their relationship with others.

This is the point, I think, of the general air of nostalgia, even of anachronism, that always surrounds the Murakami hero, whose cultural tastes are old-fashioned: he prefers jazz in the age of New Wave, Budweiser in the era of Zima, a slightly out-dated sense of *akogare*, longing, for a prior time in America, rather than the gradual reemergence of nationalism in Japan during the bubble-economy years. His morality is similarly out of date, and forms the locus of resistance, an ideal, against the tide of consumerism that threatens to wash everyone away. We note that the protagonist of "TV People" does not even own a television, while Hajime, in *South of the Border West of the Sun*, prefers vinyl LPs—preferably those with scratches—to rekindle the mood of an earlier time.

In short, Murakami's heroes still exhibit a preference for the affluent, yet simpler lifestyle of the 1950s and 1960s. Unfortunately for him, while his refusal to join what he considers to be a dehumanized society does gain him a modicum of freedom in his movements, it does not aid him in reconnecting with the real objects of his desire—friends and lovers from his past who helped him determine his sense of self during his youth. As we have seen in the previous chapter, the object of the Murakami protagonist's desire is inevitably something or someone from his past: a friend, lover, or even some object that was special to him. In all cases, the quest for the object of desire is a simultaneous attempt to establish an identity, to reconnect with some inner resource that has been lost. This can also be viewed as a movement away from language, an attempt, fruitless though it may be, to recover the thing itself, thus liberate the repressed Other.

The Internal Quest

Out of the intervention between self and self, self and other, by the Other, the Symbolic Order, emerges culture. At the same time, the price of culture is the individual, an entity born of a (non-)relationship, never quite formed yet always an object of nostalgic desire, both between the self and others, and the self and the internal Other, the unconscious Other. In this sense, Lacan argues, the drive toward culture and civilization is always a drive toward death—the eradication of the individual subject, and the permanent repression of the Other. Similarly, the drive toward language, away from the body, as noted earlier in this chapter, is also a drive toward death. Ironically, since the desire for the unconscious Other inevitably leads to the intervention of language and culture—it can take no other form—it is therefore always a movement toward the death of the individual subject.

This is also the main theme of Murakami Haruki's fiction. As noted previously, the source of conflict in these works is always the separation of the protagonist from the object of his desire. No matter what form this object takes—a friend from the past, lost lover, and so forth—the model that is actually revealed to the reader is one in which the protagonist longs for himself, his own unconscious Other, from which he has been irreversibly "alienated," to use Lacan's term. At the same time, as in the Lacanian model, the drive for the Other is always interrupted by, or transferred to the realm of, language, thus frustrating any hope of establishing contact with the Other.

But this drive for identity and the Other must be properly historicized. Readers will note from the previous chapter that in Murakami the quest for the Other is an *internal* process, made external only when excessive nostalgia makes this necessary. In other words, the Twins and the pinball machine come into being when the protagonist's nostalgia for Rat and Naoko reaches critical mass, though outwardly there may be no sign in his demeanor that this has taken place, and the emergence of such nostalgic images takes even him by surprise.

There is nothing particularly unusual in this fact alone; as I have argued above, the self has been understood as a product of both internal and external processes of signification at least since the early part of the twentieth century.[5] But it is ironic that while the intervention of the Symbolic Order is understood as the key for creating orderly interaction in society by imposing an "external" authority over the individual (even if it *does* assassinate the individual in the process!), in Murakami's fictional world this system has broken down—there is no external other with whom his protagonists can meaningfully interact.

Why is this? Simply put, it is because the peculiar "morality" of the Symbolic Order as it exists in contemporary Japan, according to Murakami's model, is designed not for developing a body of thinking individuals, but rather for creating a society of consumers whose actions and interactions will be controlled in such a way as to lead to economic and social competition, social positioning, success and failure, privileges evaluated according to the level of one's participation in that system. One might say, then, that the intervention of *this* Other has been *too* complete, cutting the subject off from those around him. In response to this, the Murakami protagonist is forced to make do with incomplete, superficial encounters with

5. Mead (1956, 201) argues persuasively about the relationship of the self to others, and to oneself internally: "It is characteristic of the self as an object to itself that . . . is represented in the word 'self,' which is reflexive, and indicates that which can be both subject and object. This type of object is essentially different from other objects, and in the past it has been distinguished as conscious, a term which indicates an experience with, an experience of, one's self." In such arguments we find grounding for Lacan's theory of the "gaze."

others, which in turn lead him to seek meaningful interaction elsewhere, to enter his unconscious realm and encounter himself, or images of himself, *as other*. This may in fact be the only viable strategy for self-construction in the contemporary moment, though Murakami's protagonists, gradually coming to understand this condition, eventually make it their most urgent quest to discover and connect with others, even if it means doing so in a collectively shared unconscious setting, constructed in their minds.[6]

In this sense we can see that his attempts to reconnect with the past and those he has lost need not necessarily be read as a gesture toward death, but an attempt to escape language and signification and rediscover the "thing itself"—Lacan's "real"—that lurks within his mind. We can, therefore, read the protagonist's attempts to enter the unconscious and interact with others as a desire to avoid the intervention of the symbolic and encounter the Other directly. This is the focus of his desire. But if this is the case, then an interesting irony emerges: while the unconscious, or "other world" of Murakami is entirely a dwelling place for the memories of the dead, or presumed dead, it is nevertheless not a world of death, but one of eternal, unchanging life.

Most Japanese critics, however, have read precisely the reverse. Yokoo Kazuhiro, for instance, as noted in the previous chapter, considers the purpose of "Shimamoto" in *South of the Border, West of the Sun*, to be to show the protagonist the world of death (Yokoo 1994, 15). But if we look closely, we cannot help noticing that nothing really ever dies or is dead in Murakami's unconscious world; that activity is reserved almost exclusively for those who inhabit his conscious world.

Certain constants signal that this is true. Time, for instance, is always somehow out of place in the unconscious, for the existence of time signals teleological movement, movement toward an end, that is, toward death. This is why, when the protagonist meets Rat in his unconscious in *A Wild Sheep Chase*, Rat stops the clock, saying only that "it makes too much noise" (*MHZ* 2:352; *WSC* 281). The real reason, however, is that time marks not only the existence of the living, but the process by which they approach death. This accounts also for the cold of the unconscious—cold that preserves, prevents decay—and also for the darkness: without light, there can be no shadows, and therefore no marking of time at all.

This, of course, responds to one of the more interesting puzzles in *Hard-Boiled Wonderland and the End of the World*: why is the protagonist

---

6. This is certainly reminiscent of the realm constructed by Saleem Sinai in Rushdie's *Midnight's Children*.

separated from his shadow? The most plausible solution seems to be that, while overall time is marked in the unconscious "end of the world" sequences—days pass, seasons change—there is little notice taken of forward progress, of irreversible change. Time is purely cyclical here, never teleological. Age remains constant and therefore does not exist as a temporal marker. The shadow is prohibited because his role is to mark time, to show, symbolically, what lies behind the protagonist in his past and, therefore, imply and acknowledge also the existence of the future. If there is a future, then there is finality, that is, death. In Murakami's unconscious world, then, death does not exist, at least not of its own accord (this is not to say that one cannot be killed, but one does not die on one's own). Even the old scientist who programmed the meltdown of the conscious protagonist's cerebral circuits understands this much:

> "There is no such thing as time in tautologies. That's the difference between tautologies and dreams. In tautologies you can see everything at once. You can experience eternity. If you close the circuit you can spin around and around in there indefinitely. That's tautology. Unlike dreams, there are no interruptions."
>
> *   *   *
>
> "In other words," I said, "immortality."
> "That's right. People who enter the tautology are immortal. Or if not true immortality, something approaching total immortality. You live forever." (*MHZ* 4:411–12; HBW&EW 284)[7]

We see an early expression of this kind of immortality in the short story, "1963/1982-nen no Ipanema musume" (1963/1982 Girl from Ipanema, 1982), in which the protagonist considers how the "real" girl from Ipanema would by now be nearly forty, have three children, and have lost her tan. "But in my record she never ages. In the velvet sound of Stan Getz's tenor sax, she would always be eighteen, always the cool and lovely girl from Ipanema" (*MHZ* 5:84). It is this inner world, the inner mind that is the real world of life, of unchanging perfection. Is it, then, any wonder that, lacking the means to interact meaningfully with others, the protagonist turns to this inner world of peace and continuity to find himself?

As we continually find in Murakami literature, the external self is always vulnerable to sudden separation from this inner counterpart and

---

7. The word "tautology" is borrowed from Birnbaum's very clever translation of *shinen*, "thought." In this instance "tautology" is exceptionally apt to describe the closed system of the protagonist's inner mind and works considerably better than the literal meaning of the term.

can thus be altered radically, depending upon the force that has acted on it. Some of the more interesting moments in the author's fiction occur, for instance, when the protagonist enters the unconscious realm, is acted upon by some force, and then emerges changed. In *The Wind-Up Bird Chronicle*, for instance, Okada Tōru enters the unconscious hotel in his mind, then emerges with a mysterious mark on his cheek, the source of miraculous healing powers. A character in *The Sputnik Sweetheart* (Supūtoniku no koibito, 1999), following a terrifying experience, finds her hair has turned white and her ability to feel sexual pleasure has disappeared. Many of Murakami's characters—usually but not always the protagonist—are transformed in some way through their encounter with the unconscious. Movement is always potentially bilateral in Murakami fiction, but it never takes place without radical transformation, and usually involves considerable trauma.

THE CRISIS OF SELF: WHAT HAPPENS WHEN "I" DISAPPEAR?

How the Other controls the formation and, equally important, the maintenance of the self, is of critical importance to us here and is an issue that receives somewhat more interesting portrayal in later Murakami literature. The critical question that is regularly asked in Murakami's writing is not merely "Who am I?" but, more apocalyptically, "What happens when 'I' am no longer 'me?'" In other words, following the radical transformation of the self into an other via the intervention of the symbolic, how does one cope with the disappearance of the self? Some characters such as Rat, as we have seen, do not cope, but simply expire. Others interrogate the issue, with varying degrees of intensity. The protagonist of "Nejimakidori to kayōbi no onnatachi" (Wind-Up Bird and Tuesday's Women, 1986) reflects on his gradual transformation from a promising young law student to an unemployed husband who keeps house while his wife works to earn their living—a situation that is still relatively rare in Japan.

> There was a time—or so I thought—that I was a normal guy, burning with ambitions. When I was in high school I read the biography of Clarence Darrow and decided to become a lawyer. My grades weren't bad, either. I came in second for "most likely to succeed" in my senior year. I made it with relative ease into a good university law program. From there things had gone completely awry somewhere.
>
> *   *   *
>
> I had simply been living as myself in a perfectly ordinary way. It occurred to me at some point that I might as well graduate from

college, and then one day I realized that I was no longer the same man I had been.

No doubt the gap initially was minute enough that it was not visible to the eye. But as time passed by that slippage grew larger, until the form that should have been me was somehow transported off to some remote place no one could see. (*MHZ* 8:148–49; see also *EV* 10–11)

Perhaps the best examples of lost identity come from the author's work centering on women or, in the case above, from men caught in circumstances that typically befall women. This is probably natural, for even in the most prosaic of circumstances a woman's "identity" is usually destined to change radically at certain moments in her life, especially with the onset of marriage and motherhood. As Dorinne Kondo, among others, has documented extensively, to marry into a family is to give up one's own roots, leave behind one's past and become wholly immersed in the patterns and structures of one's new family. "She must learn the ways of the new household (*kafū*). . . . Moreover, she cannot necessarily count on her natal family for complete support and sympathy, for once married, she is a full-fledged member of another household and is treated as such" (Kondo 1990, 134).[8]

We see not so much the tyranny of the household system in Murakami's works, but the trauma of taking on a new role in society. In "Nemuri" (Sleep, 1989), for instance, we encounter a female protagonist who awakens from a nightmare one night, and discovers that she has lost the capacity to sleep. As she pursues a wholly solitary nocturnal life—aided by the convenient fact that her husband and son are extremely heavy sleepers—it begins to dawn on her that she now has an opportunity to recover a portion of her life, implicitly the part that she gave up to assume her duties as a wife and, later, a mother. Her nocturnal activities include reading novels, eating chocolate, drinking brandy, and taking night drives in her car. She notes that "I don't normally drink though, unlike my husband, it isn't because I can't; I used to drink pretty often, in fact. But after I got married I suddenly quit altogether" (*MHZ* 8:193; *EV* 84). Later, relaxing on the couch with *Anna Karenina*, she wonders how many years it has been since she has really sat down to read carefully, painting a self-portrait of a passionate bookworm—and a gifted literary intellectual—up until some unspecified

---

8. For a more politically oriented look at women's identity via their designation as wives and mothers, see Uno 1993 and LeBlanc 1999.

point, at which she ceased to read. "Where on earth had she gone, that 'me' who was so obsessed with the books I read?" (*MHZ* 8:197; *EV* 88). The reader knows, of course, that the protagonist's passion for books disappeared around the same time as her enjoyment of alcohol. Transformed into a wife (and later mother) these modes of pleasure belong to another existence, another identity altogether. Her attention now, even when she is inclined to read, is taken up by "my child, grocery shopping, the refrigerator going out, what to wear to relatives' weddings, my father's stomach operation last month . . ." (*MHZ* 8:196; *EV* 87). Later she begins to eat chocolate, something else she gave up after getting married, presumably because her husband is a dentist and would not approve.

There is nothing particularly unusual in this situation, which simply reflects the changes incumbent on any social transformation. Rather, it is the protagonist's response to these changes that forces us to look at the ordinary as *extra*ordinary, and to query what such "normal" transformations mean to the individual. The protagonist's response to her transformation into a "sleepless" person is initially fear, followed by an almost megalomaniac glee at her emancipation. At the same time, we note that this "emancipation" is brought about through direct contact with—in fact, through envelopment by—the protagonist's unconscious, contact that does not occur without a certain risk. As I have already noted repeatedly above, the unconscious Other is never directly accessible to the conscious self with which it is associated; rather, to have direct knowledge (consciousness) of the unconscious would by definition designify the term, rendering the unconscious into consciousness. In order to circumvent this, Murakami continues to portray the unconscious as a vast, darkened storehouse in which the protagonist can only grope blindly. It is also, paradoxically, a world both of "death" (as the dwelling place of the dead, or the realm of nonconsciousness), and of eternal life (as timelessness, eternity), the realization of which terrifies the protagonist more than anything.

> Death might simply be like a deep, unconscious sleep—eternal rest, a blackout. Or so I thought.
> But then it occurred to me that this might not be so. What if death were some kind of condition totally different from sleep— what if it were like a profound awakening in the dark, like what I was experiencing now? It might just be an endless awakening there in the pitch black.
>
>   * * *
>
> Suddenly I was assailed by a violent fear. My spine chilled, like it was frozen solid. I shut my eyes tightly again. I could no longer

open them. I stared at the pitch blackness directly before my eyes.
The darkness was deep as the universe itself, without relief. I was
alone. My consciousness expanded and contracted. Realizing this,
I felt as though I could have looked straight through to the core
of that universe. But I refused to look. It's too soon, I thought.
(*MHZ* 8:218–19; *EV* 106)

However, without even realizing it, the protagonist is already moving inexorably and permanently toward that world that, like a black hole
in space, will draw her in and continue to contract around her mind and
consciousness until she is permanently trapped in a vast, yet tiny world
somewhere inside her own mind. She begins, unconsciously, to distance
herself from her duties as a wife and mother—"Out of duty I did the shopping, cooked, cleaned, played with my son, had sex with my husband. . . .
All I had to do was cut the connection between my mind and my flesh"
(*MHZ* 8:207; *EV* 95-96)—and begins to focus on a more solitary, self-centered approach. In time she looks in the mirror and is able to view herself
critically, objectively, as a different person. "I gazed at myself objectively
from a variety of angles. My eyes were not playing tricks on me. I was truly
becoming lovely" (*MHZ* 8:208–9; *EV* 97).

Is this a question of perception, or is the protagonist truly transforming into an "other" person? The answer is, both. As the title of the
story suggests, the protagonist of "Sleep" has entered the unconscious
"other" world, and we have established that nothing can exist in both worlds
in precisely the same way. Therefore by definition the protagonist must be
transformed. At the same time, having achieved a (partially or entirely)
different subjectivity, she cannot perceive anything precisely as she once
did.

But there is another important image in this scene: the mirror. As is
true in other stories as well, the mirror is used by Murakami to suggest a
two-way viewing apparatus by which one may eavesdrop on other worlds
(and by which other worlds eavesdrop on *ours!*). There is a scene in *A Wild
Sheep Chase*, for instance, in which the protagonist, standing beside the
Sheepman in Rat's mountain villa, looks into the hallway mirror and is
shocked to notice that the Sheepman does not appear in the "other" world
reflected there. In an earlier short story entitled "Kagami" (*MHZ* 5:71–79;
Mirror, 1983), Murakami's protagonist confronts his own mirrored image
in a darkened hallway, and begins to wonder which one of "him" is real,
which is in control (*MHZ* 5:73-79).

The answer, of course, is that both are real, both in control, both
simultaneously existing in separate, yet often connected, transgressable

worlds or modes of consciousness. Thus, as the protagonist of "Sleep" stares at her "own" face in the mirror, we realize that she is actually staring at the face of an other, a separate, autonomous subject, inexorably separated from, yet connected to, herself. The mirror is an exceptionally useful image in this case—as it also was for Lacan, among others—in suggesting the process of self-formation, particularly the phase at which we begin to imagine ourselves as object, caught in the gaze of an other, and then impose on this dual equation the constructed presence of the symbolic.[9] Most of Murakami's characters traverse this phase at some point in the narrative, only to be suddenly disconnected from some crucial part of themselves, forced to lead their lives as half-individuals. As we have seen again and again, the necessary, if futile, response to this is to turn inward, to seek the severed half of the self, and attempt reunification. By this time, however, the other side of the self having been transformed into an autonomous, virtually separate being, the symbolic has already moved into the breach, leaving inner and outer self able to interact only metonymically, through the use of language. Murakami protagonists can thus only *speak* the Other, give it a name, invent an image for it; they can no longer *be* the Other.

They can, however, enter into a state of (theoretically eternal) communication with the Other by retreating into the unconscious and remaining there. This is the result of "Sleep," which closes with the protagonist trapped in her car, which is being rocked and pushed by shadowy figures outside the car. What/who are these figures? Are they her husband and son, who have found her in a comatose state in "this" world and attempt to awaken her? Or are the figures shadows of her own past/self/identity (cf. *Hard-Boiled Wonderland and the End of the World*), insistently imprisoning her inside the car (symbolic of her inner mind), immobile? I am inclined to believe the former and to understand that the protagonist's transformation into a dweller of the unconscious is nearly complete.

This reading would seem to be supported by a more recent Murakami work in which a similar transformation occurs—one the reader views from the outside in this case. In *The Sputnik Sweetheart*, a peculiar love story, a

9. One of Lacan's more interesting points on this subject is that there is a period—up to the age of eighteen months, he argues—that the prelinguistic infant may confront its image in the "primordial" mode, that is, something approaching the precultural "real" discussed above. "This jubilant assumption of his specular image by the child at the *infans* stage . . . would seem to exhibit in an exemplary situation the symbolic matrix in which the *I* is precipitated in a primordial form, before it is objectified in the dialectic of identification with the other, and before language restores to it, in the universal, its function as subject" (Lacan 1977, 2).

young woman named Sumire falls in love with another woman, Myū, and finds herself transformed (willingly, but unnervingly) into someone she no longer recognizes. The love triangle is completed by the narrator himself, who plays only a minor role in the work, but whose unrequitable desire for the lesbian Sumire leads him to search for her (a familiar enough motif!) on a tiny Greek isle in the Mediterranean. Sumire predicts early on that her love for Myū "will transport me to . . . some strange, special world I've never once laid eyes on. Or maybe it will be a dangerous place" (*SK* 36).

Sumire's transformation into an other person is as startling to us as it is to the narrator. Compare, for instance, the early descriptions of Sumire with later ones:

> In the common sense of the word, Sumire was not all that attrac-tive. She had sunken cheeks, and her mouth was too wide. Her nose was small and pointed slightly upward. She was richly ex-pressive and had a sense of humor, but rarely laughed aloud. Even when she was in a good mood she always sounded like she could fly off the handle at any moment. I doubt she had ever used lipstick or an eyebrow pencil in her life, and she seemed unaware that bras came in different sizes. (*SK* 9)

We also learn in the early part of the narrative that Sumire is a fanatical reader of books and also a talented—if somewhat undisciplined—writer. In her early twenties, living on the generosity of her stepmother (her real mother having died when she was three), Sumire occupies a cheap apartment "with-out heat, a telephone, or even a mirror" (*SK* 19), and yet her life is happy because she is free to pursue reading and writing, her sole passions, more or less as she pleases. In this sense she very closely resembles the narrator, who claims a passion for reading that rivals hers. But unlike the narrator, love, to this point, has not entered her consciousness. Quite the contrary, in fact, Sumire remarks to the narrator that she understands neither love nor the sexual drive. The simple fact is that Sumire has not yet realized that she is a lesbian.

This changes when she chances to meet Myū at a wedding recep-tion for Sumire's cousin at which Sumire's father is one of the officials. The two women are dining partners and discover an attraction that is more than casual. Rather impulsively, Myū asks Sumire to come and work at her import-export company, and, willing to do anything to be closer to the ob-ject of her sexual attraction, Sumire agrees.

This is the beginning of the end for Sumire, who must radically transform herself in order to remain near to Myū. She must give up her chain-smoking out of respect for Myū's smoke-free office; she must alter her appearance, so that when the narrator first sees her in a designer dress and make-up he himself cannot recognize her. Finally—and this is the most significant of all—she gives up writing, partly because she has little time with her work schedule, but also because Myū tells her, "At this point, no matter how much time you put into it, I don't think you are capable of writing anything in an orderly way" (*SK* 54). If we now compare the transformed Sumire with the original description above, we see the contrast.

> It was Sumire, but at first I didn't recognize her. Her style was completely new. Her hair was arranged in a cool short cut; I could still see signs of the scissors used to trim the bangs that used to hang over her forehead. Over a navy blue dress she had draped a cardigan. Mid-size heels in black enamel. She even wore stockings. Stockings? And while I am no connoisseur of women's apparel, even I could tell that everything she wore was top quality. Dressed up like that, Sumire looked more beautiful, more refined, than ever. (*SK* 45)

Yet, the narrator prefers the old Sumire, perhaps sensing even now that this transformation is more than a matter of surface coverings, one that will lead her away from him and the friendship they have shared. In so altering her appearance and behavior, Sumire has moved herself closer to the object of her desire, and indeed become the ideal assistant for Myū. Having given up her passion for writing, however, she is no longer the same Sumire; she has already begun her journey to the "other" world she predicted earlier, from which she will never return as herself.

LOVE, DEATH, AND TRANSFIGURATION

We could ground Sumire's crisis of identity in several events, but two in particular strike me as crucial. First is the death of her mother, who leaves her with a father who is as handsome as Sumire is plain. Never does Sumire complain about her father's treatment of her—indeed, he is solicitous to a fault, and even remarries to a woman very similar to her real mother, so as to make the transition easier for her. But her occasionally bitter remarks about her father's good looks are a not-too-veiled expression of identity crisis: her mother is gone and she bears no resemblance to her father, so who, really, is she?

The second event is her rejection by Myū when she attempts to make love to the older woman. Here, too, Myū's inability to return Sumire's sexual affection in kind is neither cruel nor intentional, but inevitable, for Myū's sexual drive was destroyed in what can only be described as an "out of body" experience some years previously. Nevertheless, the event leaves Sumire in a state of complete crisis, utterly alone, and she disappears for good immediately afterward.

The solution to the problem of where Sumire has gone and why lies, I think, in understanding the symbolic connections between the loss of her mother, on the one hand, and her desire for Myū on the other. As the narrator, who has come to investigate her disappearance, goes through Sumire's files on a computer disk, he encounters her account of dreaming of her mother. That the movement toward the Other has already begun is indicated in the fact that Sumire narrates her own story in the third person. In the dream, she imagines that her dead mother has come back to her, intent on conveying something of the utmost importance to her daughter.

> Sumire climbed a long spiral staircase to meet her mother, who had died long ago. Her mother was to be waiting for her at the top. Her mother had something she wanted to tell Sumire. It was an important something that Sumire needed to know in order to go on living. (*SK* 202)

This "something" can only be the answer to Sumire's most pressing question, the same question all Murakami protagonists ask: "Who am I?" Unfortunately—but inevitably—Sumire never receives her mother's message. At the very moment of speaking, her mother is sucked down into a dark hole at the top of the tower, whisked away at the very moment of conveying Sumire's birthright. Sumire herself is then trapped at the top of the tower and waits in vain for someone to rescue her.

Two things should strike us about this dream: first, the explicit use of conventional sexual imagery like the tower (the phallus) and the hole (the vagina) to suggest both Sumire's origins and her desires; second, the fact that the power to convey the "birthright," the secret of her identity, is entrusted to the mother rather than the father, in a reversal of convention. At the same time, we see the futility of this gesture: the intervention of the tower is the intervention of the symbolic, which encapsulates and obliterates the mother. Thus, while initially appearing to challenge the dominant patriarchal conventions of power and control, Murakami creates in these images a model in which the phallus is finally reinforced as the ultimate power of identification and control.

Or is it?

The fact that this dream emerges now, as Sumire pursues her relationship with Myū, leaving bits and pieces of her former self behind all along the way, is natural, for she is less certain now than ever who she really is. In purely psychological terms we may surmise from it that her unconscious is calling out to her, inviting her to reconnect with her past, therefore with herself. But there is also a metaphysical side to this, for the "mother" in Sumire's dream is not merely a representation of her "real" mother, whom she remembers only from photographs; in fact, her dream mother bears no resemblance to the photographs she retains of her mother. Yet, Sumire immediately knows who she is. This is because, returning to the model of the magical universe posited in the previous chapter, Sumire's dream mother is truly "alive" in the sense of being composed of a fragment of memory. In this sense Sumire's dream mother is no different from Rat or Naoko, save that Sumire knows immediately who she is in her dream form.

It is not difficult, in this context, to understand Sumire's desire for Myū, or to fathom the seriousness of the crisis that develops in response to Myū's rejection of her sexual overtures. Clearly, like her desire to recover her mother, Sumire's desire for Myū is a means of retracing the steps back to her own birth, the origin of her autonomous existence. Her sexual desire for Myū, in other words, specifically for Myū's breasts and vagina, both connected simultaneously with sexuality and motherhood, may be read as representative of her desire to return to a point prior to her mother's death, thereby recovering the potential for her mother (as Other) to instill her sense of identity. But, equally important, her desire to enter into Myū's body via the sexual orifice also suggests a desire to return to the presymbolic, to recover her original self prior to the imposition of language and the symbolic. In other words, we may read in Sumire's actions a desire to reconnect with something more real and eternal than the symbolic, for (as I have repeatedly shown above), the products of language are time, the teleological structures leading from our beginning (birth) to our end (death), and our removal from the object of our desire via metonymy. Thus, rather than simply reaffirming the phallocentric ideology of power and identification, Murakami provides an alternative: to take the active role, dive into the unconscious and live one's life out in that realm of timeless eternity. He also returns to an important theme seen in *The Wind-Up Bird Chronicle* and *South of the Border, West of the Sun*: the possibility of approaching the Other through physical contact, especially via the sexual organs.

It is, therefore, not difficult to surmise what has happened to Sumire when she disappears. Rejected by Myū, who represents her conscious ability to recover, though only symbolically, her identity and the source of her birth, Sumire elects instead to commit herself to the unconscious world whence her mother came to her in a dream, and to which she returned, her mission as messenger unfulfilled. How this transition is made is never revealed, nor is it important. What is important is that Sumire, having systematically given up her earlier identity for love—an identity that, while not perfect, was at least familiar and comfortable—retreats to the world of the unconscious Other in order to reconnect with herself permanently.

Like so many protagonists in Murakami fiction, then, flight turns out to be the answer to the pressing question of what to do when the self disappears. In that sense, *The Sputnik Sweetheart* turns out to have much in common with *A Wild Sheep Chase* and *Hard-Boiled Wonderland and the End of the World*, in that the protagonists of those works, as well, find the contemporary world and its imposing structures too much to manage, and finally run for the hills—either the pastoral hills of Hokkaido, or the darker, rather more mysterious ones lurking inside the mind. It also proves to have something in common, in this sense, with Murakami's most explicit anticonsumerist novel to date, *Dance Dance Dance* (1988).

Dance Dance Dance: The Repression of the Other

One is tempted to describe the cultural economy presented in *Dance Dance Dance* as "predatory"; shrouded in a cloak of pleasure, sexual and material gratification, the dominant consumerist culture of Tokyo that forms the landscape of this novel systematically displaces and deflects into more profitable avenues the process of desire and gratification in its participants. This economy, a novelistic representation of the very real phenomenon of the cult of consumerism, maintains and nourishes its growth by controlling—especially through the mass media—the desire of its participants, replacing desire for the Other with desire that better suits the production system in place. In the process of doing so, it necessarily creates a new version of the symbolic, one that, as argued in the previous chapter, supports a national goal of economic growth. The novel also suggests, however, that the modes of gratification used by this economy are illusory, vulnerable, and hollow.

Dance Dance Dance stirred up a fair amount of controversy when it first came out, not so much because of its portrayal of what may in fact *be* the dominant cultural paradigm of contemporary Japan, but because, in general, the work's principal thrust was missed by most critics, in some cases obscured by the slow pace of a work that was, after all, a sequel to the best-selling *A Wild Sheep Chase*. Jay Rubin (1992, 498) complains, justifiably, that Murakami spends too much space simply "killing time," waiting for something to happen, while the reader also waits. Kuroko Kazuo (1993,87) criticizes the novel's hero as yet another "chic" urbanite who remains isolated from his society. Fuse Hidetoshi, on the other hand, views *Dance Dance Dance* positively as a work that presages Murakami's growing concern for contemporary man's increasing aloofness from real events going on around him, noting that the author deliberately differentiates the world of the protagonist (and by extension, us) from a darker "other" world in which people die in horrible traffic accidents, and young prostitutes are brutally murdered: "In this world of modern civilization, in which the borders [between these two worlds] have become solidified, we have all but forgotten the existence of the 'Other.' Murakami's presentation of these corpses is supposed to help us to rediscover that 'other' world" (Fuse 1995, 205-6). Similarly, and perhaps with the most acute observation, Yokoo Kazuhiro sees in this novel early signs that Murakami is about to enter a new phase in which he seeks, through his literature, the rebirth of the individual self (Yokoo 1994, 35).

Most closely linked with this in *Dance Dance Dance* is Murakami's critique of *kōdo shihonshugi*, roughly translated as "rapid capitalism," a term that shares some broad characteristics with Fredric Jameson's explication of "late capitalism," a concept that originated with the Frankfurt School. It is important, however, that we do not attempt to equate the terms "late-model capitalism" and "rapid capitalism" too closely, though certain obvious similarities exist. Both refer, for instance, to the matter of capitalism's tendency to commodify "hitherto uncommodified areas," meaning, in Jameson's case, the infiltration of the Third World (and by extension our own utopian visions thereof), and of the unconscious. "One is tempted to speak in this connection of a new and historically original penetration and colonization of Nature and the Unconscious: that is, the destruction of precapitalist Third World agriculture by the Green Revolution, and the rise of the media and the advertising industry" (Jameson 1991, 36). In Murakami's terms, too, the infiltration of the mass media into the popular consciousness is certainly a major theme, and even late capitalism's movement into the Third World is given some limited expression—particularly in one of his most recent books, *Kami no kodomotachi wa minna odoru* (All the Gods' Children Dance, 2000), in which a traveler to Bangkok reflects on the contrasts between the city itself and its surrounding countryside.

For the most part, however, Murakami's "rapid capitalism" has tended more to depict the intrusive commodification of areas of human relationships that had previously remained aloof from the consumerist ethic—friendship, love, even family roles. Rapid capitalism, responding to the gradual dehumanization of the population that feeds it, naturally creates a demand for these emotional "goods" and then works to provide them by recruiting professionals to fulfill those needs.

In this sense, then, "late-model capitalism" and "rapid capitalism" do resemble one another. The fundamental differences between them, we might say, are ideological: Jameson's use of the term "late-model" reflects the Marxist assertion of a deterministic progression to all economic and historical development—"late model" capitalism must inevitably follow the previous stage of "monopoly" or "imperialist" capitalism. Jameson's Marxist analysis, in other words, requires him to accept the evolutionary notion that late capitalism is not only the dialectical result of the preceding stage but a more highly evolved, therefore "better" stage, an idea with which he is not overly comfortable: "the dialectic requires us to hold equally to a positive or 'progressive' evaluation of its emergence, as Marx did for the world market on the horizon" (Jameson 1991, 50).

Murakami, on the other hand, is not prepared to understand the progression of the Japanese economy from "monopoly" to "rapid" capitalism as either deterministic nor necessarily as a more highly evolved form. This is not because Japanese rapid capitalism is not a product of some earlier form of capitalism, however; rather, it is because Murakami is uncomfortable with any notion that declares an inevitable—a *natural*—progression, implying either deterministic progress or teleology—a logical ending point—that must lie ahead, always ahead, of each social, economic, or historical moment of development.

Rather, Murakami's vision of rapid capitalism is probably more comfortable with ideas such as the seemingly random mutations described by Baudrillard's "systems of code," by which he claims the world operates in the postmodern era. Presumably writing in response to Marxism's claims of determinism and evolution, Baudrillard insists that the world is guided more by a kind of "chaos theory" than by any predictable mode of progressivism. "Cybernetic operationality, the genetic code, the random order of mutations, the principle of uncertainty, and so on: all of these replace a determinist and objectivist science, a dialectical vision of history and consciousness" (Baudrillard 1988, 122).

Yet we must be very careful with terms like "random" in dealing with Murakami's vision of the world. The metaphor of cybernetics, of manipulation and mutation of genetic codes, is more than sufficient to give us a model of the managed, yet "trial-and-error" nature of the Japanese economic system, one that lives and feeds, as noted above, solely to perpetuate itself and adapts with remarkable speed and agility to changing market needs. At the same time, this system is so managed, so well controlled, that one could neither describe it in terms of Jameson's Marxist determinism, nor in Baudrillard's postmodern metaphor of random chaos.

Rather, our focus should be on the term "rapid," the use of which does not preclude rapid capitalism's participation in what Jameson calls "the dissolution of an autonomous sphere of culture" (1991, 48). Rather, like Jameson's late-model capitalism, the dominant theme of rapid capitalism is the control of desire in the marketplace, control that is maintained through speed and versatility on the part of the industrial production sector and the mass media to meet the needs of the market.

The term "rapid capitalism," then, does appear to carry with it certain overtones of the earlier *kōdo seichō*, or "rapid growth" period of roughly 1955–73, and thus contains a superficial sense of chronology with previous, less-developed economic moments. More importantly, however, its real grounding echoes other trendy terms of recent years, such as *kōdo jōhōka shakai* ("rapid information society"), which emphasizes the need, due to high-speed accessibility of information, for specialists in the art of processing and disseminating that information. It also alludes to the multiplicity of ideas that become potentially (and confusingly) available in such a context. We might also think of the implementation of the *kōdo jōhō tsūshin taisei* ("rapid information transmission system"), which has taken concrete shape within the past few years in NTT's implementation of the high-speed digital ISDN network, combining telephone and internet service, among other things.

"Rapid capitalism" shares certain aspects of these concepts, particularly in its emphasis on maintaining an "edge" in the marketplace by reacting quickly to market changes, tapping into new desires in the community (or, alternatively, *creating* those new desires), then fulfilling them. At the same time, "rapid" and "new" imply, of necessity, *mass* consumption. The age of the individual consumer (if such a thing ever really existed) has given way to consumer groups, market shares, and disposability that encourages us always to replace used goods with the latest concoction of the production system. One hardly need add the importance of the mass media in moving such an economy forward.

Certain observations can be made about rapid capitalism in this context. First, we should acknowledge that although the system is geared *away* from the individual, it nevertheless creates the illusion of a seemingly endless variety of choices available in to the individual in the marketplace. One can, therefore, become caught up in the fantasy of making his or her own choices, unaware of being constantly *driven* by unseen, largely unknown forces. (Only in recent years have we at last come to realize how the personal computer industry has flourished for the past two decades by creating an "arms race" of sorts, in which hardware and software developers continually outdo one another, forcing the consumer to keep up by regular upgrades to newer and more powerful equipment.)

It is also important to point out that *rapid* refers not only to production but to consumption, as well, and that in order to remain viable new products, or clever ways of re-presenting old products, becomes an important facet of the system. Tatsumi Takayuki argues that rapid capitalism refers in large part to the use of high-speed communications as a means of breaking down cultural barriers, thus "naturalizing" both imported and domestic culture for the mass audience (1998, 93), something he views as inevitable in the post-rapid growth era of high technology. There is, however, an even more revealing phenomenon that has developed out of the same impulse—the impulse toward opening and maintaining new markets—and this is the expansion of the "role playing" industry. In recent years we have seen—especially in Japan—considerable growth of the service industry specializing in the creation of live fantasies. Some of these are prosaic, others concern various social moral taboos. As might be expected, the predominant area in which this becomes a viable industry is that of adult entertainment, and already the term *imēji kurabu*, shortened to *imekura*, has made its way into contemporary Japanese parlance. In such clubs, which are now widespread throughout Tokyo, the (typically male) customer pays for an elaborate enactment of some sexual fantasy (popular scenarios include raping office girls, having sex with school girls, and fondling women on trains, reflecting the real-world phenomenon of the *chikan*, or train pervert). Ultimately this may be viewed as just one more variety of prostitution, and indeed it is, but the lengths to which some clubs will go to make the fantasy seem real are at times astonishing.[10]

This, of course, is not an unexpected expansion of the adult industry, which through the video and print media—to say nothing of various live establishments—has long specialized in the satisfaction of "taboo" sexual desires within the relatively controlled environment of the pornographic film or live sex club. Even outside the sexual arena, role playing establishments have provided Japanese with an escape from their everyday personae. The most common example of this is probably the theme bar or coffee

---

10. Shimada Masahiko's 1990 novel *Rokoko-chō* (Tokyo: Shōeisha) plays on this kind of sexual fantasy. In an amusement park hidden in the heart of Tokyo, professional "rape girls" walk the streets, waiting to be "raped" by customers, who then pay them.

shop, where customers can slip into another persona and "become" something otherwise impossible in the rigid structure of their daily lives.

Rather more interesting—and certainly more revealing—than what goes on at sex clubs, however, is the expansion of the role-playing industry into areas previously understood as "everyday life"—again, the infiltration of capitalism into new areas previously thought to be immune to the desires of the market. The new urban fantasy seems to be for a stable home, parents, people who care about one, suggesting the very kind of "gap" in Japanese society that Murakami frequently notes in his essays and nonfiction, as well. In an essay on the disappearance of the traditional family in Yoshimoto Banana's novels, John Treat remarks that a company was created in the early 1990s "which rents out, by the hour, 'families' on behalf of Japanese themselves too busy to carry out the social obligations associated with being good sons, daughters-in-law, grandparents, etc. Its success attributed to 'disintegrating traditional family ties,' Japan Efficiency Headquarters is testimony to creative entrepreneurship and its ability to commercialize, even commodify, the most basic human 'relations'" (1993, 374n.43). This example would seem to suggest that Japan has come full circle, from fantasizing its way *out* of the home, to refantasizing the *reconstruction* of the home.

Murakami is obviously not alone in his perception of the constructed, commodified nature of relationships in contemporary Japanese society. One of the best examples of such a perception may be found in Shimada Masahiko's 1989 novel, *Yumetsukai* (translated as Dream Messenger, 1992), in which the protagonist, an international orphan named Masao/Matthew, is raised in an orphanage in New York that rents its children out to couples who, for one reason or another, wish to simulate the presence of children in their homes. The "dream messenger" of the book's English title has to do with the existence of a "guardian spirit" that each of the children at the orphanage carries with him, whose function is both to instruct and protect the child, and to establish meaningful contacts both among the spirits and their own children.

At the same time, Shimada's vision of Tokyo shares much with that of Murakami, particularly in its characterization as a city of facades, but little depth. One character in the novel, a writer named "Kubi" who has been literally purchased by a wealthy woman in need of fashionable companionship, describes Tokyo as a city of exhausted, miserable people who have lost their spirit:

> Kubi sought out comfort in a bar, eager for a cure for his depression. Amid the odor of raw fish and fried food, he nursed his beer

and listened. In between the slurps and clinking glasses, he heard another sound, a chorus of *"Shigata ga nai!* What can you do?" There were as many voices repeating this refrain as there were people in the bar. And everyone had the look of exhaustion. It made Kubi sick.

Before him he saw the entire country, Japan, millions of people, drinking, spewing out their complaints, their misery and jealousy and fatigue enveloping them like a mist. (Shimada 1989, 192–93)

Other characters give themselves over to what Tokyo has become: a gigantic banking center, where money is at the heart of every relationship, every action, and every desire. Yet with the exception of Kubi, who hopes to develop an autonomous zone outside of Japanese territorial waters for dissidents and nonconformists aboard an abandoned oil tanker, this image of Tokyo is not unattractive. Even the commodification of Tokyo's residents does not carry the sinister quality that it seems to in the Murakami universe. Maiko, a financial expert hired to help locate Masao/Matthew by his mother, assumes that this is simply the way of the world now. "In fact, she had for all intents and purposes changed into money herself, her brain in tune with the electronic flow that sent money shooting off at the touch of a computer key. The world, after all, revolved around money. Politics, science, technology, fashion, rumors, human relations—all manifested themselves in this ebb and flow of money" (*DM* 30–31).

Masao/Matthew himself, his name suggesting the fluidity of his identity, seems to experience no real difficulties in his multiple identity. "I can change from stranger to friend, from friend to brother, from brother back to stranger," he tells himself. "A nonentity on an endless journey, selling my time and affection to the people I meet—that's me" (*DM* 175). And yet, at times we have the sense that Masao/Matthew would like to be able to "come home," that is, pull together a singular identity from the fragmented multiple selves he has become. Unfortunately, as an orphan, he has no clear memory of his own past, and his work as a rental child has only made things more difficult.

I don't know who created me, and I've never been the child of any one particular set of parents for very long. I was always being broken up, the parts presented to a new set of strangers, so arranging my memories into a single personal history isn't easy. Still, I can't stop trying.

With Mikainaito's help, I try to piece together this jigsaw puzzle of myself. Fragments of memories come together in dreams. Only dreams will work. Life stories and myths are not enough.

Dreams put the past in order, even help me see into the future. (*DM* 59–60)

But others are less enamored of what Japan—particularly Tokyo—has become. One character has his wife murdered for the insurance money, and when confronted on the witness stand in court, he blames money. "His statement was more like the confessions of a fanatic religious follower. For forty minutes he mumbled about the curse of money, and the curse on himself for having fallen slave to it. Over and over he begged to be executed. Only death could sever him from the filth of money, he screamed" (*DM* 44). Still another, a rock star named Tetsuya, becomes commodified by his fame, and in turn ends up completely isolated, starved for human contact. "Even when he struck someone, Tetsuya wasn't very macho—he hit them because he was starved for love. He didn't feel loneliness with his mind; he felt it with his body. Each sinew and muscle in his body strained for warm contact" (*DM* 175).

Tetsuya's violent response is eventually channeled while on stage into his calls for revolution, for the people of Tokyo to destroy the city. His violent reaction against the dehumanization that Tokyo represents is echoed in the increasingly revolutionary thoughts of Kubi, who fantasizes that "If only he could hand out hammers to the crowd and get them screaming 'Destroy Tokyo! Destroy Tokyo!' the city'd be in ruins overnight" (*DM* 191). No less radical is his vision of Tokyo divided into a multitude of autonomous zones, each representing a different theme, for he reasons that Tokyo's great flaw—and by extension, that of Japan in general—is its vaunted homogeneity.

> Tokyo is a city where thinking and looking the same as everybody else is the norm. If you wanted to start a revolution here, you'd have to build several different countries inside the city. It was the only way not to end up with what you have now—Japanese doing their best to be like foreigners, and foreigners pretending to be Japanese. (*DM* 191–92)

One of Shimada's characters blames this homogeneity on the dominance of rice culture, of "a race of farmers and the special malice found in communities bound together by rice cultivation" (*DM* 224) that leads them to form in-groups based on sameness, and to exclude others based on their difference.

In the end, I think *Dream Messenger* presents an ambivalent perception of the fragmentation of identity in contemporary Japan, and its subsequent replacement with a money- or consumerist-based identity as participant in the rapid capitalist economy. At the same time, we can hardly help noticing that participation in this economy is always voluntary, attracted by the rewards of comfort and pleasure.

In *Dance Dance Dance*, Murakami creates a similar social economy, in which the protagonist's commodification, his transformation into a role player—friend, elder brother, and so forth—is made inevitable by the relationships into which circumstances force him. His marketability is the result of both a gap or lack perceived by those around him (what is lacking will be discussed in a moment), and the acceptance of a social and cultural economy that now puts a price on virtually everything, including, as Treat points out above, "the most basic human 'relations.'"

It is worth noting that, initially, at least, the protagonist's relationship with that system is integral; he is a part of the mass media aspect of it, a fact that inspires in him a certain cynicism. A player in the contemporary "high-speed information" aspect of rapid capitalism, representing the realization, so to speak, of the *jōhō shakai* (information society) dream of the late 1960s, the protagonist of *Dance Dance Dance* reveals the disappointments of that dream. One might describe his era as a "postinformational" one, in which the speed and technology of the media have led not to a better-informed public, but instead to one overwhelmed by both meaningful and meaningless images, but never quite capable of determining the difference. Initially this does not seem to bother him particularly.

> I *did* wonder sometimes if this wasn't wasting my life. But even if my life was being wasted along with all that pulp and ink, I didn't necessarily have any business complaining. We live in a rapid capitalist society, where waste is the highest virtue. Politicians call this "the refinement of domestic demand." I call it "meaningless waste." It's just a different way of thinking. (*MHZ* 7:33; *DDD* 12)

Acknowledging his role in the spread of meaningless propaganda in a society glutted with messages from all sides, he describes his work as *bunkateki yukikaki*, "cultural snow-shoveling." The meaning of this term is admittedly unclear, and Kuroko has gone so far as to suggest that the protagonist's irony itself is ironic, that Murakami's cynical posture toward the work of the public relations writer merely reaffirms his admiration for the "knowledge/culture élite" that is inexorably separated from the "real world of workers' unions and manual labor" (1993, 86). I would, however, offer a different reading: Murakami's critique of the rapid capitalist system absolutely rests upon his deconstruction of the opposition of physical and cultural labor. By conflating the two, he effectively narrows the gap between the educated bourgeoisie and the working class. If this gesture is cynical, it is because rather than elevating physical labor to the level of cultural labor, or better still above it (as some Marxists have done), Murakami *lowers* the cultural to the level of the physical, denigrating both. This, I think, is what really infuriates Kuroko, who would prefer to see Murakami challenge the current hierarchy that privileges the intellectual over the physical, rather than merely deconstructing it.

But the protagonist's cynicism and indifference to the society around him should be attributed to the deep disillusionment he experienced at the end of *A Wild Sheep Chase* with the death of Rat. It is the same disillusionment that leads to his total complicity with the dominant rapid capitalist culture around him, thus completing the allegory of "Rat = Zenkyōtō," and "protagonist = student activists."

This is the real thrust of *Dance Dance Dance*, which begins with a proposed quest for the "girl with the ears" who disappeared at the end of *A Wild Sheep Chase*, but whose narrative somehow never quite achieves the same sense of focus or purpose as its predecessor. The protagonist, dreaming that he can hear his missing girlfriend (who has now acquired the name "Kiki," a pun on the verb "hear") decides to return to Hokkaido and seek her. Yet the quest itself turns out to be secondary, as suggested by the fact that it all but disappears before the end of the work. The more important aspect of the visit to Hokkaido is that it facilitates encounters with a variety of other characters who are integral to the exposition of the protagonist's involvement with the rapid capitalist economy that surrounds him.

Among the fairly large cast of characters, those who stand out are "Gotanda," "Yuki," "Makimura Hiraku," "Yumiyoshi," and the "Sheepman." Gotanda is a famous film star whom the protagonist recognizes as a classmate from his junior high school days, and whose role is that of a pampered "victim" of rapid capitalist commodification of the self. Yuki is a pretty, precocious thirteen-year-old clairvoyant who leads the protagonist to her father, Maki-mura Hiraku, himself a famous media personality who serves as spokesman and advocate for rapid capitalism. These characters contrast with Yumi-yoshi, a comparatively simple hotelier who manages to restore, to some extent, the atmosphere of pastoral simplicity to rapidly urbanizing Hok-kaido. Finally, there is the Sheepman, who holds everything together at the center of the protagonist's inner consciousness. The Sheepman, as will be recalled from the previous chapter, began his existence as a peculiar image created from the protagonist's desperate desire to connect with his inner self, represented by Rat, in the final chapters of *A Wild Sheep Chase.* We might look upon him as simultaneously a representation of the self—the part of the protagonist that is associated with Rat and counterculture—and also of the Other, in the symbolic sense, the sheep signifying the repression of the state, or dominant cultural paradigm. Indeed, taken to its logical conclusion, the absurd character of the "Sheepman"—from his grotesque appearance to his confused and diffuse personality—shows the peculiar reality of combining mainstream and counterculture in a single body: that of contemporary Japanese society.

In *Dance Dance Dance,* however, Murakami creates a somewhat different persona for the Sheepman, transforming him from the dialectical (synthetic) representation of establishment culture and counterculture into a benevolent character, a friendly, bucolic wise man standing guard over the protagonist's core consciousness (a dimly lit, dusty room filled with old junk), helping him to understand his quest.

In a general sense we can see *Dance Dance Dance* as a novel depicting radical change—modernization, urbanization, a new, chic sophistication—almost everywhere we look. Even Hokkaido has lost much of the charm that, in *A Wild Sheep Chase,* derived from its unsullied atmosphere. Some of the appeal of Hokkaido in that novel lay, no doubt, in its depiction—real or imagined—as a pastoral realm in which state control was still relatively remote, and thus served as an effective foil for the urban turmoil of modern Tokyo. This was the one possible setting in which the power of the Sheep and its sophisticated organization might conceivably be neutralized, as indeed it was. Even the shabby "Iruka Hotel," where the protagonist and the "girl with the ears" link up with the Sheep Professor, has the atmosphere of a safe house, a place the modern world does not and cannot touch.

Yet this is only an illusion, as the protagonist repeatedly learns. These enclaves of protected space against which the rapid capitalist market seems to have no power, where the protagonist imagines he might find a pristine, private space, even connection with the Other, are mythical, romantic, sentimental. Jameson (1991, 200) is clearly impatient with such fictions when he writes that "the 'realisms'. . . that evoke some pastoral withdrawal from the market into some other (imaginary) inner-worldly space are all weak and sentimental fantasies." Rather, the nature of the postmodern moment for Jameson is that even such enclaves of "primordial space," once imagined to be sacred, have now been infiltrated by the logic of the market.

Murakami's implicit agreement with this argument is reflected in the extraordinary, but predictable, alteration of the Hokkaido landscape in *Dance Dance Dance,* as the "Iruka" Hotel is replaced with a modern luxury high rise, now given the English name the "Dolphin Hotel," suggesting a more cosmopolitan feel. Gone are the angry Sheep Professor and his cowering son, replaced by a large, efficient, professional staff, including Yumiyoshi. The "Iruka" is not actually gone, however; rather, as the name might imply, it remains a part—a magical, unconscious part—of the new "Dolphin," one that remains to house the core consciousness of the novel's protagonist. There, in the dank, musty corridors of the old Iruka Hotel, the protagonist reencounters the Sheepman, who explains that the older hotel has been preserved as a place solely for him, to permit his connection with both past and future. Obviously, the metaphor refers to the inner consciousness as older, housing memories of the past, surrounded by the facade of the present reality. The old Iruka Hotel, then, is his "black box" in *Dance Dance Dance*. This is clear from the Sheepman's assurances to the protagonist that this one place, at least, is entirely his, and that it always will be here for him.

> "This is your place. That isn't going to change. You're connected with this place. This place is connected with everything. This is your hub."
> "Everything?"
> "The things you've lost. The things you will lose. All those things are connected to this place. Everything is centered right here." (*MHZ* 7:128; *DDD* 83)

It is the theme of constancy in this passage that is important, for as we have seen, flux and change—particularly the radical transformation of the self or identity (such as that seen in *The Sputnik Sweetheart*) is the beginning stage of severe crisis for Murakami protagonists.

FLUX AND CHANGE IN THE RAPID CAPITALIST WORLD

Yet flux and change are, as noted above, definitive parts of the rapid capitalist system. As such, stability and continuity, where they lead to stagnation of consumer activity, are problematic, discouraged wherever possible. Individualism is an anachronistic and counterproductive concept, having been replaced by market-driven systems of thought and behavior that allow the consumer a wide variety of choice, but only insofar as he or she stays within the parameters of the selection menu.

In any society, what is "acceptable"—the dominant morality—is transmitted from older members of the society to younger ones, either through direct teaching or by example and observation. This has not changed in the contemporary era, but, as in most modern societies, morality in *Dance*

Dance Dance (again reflecting real-world practice) is transmitted to a mass audience through the mass media, whose pervasive effects throughout society are also noted by Lacan (1978, 274). What is lost in the sense of personal connections in the modern era is gained in efficiency.[11] Not surprisingly, the most prominent spokesman and advocate in the novel for this era of greater efficiency is Makimura Hiraku, a high-profile mass media star. Taking issue with the protagonist one day for his stubborn adherence to a unique, individual system of principles, Makimura accuses him of being behind the times.

> "A system," he said, touching his ear again. "Things like that don't mean much anymore, though. It's like putting together one of those old home-made tube amplifiers; instead of spending all that time and trouble, it's cheaper just to go to the hi-fi shop and pick up a new transistor amp—you get better sound, too. If it breaks down, they come and fix it for you, and when you get a new one, they'll come and take the old one away. There's no place these days for 'thought systems.' There used to be, but now things are different. Now you just buy whatever you need. Even ways of thinking."
> "Rapid capitalism," I summarized.
> "Bingo," he confirmed. (*MHZ* 7:297–98; *DDD* 204)

Makimura's argument is interesting in its implication that thought systems are interchangeable, available on a trial basis, and wholly disposable—similar in this respect to the spirit of Ōe's critique of contemporary writers in "A Writer's Dilemma," as well. What does this mean for the fate of identity in rapid capitalist Japan? Obviously, insofar as we construct ourselves according to an ideology, a set of beliefs that remain more or less constant, when thought/belief systems become as interchangeable as the operating system on a computer, the potential for radical alteration of the identity (resulting in identit*ies*) is all but inevitable.

This is not science fiction or fantasy; it is reality. To return to Lacan's expression *à la dérive*, we might say that today more than ever the subject is adrift. Clearly this is not a recent development, but one could argue that knowledge of the unconscious becomes that much more tenuous in an era when the unconscious itself is no longer permitted to develop in the context of individually formulated opinions; instead they are ready-made, prefor-

---

11. Andrew Painter (1993) has written at some length on the Japanese popular media's attempts to humanize and make familiar some of its television personalities, especially by making them do silly things on camera for an appreciative mass audience.

mulated and slipped into place within the unconscious like so many memory modules.

It is also notable that while no one has direct knowledge of his or her unconscious, this does not diminish the impact of the unconscious on our formation of identity. As noted above, the connection is a linguistic one, and rarely comprehended by the subject. Indeed, perhaps the reason contemporary human beings cope at all with so many distinct thought systems is the awareness, more now than ever before, that language itself is unstable, artificial, and generally inadequate to signify even the concrete objects we see with our conscious eyes, let alone the disorderly jumble of images and memories in our unconscious minds. From that point it is a minor matter to remind ourselves not only that a variety of viewpoints exist on any controversial issue, but that more than one of them may be "correct." In other words we cannot declare, as Mead did forty years ago, that "anything you say that has any meaning at all is universal" (1956, 211).

This is relevant because both situations—the dislocation of language and Murakami's "rapid capitalism"—derive from the same source: the postmodern, which if not a system, exactly, is at least a mode of discourse by which absolutes are undermined, specificities and exceptions explored. However, whereas the former—a philosophical and historical impulse—may be defended as an opportunity to revive the lost "texts" of the periphery, the postmodern impulse applied to the economic sphere clearly creates a new periphery. The distinction is actually a reenactment of the distinctions that have remained evident throughout this century between the academic and the economic. The one is driven by the imagination, the other by the market. To some extent a merger between the two drives is conceivable—the result would certainly strike us as postmodern!—but ultimately such a liaison would be doomed to fail, for the late-model capitalist market rejects what is unprofitable, as specificities inevitably are, given the cost of producing them. We might consider (to return to my computer metaphor) Gateway Computers' advertised offer some years ago, to "let us build you a computer," implying that a unique unit will be constructed. But when one goes to order such a computer, one simply finds a check-list of desired features that can be selected, each with its own cost. This is not infinite choice; one cannot, for instance, select components not on the list. Gateway cannot reinvent the computer for me; the cost would be prohibitive. Nevertheless, Gateway manages to give the impression that its computers are created individually, one by one, for each customer. Such innovations are growing increasingly common in the real marketplace—Saturn Corporation implemented a similar scheme some years ago by allowing buyers to "order" their cars—but this finally only expresses our nostalgia for a (perhaps mythical) time when products were produced by skilled individual craftsmen to the precise specifications of the consumer.

To return to *Dance Dance Dance,* we see in Makimura Hiraku an apologist of precisely this kind of economic system, urging the protagonist to forget about real specificities and join the system of prefabricated identity.[12] But herein the postmodern rapid capitalist economy creates a new periphery, for one either participates or one is left outside the market. (One hardly need add that this is a very *large* center, and a very limited periphery!) As I noted above, the major theme of *Dance Dance Dance* is that of co-opting the protagonist, who is drawn into the economy both as consumer *and* consumed; the distinction grows particularly difficult to discern in this novel.

If Makimura Hiraku is a spokesman for the rapid capitalist system, the movie star Gotanda is a product of it. Living in a world of appearances, Gotanda is a manufactured man, a living image whose personality must be carefully managed in order to maintain his marketability. His life is one of luxury—he lives in Minato-ku, one of Tokyo's most affluent areas, drives a Maserati, and enjoys the services of Tokyo's most exclusive call-girl establishments. Yet we see almost immediately that for all this apparent luxury he has sacrificed the true object of his desire: normality, control over his movements and desires. And in a reversal of conventional morality that is almost funny, we learn that the true object of Gotanda's desire is his ex-wife, with whom he still enjoys cordial relations. Forbidden to sleep with his ex-wife because it might taint his image as a sex symbol, Gotanda is encouraged instead to engage openly in the consumption of professional women. His movements are strictly controlled by an entity he calls simply "the Company" (*kaisha*), reminiscent of "the System" that managed the protagonist of *Hard-Boiled Wonderland and the End of the World.*

We can hardly help making connections between Gotanda's empty life of luxury and the "white utopia" offered to Rat in *A Wild Sheep Chase.* In a monologue to the narrator that suggests the conflation of the roles of movie star and prostitute, Gotanda complains bitterly that his life is virtually owned by the Company:

12. One is not unaware that the protagonist's nostalgia for an era of "free thought" is no less managed than the system Makimura describes; for instance, were the student activists of the 1960s really creating their own thought systems, or were they, as Murakami himself has argued more than once, just copying what everyone else was doing?

"I'm sick of my life. I *want* to lead an orderly, normal life, but it's no use. All I do is get pushed around by the Company. I'm just a dress-up doll to them, but they've got me so deep in debt that I can't say a word. If I say I want to do something this way or that, nobody pays any attention." (*MHZ* 7:436; *DDD* 290)

What Gotanda faces is the total suppression of his identity for the sake of the dominant Symbolic Order of contemporary Japanese society, grounded in consumption and marketability. The new symbolic in this not-so-fanciful society suggests that what cannot be bought or sold with money—love, friendship, knowledge—must either be commodified (sex, companionship, information) to suit the system, or discarded as an unhealthy waste of resources. This is eventually to become the fate of the protagonist as well, but the underlying message here is that ordinary Japanese, whose easy access to technological gadgetry creates the impression of an affluent, liberated lifestyle, are actually no better off than Gotanda, for their every move is somehow managed by the rapid capitalist system.

Other characters express similar sentiments. One of Gotanda's high-priced call girls tells the protagonist that common courtesy among members of her profession prohibits attempts at forming intimate human attachments, either with customers or other prostitutes. It is an unspoken taboo to speak of one's own background or history, reminiscent, perhaps, of Shimamoto's refusal to disclose anything about herself to Hajime in *South of the Border, West of the Sun.* "We don't ask for anything more than what someone tells us on her own," one call girl tells the protagonist of *Dance Dance Dance.* "For us there is no real life. I guess you could say we're just symbols, part of an illusion" (*MHZ* 7:228; *DDD* 156). The protagonist himself becomes part of that illusion simply by being what he is: a generous, friendly sort, a good listener, and most importantly, a man to whom wealth means very little. He is eventually "hired" to become an avuncular figure to Makimura Hiraku's daughter, Yuki, whose own parents have no time for her. In exchange, Makimura attempts on several occasions to pay the protagonist for his time, but is repeatedly turned down. However, the protagonist does agree to accompany Yuki on an all-expense-paid vacation to Hawaii and even accepts the services of a prostitute ordered and sent to his room by Makimura via long-distance (taking the notion of "room service" to an all-new level). Only after Yuki becomes upset with him for this last does the protagonist come to realize that for all his resistance to becoming a paid companion, this is exactly what has happened.

The parallel between his "job," Gotanda's work and the image of prostitutes that continually resurfaces in the work, now becomes quite obvious: for a fee remitted in barter goods and services, the protagonist rents himself out as a professional friend. Like Gotanda and the other prostitutes, he becomes a symbol, an image, in exchange for which he basks in a new affluence. Before he knows it, his relationship with Makimura and Yuki has been infiltrated by wages.   Even his relationship with Gotanda takes on this shape, as the protagonist unthinkingly accepts gifts in exchange for his friendship. As a commodity, part of an exchange with other commodities, Gotanda is incapable of responding to the protagonist with the same kind of friendship he receives and thus must barter the material goods and services he possesses in excess for emotional support that only the protagonist can provide. In exchange for friendship and humanity, Gotanda provides fine meals and expensive call girls to which the protagonist's social and financial position deny him access. And just to make certain the point comes home, Gotanda asks to swap vehicles: his Maserati for the protagonist's battered little Subaru.

But what does Murakami's hero gain from these gifts? He is afraid to drive the Maserati for fear of denting it; his one night with a prostitute costs him three days in a police interrogation cell after she is murdered; and the object of his quest, Kiki, is still far out of reach. Gradually, by participating in the commodity side of the economy (as opposed to the media side), the protagonist comes to understand what he has been helping to promote through his advertising copy. Perhaps it is recognition of his own role in this traffic in humanity that leads him to seek a return to a less-commodified humanity, and, finally, to convey his own notion of morality to Yuki, whose generation will either resist the current economy, or preserve it forever. "All I'm trying to say is that *you can't buy friends with money. And you sure as hell can't put them on an expense account.*" To which Yuki replies, perhaps answering the implicit question above, "That's a terrific theme for a fairy tale" (*MHZ* 7:460–61; *DDD* 306).[13]

COMMODIFICATION OF THE INDIVIDUAL

Feminists have argued for decades about the dehumanizing process of appropriating the female body, either for sale as an instrument of pleasure (in the form of prostitution) or as an instrument of (re)production. Gayle Rubin

---

13. One of Shimada's characters expresses a similar sentiment to Masao/Matthew in *Dream Messenger*: "I want to love, and be loved, by lots of people. People I haven't even met yet. Whores trade love for money; well, I want to trade love for love. The kind of love I want means buying with your body and heart what you can't buy with money" (158–59).

(1975, 157–210) argued more than twenty years ago, echoing Marx, that as an object of barter, a woman's value became apparent only in the context of the capitalist schemes of economic production. Rather than valuing her as an individual, a human being, she is instead placed within an economic framework and used as object, never subject. Her sexuality is the final issue, and under "moral" circumstances is reserved and used for production purposes; at other times, all things being equal, she is used as a device by which male sexuality is satisfied, her body, in the words of Luce Irigaray (1981, 99–106), becoming a sheath by which the penis is massaged.

Identity under these conditions is a tenuous and difficult matter indeed. Is there any identity for the object, for those whose existence is managed in such a way as to maximize market and production value only? Despite fairly substantial differences in methodology, most feminists will probably agree that what is needed most is a sense of unique female identity that values the female *as* female, whether based on current cultural and social structures or something radically different. Most would similarly agree, I suspect, that any entity systematically peripheralized, excluded from the subjective position, will be left without the essential materials to construct identity or self.

These issues are worth raising because it becomes clear through *Dance Dance Dance* that Murakami enacts a model of contemporary society in which exploitation is not limited only to females, nor only to the members of the sex industry, but now includes the so-called "cultural élite" as well. At the same time, the various stigma traditionally attendant upon such exploitation are removed, until living icons and manufactured signs such as Gotanda and his prostitutes become "normal"—even respectable. In such a model the potential for the commodification of the subject is enhanced dramatically. This necessarily results in the transformation of structures of desire, as we have repeatedly seen, for by definition an object does not desire, but is desired. This leads to the necessary construction of at least a mask of subjectivity for Gotanda, for, as will be readily apparent, no economy can function in the absence of desire, and thus desire must be manufactured and implanted into the constructed subject/object. As I have attempted to show throughout this chapter, such a system of constructed subjectivity and manufactured, implanted desire merely obscures the fact that true identity is suppressed, replaced by the simulation of desire. Yet it is a system that has proved remarkably effective in maintaining consumer participation in the rapid capitalist system, for its rewards are affluence and full participation in the consumerist economy.

CONCLUSION

A number of useful conclusions may be drawn from the analyses above. First, I would reiterate the theme of my introduction above, that Murakami's decision to write about his society beginning with the year 1970 was no accident; rather, as the author himself understood from the beginning, 1970 is a watershed in the history of Japanese identity. Historically, the renewal of the U.S.-Japan Security Treaty in 1970 has come to symbolize the beginning of the end of the student counterculture movement known as Zenkyōtō, of youth-powered mass activism in general. Virtually overnight the movement lost its momentum, degenerating into a number of splinter groups that never approached the kind of political or social potential that the movement as a whole had promised. I would also reiterate my point that, even if the motivations of the Zenkyōtō movement were unclear—even if we *can* interpret its final years as a kind of mass suicide—it was nonetheless an important source of goal orientation among young Japanese between the ages of eighteen and twenty at that time, the demise of which created disarray among that age group in terms of identity formation. In the absence of the Zenkyōtō movement, on what were they to ground their sense of self? Perhaps more than any other period in modern Japanese history, the sudden collapse of the student political activism was a catastrophe for the development of the individual self in Japan, amounting to a sinkhole that opened beneath the psychological structures of Japanese youth at a particularly critical moment in their development as adult social beings. Moreover, I would argue that this lack of basic tools for self-formation has continued unabated, supported and maintained by an affluent standard of living among the majority of Japanese. In short, the achievement of affluence in the 1950s and 1960s has proved to be the downfall of individual selfhood in post-1970 Japan.

This is an issue that deserves further study over time. What will be the long-term results of a society based on a goal that has already been largely achieved, and in place of which no new national goal has been produced? How long can Japanese young people be persuaded to put themselves through the hell of the Japanese examination system, seeking out a place on the cogwheels of Japanese business and industry, struggling to maintain the same affluent society into which they were born? One of the issues of the 1992 U.S. presidential campaign between George Bush and Bill Clinton was how to prevent members of "Generation X" from winding up *worse* off than their "baby-boomer" parents. Is this going to become the new path for generations to follow throughout the industrialized and postindustrialized world? And if so, will that be enough to generate a sense of individual self-worth, or to define individual and collective goals?

If self-identity is grounded in the structure of desire between the self and others, and finally to the (imagined) relation to the Other, the Symbolic Order, then what happens when the symbolic is appropriated in order to maintain economic growth, but not spiritual or emotional growth? We live, Lacan said, in a postreligious society (MacCannell 1986, 125); more accurately, one might say that we have until quite recently existed in the awkward space between religion and secularism, in which we value secular morality (liberty, democracy) that is, however, grounded in anti-quated spiritual beliefs. But have we yet come to understand that even secular morality is gradually giving way to the "morality" of consumption? Have we realized in the non-conflict-oriented post-Cold War era that we have eliminated much of the strength of our declarations about concepts such as liberty and democracy? As historical events have shown, in a world no longer divided into hemispheres of "good" and "evil," we are now lim-ited either to nostalgic ruminations over these ideals, or to the creation of and participation in more limited conflicts such as the Gulf War or, more recently, the civil war in the Balkans. Jean Baudrillard expresses a similar concern about the post-Cold War world in *The Illusion of the End*:

> Entire peoples are rushing towards a "historical" objective of lib-erty which no longer exists at all in the form in which they imag-ine it, towards a form of "democratic" representation which has also long been dying from speculation. . . . The democratic illu-sion is universal, linked as it is to the zero degree of civic energy. All we have left of liberty is an ad-man's illusion, that [is], the zero degree of the idea. . . . (1994a, 36)

If we are engulfed, as Baudrillard suggests in the same piece (38), by the "liberal virus, our compulsion for objects and images," then for what issue are we, as contemporary postindustrial beings, to exert ourselves? What will become our *raison d'être*, and what kinds of identities will we manage to build on top of it?

For years Murakami has expressed his wonder at Japanese white-collar workers' willingness to continue their participation in the industrial and economic mechanism that drives Japan, battling their peers for the smallest chance to get ahead. He wonders at their seemingly passive accep-tance of radical transformation in the autumn of 1970, when tens of thou-sands of student activists returned to their classrooms, or, trading in their staves and helmets for briefcases and business suits, joined the society against which they had struggled.

We are left to consider, as Murakami has, whether in capitulation these former activists truly found a realistic groundwork to replace the goals and the drive of student counterculture? Is the competition to get ahead in the workplace, or the race to own a better car, television, or home, adequate substitute for the fulfillment of an ideologically charged, intellectually stimulating worldwide political movement?

It is worth noting, in closing this chapter, that while Zenkyōtō in its immensity dissipated thirty years ago in the summer/autumn of 1970, the image of the movement lives on in contemporary anti-AMPO demonstrations in Hibiya Park. Comparatively small units of students sometimes do still assemble to march with placards and staves, chanting in unison for an end to AMPO. Yet one cannot help wondering, do these young people seriously believe they will have some effect on the political-military relationship between the United States and Japan? Or, as one is tempted to believe, following Baudrillard, do they merely attempt to recapture some sense of purpose in their lives, and achieve self-definition by that means? If so, one can only lament that their identity will ultimately be no more than a borrowed illusion.

Chapter Four

Historiography, Ideology, and the Politics of Representation

"What is the ontological nature of historical documents? Are they a stand-in for the past? What is meant—in ideological terms—by our 'natural' understanding of historical explanation?"
—Linda Hutcheon, A Poetics of Postmodernism

This chapter follows up the discussion in the previous one about self-formation and the force exerted by the symbolic in that process. Until now I have confined my discussion of Murakami's literature primarily to the realm of the psychological, the ontological, and the aesthetic. As has become clear in each of these sections, however, one is never free from the highly politicized issue of identity in Murakami's work, nor even very far from it. Certainly this is a major issue connected with the author's use of magical realism, as well as an undeniable grounding for his psychological portrayals. In this chapter I would like to turn more concretely to the political side of Murakami literature by discussing his approach to three major concepts: representation, ideology, and history.

It would be safe to say that the relationship between these three issues becomes truly apparent only when they emerge into postmodern debate. What is "history" in postmodern discourse? This is no simple matter. "History," in and of itself, no longer exists. Instead one speaks of histor*ies*, but more important, even, than these is the matter of *writing* history that, as I noted in my introduction, is always a political act. The writing of history always concerns selections and interpretations that, as Hayden White (1987, 24) points out, include the writer's subjectivity: "Where, in any account of reality, narrativity is present, we can be sure that morality or a moralizing impulse is present too." In other words, objectivity in historical writing is no longer possible.

Hutcheon argues similarly that one of the chief projects of the postmodern is to undermine the notion that "history" is somehow more real or true than "fiction" by virtue of its reliance on fact. Whereas White's critique of historical validity is grounded in the inevitable subjectivity of the author, however, Hutcheon's is based on the unreliability of the medium of language itself. Because facts must be expressed as language, or text, she argues, they are no more certain or true than fiction, which uses the same medium. That is to say, insofar as "reality" must be, finally, comprehended through the filters of language, culture, and experience, there can be, as I argued in my introduction, no such thing as autonomous, external "reality."

> The twentieth-century discipline of history has traditionally been structured by positivist and empiricist assumptions that have worked to separate it from anything that smacks of the "merely literary." In its usual setting up of the "real" as unproblematic presence to be reproduced or reconstructed, history is begging for deconstruction to question the function of the writing of history itself. (Hutcheon 1988, 95)

Hutcheon's interrogation of history goes beyond the mere question of whether we can ever get to "the Truth" to question more importantly the effectiveness of language, the written text, to substitute for history itself: "What is the ontological nature of historical documents?" she demands. "Are they a stand-in for the past? What is meant—in ideological terms—by our 'natural' understanding of historical explanation?" (Hutcheon 1988, 93).

Essentially this calls into question concepts like "fact" and "reality" and asserts that any notion of viewing historical discourse as more real or objective than other modes of discourse (fiction, for instance) is ultimately a fallacy; nothing can be known, given meaning, without first representing it—through language, a conceptual framework, cultural boundaries. This is not true merely because to read history is also write it, as White argued nearly three decades ago, though that certainly is one step in the argument (White 1973, see esp. 2–42). But representation becomes integrated with history when it is realized that all perception, interpretation, and conveyance of the past is finally an act of language and textualization, and such gestures are always political at some level. I do not say that it is always an act of *individual, subjective* politics, however; but cultural ideologies have it in their power to influence how we view, interpret, and represent a political drive, even if only through our decision to accept or reject them. In short, culture is always dependent upon the politics of ideology and the symbolic. Thus one may say, as I did in my introduction, that any decision to represent the past (or indeed the present), either as a closed narrative or an open-ended one, is itself a political act.

There is no escaping the reality that interpretation and representation are a means to power—the power and right to speak. If knowledge is power, then the ultimate power comes from the appropriation of the right to *generate* knowledge by selecting, interpreting, and creating the historical past in textualized form. In this context the connection with ideology becomes fairly obvious. If ideology is the groundwork of culture, the bedrock in which our actions, ideas, and thought systems are anchored, then the potential power to be gained from controlling historical discourse is almost unlimited. That is to say, once one undermines the notion of a singular history, a series of events that happened and have been handed down to us, one opens the possibility that our cultural foundations are set in shifting, unreliable sand rather than unshakable rock. In some cases, as Hutcheon argues, the clear and obvious goal of the historiographer is to recover peripheralized, "decentered" histories. At the same time, in ontological terms, postmodern discourse has been concerned with showing that other forms of discourse—most notably fiction—have as much claim to veracity as historical discourse. As Brian McHale (1992, 152) writes, contrasting conventional historical writing with the politically slanted postmodern variety,

> Where the classic historical novel sought to ease ontological tensions between historical fact and fictional inventions, and to camouflage if possible the seam along which fact and fiction meet, postmodernist historical fictions . . . aim to exacerbate this tension and expose the seam. They do this, for instance, by contradicting familiar historical fact, by mingling the realistic and fantastic modes, and by flaunting anachronism.

But the purpose of such writing is not so much an attempt to elevate fiction to the level of truth as to reduce the status of historical discourse to that of linguistic representation, to acknowledge its dependence on language—on interpretation and representation. In short, the postmodern mode suggests that the historical past cannot be concretely known except through the tenuous and always subjective, always politically implicated terms of language.

In brief, I wish to argue in this chapter that the notion of objective history has been successfully challenged by postmodern writers throughout the world, and supplanted by an acknowledgment of the writing of subjective histories. Among English-speaking writers, Salman Rushdie, Ian Watson,

John Fowles, D.M. Thomas, E.L. Doctorow and Toni Morrison are names that come up frequently in this regard; in Japan such writers are fewer, their experiments being of a somewhat different nature, but I think one could write convincingly of the historical experiments of Oda Makoto, whose representation of the atomic bombing of Hiroshima is unlike anything else yet written; of Murakami Ryū, who, Stephen Snyder astutely points out, writes nostalgically of a "future" past (1996, 69–83); of Ōe Kenzaburō, whose novel *The Silent Cry* is a useful exercise in the questioning (and blurring) of historical versus mythical truth-value, and whose narratives are nothing if not subjective. One might also look at Kaikō Takeshi's vividly personal accounts of his correspondent's life during the Vietnam War, for while the events and characters described in the work are certainly realistic, we are not always assured that they are "real."

I believe that the historiographic efforts of Murakami Haruki are comparable to those writers noted above. Like many of them, Murakami's talent here lies in his ability to mingle the elements of fantasy, of magical realism, of historical and fictional narrative, into an imaginative presentation of "real" historical moments. In doing so, he succeeds, at least to a point, in recovering the "lost" voice of his own generation.

Murakami's play with history has captured the attention of critics almost from the beginning, and a number of interesting, if sometimes rather directionless, debates have been carried on about this. I noted in the introduction above, for instance, Aoki Tamotsu's attempt some years back to present in a more positive light the Murakami hero's absorption in popular culture as a peculiar kind of historical awareness, an awareness that effectively provokes a nostalgic response from the reader. I have also noted the attacks of Kuroko Kazuo, who finds too little awareness of historical "reality" in Murakami, and Katō Norihiro's complaint that the author excessively romanticizes the past—especially the 1960s.

Some of this body of criticism also focuses on Murakami's linguistic representation, not merely of the historical past but of reality in general. As noted above, Karatani Kōjin (1990a, 1990b) suggests that the author has carried out a sustained campaign to de-specify historical discourse by removing concrete, proper referents from the events to which they are connected, arguing in particular that Murakami's unwillingness to attach proper names to his characters designifies them until they simply "disappear into language in general" (Karatani 1990a, 297). We might view the author's propensity for linking popular song titles to significant years in a similar way; the defining event of 1963 is not merely Kennedy's assassination but is also the release of Stan Getz's hit song, "The Girl from Ipanema." One cannot help feeling sympathetic to Karatani's critique.

But Murakami's mistrust of our ability to represent the historical past in language is neither unique nor misplaced. Much of the literature on postmodernism is concerned with understanding and redefining the role language plays in our discourses on cultural productions. Brian McHale (1987), expanding on the term "realeme," coined by Itamar Even-Zohar, labors to protect an increasingly untenable assumption that there is a "real" history against which the various histories of postmodern fiction may be compared. The matter of *which* history is "the" history is, of course, something that McHale has considered, but he appears more willing than others—Hutcheon, for instance—to accept that there is something called "the past" that exists as a monolithic body of fact. Moreover, it is a body of knowledge that we can know intuitively, and that thus allows us to make comparisons between "real" history and "invented" history. "Slippery though they may be, we do operate with intuitions about what is accepted historical 'fact' and how far any fictional version deviates from that 'fact'" (McHale 1987, 86). McHale even attempts, perhaps revealing a structuralist desire to categorize according to the norms of differentiation between center and periphery, to construct a series of rules by which the degree of deviation from "true" historical fact may be judged.

Much of this is mitigated in McHale's more recent work, *Constructing Postmodernism*, in which he acknowledges the critical importance of "a delicate balance to be maintained between advocating a particular version of constructed reality and entertaining a plurality of versions . . . " (1992, 1–2). Lest one imagine that this refers solely to his earlier tendency to read postmodernism as "a kind of fixed essence that Alan Thiher rightly denies to it" (1992, 1), he more recently appears prepared to approach the notion of reality, within the peculiar aesthetic parameters of the postmodern, as something equally slippery. That is to say, McHale now concedes, at least to a point, that claims of knowledge about what is "real" and what is, by contrast, "unreliable," is a question best left to modernist criticism (1992, 64). In postmodern writing, however, "versions" of reality must be accounted for through the interactive workings of disparate discourses, of interpretations and perspectives. Because language is neither uniform nor always effective, however, and interpretation always subjective, the subjectivity of such discourses more or less ensures that no single "reality" can exist; there can only be reali*ties*.

> The categories a discourse carves out, the relations it establishes
> among them, its characteristic patterns of linking elements, and

so on—all these encode a particular version of reality, and the different version of reality encoded by different discourses must inevitably be, to some larger or smaller degree, mutually incompatible, incommensurable. Consequently, discursive parallax, in cases where discourses cannot be attributed to personified sources within the fictional world, implies an *ontological* parallax, a parallax of worlds. In effect, to juxtapose two or more free-standing discourses is to juxtapose disparate worlds, different reality templates. (McHale 1992, 54)

Fredric Jameson has also demonstrated concern over the alleged subversion of "genuine" history by postmodern literature's willingness to mix the genres of history and fiction writing. Writing of Doctorow's novel *Ragtime* as "a crisis in historicity," he describes the "poignant distress" one feels at being confronted with "the disappearance of the historical referent" (Jameson 1991, 24–25). But Jameson's "distress" also betrays the assumption that there is such a thing as a knowable, recoverable past, "genuine" history, a notion that conflicts with François Lyotard's argument (responding to Jürgen Habermas's contention that modernity is merely an "unfinished project") that the totalizing "grand meta-narratives" of modernity are no longer the dominant paradigm (Habermas 1983; Lyotard 1984). Hutcheon, however, counters that "the historical referent is very present—and in spades" in *Ragtime*, and that "it is [the] mixing of the historical and the fictive and this tampering with the 'facts' of received history that Jameson objects to" (1988, 89).

It is not only the mixture that bothers Jameson, however, but its attendant implication that history is being tainted by nostalgia, that by fictionalizing the past Doctorow invites us to partake of a "safe" past, contained in the narrative and thus incapable of disturbing us with what really *ought* to be disturbing: the injustices of the 1920s toward minorities, women, and so-called political "subversives." I think Hutcheon is probably right, however, in pointing out that this imagistic perspective of the 1920s, while partially fictionalized (as in the internal narrative of Coalhouse Walker), is nevertheless "always ironically turned against itself—and us" (1988, 89).

A similar argument is applicable in the context of Murakami's unwillingness to term historical periods or significant historical events by their "proper" names. As noted above, in what may be a unique gesture of cultural signification, Murakami presents his own historical formations based on popular culture icons, while cross-referencing them with the "major" events of the same period. "1969" is simultaneously the year in which Japanese universities were crippled by student strikes and violent confrontations with riot police, and also emblematized by the Rolling Stones and

Deep Purple. "1970" is both the year of Mishima Yukio's celebrated *seppuku* and of a very personal crisis for Murakami's protagonist—the disappearance of Rat. He invents the year "1934" as that in which the first pinball machine was created then adds nonchalantly that it was also the year Hitler seized power from the Weimar Republic (*MHZ* 1:139).[1] There is no privileging of one event over the other, nor is any attempt made to judge the relative importance of the two occurrences. We may read here the essence of Karatani's conception of "landscape," in which background is pushed to foreground, and "the very 'history' contained within proper names is overcome. It is here that 'landscape' appears" (1990a, 300).

Karatani's conception of landscape in this respect is clearly linked to postmodern conceptions of historiography, which similarly undermines the "history" that is metonymically contained (or perhaps imprisoned) within accepted and acceptable proper names, rejecting the objectivity that such terms provide in favor of subjectivized narratives, grounded in the individual and his or her experiences—from the world historic to the cultural. Karatani's own strategy has been to displace the Western calendar in favor of that organized according to Japanese imperial reign names, a practice that has yielded surprising insights about the nature of Japanese history and historicization (1993a). His attempt itself is historiographic in nature, that is, it attempts to revisit history from an alternative (subjective) point of view, with the express purpose of uncovering a new story, or a new reading. Such an approach is consistent with Hayden White's (1973, 1987) contention that the historian's methodology is—and always must be—concerned not merely with presenting facts, but with confronting the issues of selection and presentation. History is not simply "there," waiting for us to "uncover" it, he argues, nor is there any "natural" sense of beginnings and ends in historical events. All of this must be constructed by the historian through narrative. "What I have sought to suggest," writes White, "is that this value attached to narrativity in the representation of real events arises out of a desire to have real events display the coherence, integrity, fullness, and closure of an image of life that is and can only be imaginary" (1987, 24).

The questions confronting the historian today, then, are similar, if not identical, to those confronting the writer of fiction: How are the events to be selected and narrated, by whom shall they be narrated, and most importantly, for what purpose? Such questions naturally foreground the

1. Murakami is, however, off by one year; the Weimar Republic ended in 1933, following
   Hitler's ascendancy to the Chancellorship.

inevitability of a political agenda in the practice of writing both history and fiction.

The project of postmodern historiography for the past twenty years has been to recover narratives that have been suppressed, overlooked, deemphasized. Its particular focus in recent years, according to Hutcheon (1988), has been to rediscover the narratives of women and ethnic and racial minorities (Hutcheon 1988, 95). At the same time, historiography's strength has been to avoid the vacuum of so-called "objective" history, in favor of an approach that acknowledges the influences of the contemporary on our understanding of the past, for "the writing, reception, and 'critical reading' of narratives about the past are not unrelated to issues of power, both intellectual and institutional" in the present moment (Hutcheon 1988, 98).

An additional contribution of the postmodern to the project of historiography has been the so-called "historiographic metafiction" of writers like E.L. Doctorow, Toni Morrison, Ian Watson, and Salmon Rushdie. Through the works of these writers we may view historiographic metafiction, perhaps somewhat paradoxically, as a return to *earlier* methodology, for it is only since the late nineteenth century that literature and history have been considered mutually exclusive disciplines (Hutcheon 1988, 105). The double task of historiographic metafiction is to reveal "new" versions of past experience, and to highlight its self-consciously subjective approach toward the reading of that experience. Brenda Marshall (1992, ch. 6) points to Morrison's 1987 novel *Beloved* as an example of a work that combines the narrative of the enslavement of Africans in the United States with the "magical realism" that has become an essential and definitive part of postmodern expression. Rushdie's *Midnight's Children* (1980) similarly displaces conventional, "objective" history in favor of the subjective, admittedly limited viewpoint of a single person—the narrator of the novel. Doctorow's *Ragtime* (1974) offers an eclectic cast of fictionalized "real" historical figures—Emma Goldman, J.P. Morgan, Harry Houdini, and Sigmund Freud—and also purely fictional characters (the nature of historiographic metafiction is that *all* characters, whether known to us or not, are "introduced" for the first time).[2]

It is, then, the goal of historiographic metafiction, in its juxtapositioning (though never its reconciliation) of historical and literary discourses, to enact a deconstruction of "history" as the holder of ultimate

2. Both Rushdie and Doctorow are treated in Hutcheon 1988; Doctorow is further taken up in Jameson 1991.

truth, undermining traditional modes of evaluation that have left fiction in the secondary position. Rather, in emphasizing the fact that the two disciplines (or genres, as Hutcheon terms them, further narrowing the gap) utilize many of the same conventions—"selection, organization, diegesis, anecdote, temporal pacing, and emplotment" (Hutcheon 1988, 111)—historiographic metafiction demarginalizes fiction, not by demonstrating a higher truth-value in works of fiction, but in underscoring the construct of higher truth-value traditionally assigned to the historical process: "Postmodernism deliberately confuses the notion that history's problem is verification, while fiction's is veracity" (112).

But we are equally aware of the crisis that this kind of narrative represents. In self-consciously relativizing its interpretive strategies of past experience, simultaneously maintaining and critiquing the possibility of representing that past through language, historiographic metafiction saws at the very branch on which it sits; that is, it mistrusts language, finds fault with historical textuality, but at the same time admits that language and textuality are the only media available by which to engage in such discourses. The past, as both McHale and Hutcheon emphasize, can never be more than text, language, and this is how we are forced to conceive of it. McHale's and Jameson's persistent attempts notwithstanding, the past "exists" only as a construct of language, and as such is by definition only as real as any narrative rendered in the same way. Indeed, one can go even further, as Baudrillard does, and argue that "reality" in the hands of the mass media has been erased, its replacement with the so-called "simulacrum" only partially hidden from us.[3] There is no particular reason why this argument should be limited to present reality; if the mass media can "mask" its (re)construction of a simulated reality, why not also a history? Indeed, this is precisely what has occurred in postwar Japan with the mass media's ever-delicate handling of Japanese war responsibility in the Second World War. One cannot help but be astonished at how the media image of Japan presented to the world somehow expresses simultaneously repentance

---

3. I mean, of course, to suggest a relationship between reality and meaning, or the "implosion of meaning," as Baudrillard (1994b, 82–83)refers to the metonymical tendency of mass media productions of historical events to take the place of the events themselves: "Just as the extermination of the Jews disappeared behind the televised event Holocaust," reality is now presented to us in images in which the medium and the message are conflated. "Strictly, this is what implosion signifies. The absorption of one pole into another, the short circuiting between poles of every differential system of meaning, the erasure of distinct terms and oppositions, including that of the medium and of the real." See also in this regard "Symbolic Exchange and Death" in Baudrillard 1988.

(toward the West) and denial of war atrocities (toward the rest of Asia) (see Hidaka 1984; Honda 1993).

HISTORIOGRAPHY IN POST-1970 JAPAN

I wish, nonetheless, to argue that historiographic metafiction as Hutcheon describes it (see above) above does not maintain a high profile presence in Japanese literature. This is not to suggest that historiographic experiments in fiction do not exist; the writings of Oda Makoto, Kaikō Takeshi, and indeed, Murakami himself, are proof of this. But if we are to examine historiography and the critique of historical representation in general in Japanese literature, we are clearly faced with some necessary redefinition of the terminology.

Let us begin with some of the specific determinants of historiographic metafiction. As Hutcheon notes, the genre is rather vaguely interposed between the genres of history and fiction, becoming wholly neither one nor the other. This is, however, not definitive of "metafiction" so much as of historiography itself, which acknowledges its subjectivity, foregrounds the subjective nature of its selection of "texts" used to produce its narrative, and seeks to recuperate "lost" or "marginalized" texts.[4]

Metafiction, on the other hand, is what results when the author underscores the questionability of his or her sources by clearly and obviously mingling the conventionally factual with the openly fictional, demonstrating not only that his or her own unique history is inevitably flawed, but that all histories will be so. "What is foregrounded in postmodern theory and practice," writes Hutcheon, "is the self-conscious inscription within history of the existing, but usually concealed, attitude of historians toward their material" (1989, 74). In other words, historiographic metafiction is unapologetically open about its nonobjectivity, but also its potential (and its prerogative) not always to "get it right" beyond the scope of their own limited perspective.

This is the stance we find, for instance, in *Midnight's Children*, whose narrator presents a history of India that is unique because it is grounded in his own, unequivocally unique life experience. We are given a narrative that is grounded partially in the external events, but more in the author's unique personal situation at the time he writes: his wife's reactions to the writing process are entered into the record, as is a brief bout of fever.

4. In this sense, historiographic metafiction shares something in common with the "literary journalism" of the late nineteenth century, and with the so-called "New Journalism" of the 1960s. Both of these terms will be discussed shortly below.

Certain scents, certain flavors (especially green chutney!), comments by a small, anonymous army of neighbors, all affect Saleem Sinai's choice of what to narrate, when to do so, and how. In Murakami's *The Wind-Up Bird Chronicle*, on the other hand, as we shall shortly see, this questioning of sources amounts to certain eccentricities in the narrative: the fact, for instance, that Okada Tōru is referred to as "Mr. Wind-Up Bird" by one character in the story, while another, wholly separate character creates a narrative that he entitles the "Wind-Up Bird Chronicles." We cannot help but wonder whether these connections are real, imagined, or coincidental? What are we to make, then, of the "histories" they seem to contain?

Historiographic metafiction rhetorically asks the question, Is this a valid way to write history? The answer is yes, because it merely offers one among many valid perspectives. What historiographic metafiction sets out to do is to highlight the subjective, usually political agenda that lies beneath all attempts to narrate the past, thereby denying objectivity, the centrality of so-called "neutral" history. A by-product—but I think not the central purpose—is that the gap between fiction and history created by the latter's claim to superior truth value is narrowed considerably.

But this, despite definite similarities, is not really what is happening in Japanese literature. There is no question that historical fiction is produced, even historical fiction that seeks to recover lost texts. What is missing is the intentional undermining of the historical source. With few exceptions—Ōe's work of the late 1960s comes to mind—we do not see Japanese authors self-consciously calling into question their methodology, sources, or truth value. Instead, Japanese writers produce texts that resemble historiographic metafiction, and even serve many of the same goals, yet are not necessarily a response to the issue of truth value, nor self-consciously aware of their conflation of the two genres of history and fiction. Instead, the issue is one of perspective, the methodology something I would like to call "relief historiography." This term, which I have adapted from the idea of relief sculpture, is meant to suggest that the outlines of the historical past, the outer limits of the historical moment under discussion, are displayed in such a way as to invite the reader to envision an image of the interior narrative. Quite literally in the gaps, the spaces that are opened up by the discourse, a historical period or event is evoked in relief. It is a method whose effectiveness no doubt lies in the fact that it requires the active participation of the reader's imagination. A useful example of what I mean by the term "relief historiography" may be found in Oda Makoto's novel *Hiroshima* (1984), a work that, as its title will suggest to most readers, concerns the atomic bomb. Yet, while *Hiroshima* is about the nuclear annihilation of that city, its primary setting in the Los Alamos desert of New Mexico deflects us from that initial image. In fact, it could be argued that Oda's work is more about racism in America—racism that led the U.S. government to test its doomsday weapon on Native American land, to look the other way when members of the indigenous population were injured by the testing and its aftermath, and finally to use the weapon on human, civilian targets. Even the scenes of *Hiroshima* that take place in Japan are largely peripheral to the central theme of the work, leading us to the recovery of an entirely different angle of nuclear catastrophe. We understand from this work not only that without Los Alamos there could have been no Hiroshima, but also that the victims of the U.S. nuclear program were not limited to those attacked in the nuclear strikes of August 6 and 9, 1945. John Treat notes also in *Writing Ground Zero* (1995) that *Hiroshima* "is not a novel properly 'about' Hiroshima at all. Only a very few pages speak of August 6, and even those are from a non-Japanese perspective. . . . Oda attempts to dislodge talk of the atomic bombings from the Japanese victims' perspective and shift it, imaginatively, elsewhere" (Treat 1995, 373–74). Not surprisingly, such an attempt to open up the historical past can be offensive and even traumatizing to those personally involved in the events in question, and Treat notes that *Hiroshima* was construed by some readers as "trivializing" what may well have been the twentieth century's most historically unique and significant event (ibid.).

What I wish to emphasize about this, however, is that even though *Hiroshima* is not specifically about August 6, 1945, it nevertheless narrates the events of that date effectively by presenting the peripheral events before and after the actual bombing. The reader gains a detailed fictional account of who lived in Los Alamos prior to the start of nuclear testing, and also the effects afterwards—radiation contamination, birth defects, a major cancer outbreak, and so forth. This, too, is part of the history of the Hiroshima experience, a useful one in the innovative way it permits readers to grapple simultaneously with the issues of nuclear weapons, the specific moral question of using the bomb on Hiroshima itself, racial bigotry, and governmental callousness. It may well be that this dilutes the power, as an event, of the Hiroshima bombing itself, but I think that becomes potentially one of the more definitive signs of postmodern historiography. By opening up the past to a wholly subjective perspective, the author is liberated in his or her choice of what is truly central to the discourse.

As noted above, Murakami has also concerned himself with writing what I call "relief historiography," both in his fiction and nonfiction. Prominent fictional attempts include works like *A Wild Sheep Chase, Hard-Boiled*

Wonderland and the End of the World, *The Wind-Up Bird Chronicle*, and even *Dance Dance Dance;* in the nonfiction area, *Underground* and *At the Place that Was Promised: Underground 2* stand out as narratives with significant historical content derived from subjective sources.

The methodology employed to this end by the author varies in his fiction from parody and allegory to historical fictionalization. In *A Wild Sheep Chase*, for instance, Murakami superimposes the political structure of the late 1970s onto the historical events of one decade earlier, the death of the counterculture movement of the late 1960s. One may see this as parody, but I would prefer to understand the double gesture as a method of writing both histories at once, the events that occur with Rat both real and symbolic of the earlier, collective destruction (or suicide) of Zenkyōtō. A similar methodology is used in *Hard-Boiled Wonderland and the End of the World*, except that the real-time present of the novel is set in the not-too-distant future. As in *A Wild Sheep Chase*, however, disparate historical moments are permitted to collide, commingle, and influence one another. One could even read *Norwegian Wood* in this way, though the "present" time of the novel—eighteen years after the events narrated in the main text—is, in my opinion, poorly handled by the author, too peripheral to produce the "double exposure" effect we have in the novels that come before it.

In other cases, Murakami simply narrates a historical moment that interests him, presumably as part of his critique of the dominant state ideology in Japan. The most recent example, his portrayal of the Imperial Japanese Army's activities in Manchuria and Outer Mongolia, closely resembles the fictional "mini-histories" of Derek Hartfield, pinball, and the mythical sheep: all are designed, at some level, to reveal a crisis of some kind, be it psychological or political in nature.

RECONSTITUTING THE 1960s IN *A WILD SHEEP CHASE*

A few comments on the historical subtext of *A Wild Sheep Chase* will help to illustrate this point. As I noted in the introduction to this book, *A Wild Sheep Chase* is all about the 1960s, despite the fact that the 1960s are never really narrated. Instead, we see a kind of semioticization of the era, either through language or, more commonly in Murakami, through the manipulation of nostalgic images that *are* pure signifiers, pure language itself. I have already discussed the nostalgic image in terms of reconstructed desire vis-à-vis Jacques Lacan; here I wish to understand the Murakami image, nostalgic or otherwise, purely as a signifier of the historical landscape.

As I noted earlier, the idea of textualization is central to postmodern expression, and refers, in its simplest terms, to the reliance on language to represent objects and events. This is the critique of representation. That is to say, postmodernism's understanding of the textual forces us to ask what the past really is, and how it relates to the documents, or the language, that we use to represent it. This is the implicit question behind postmodern historiography as well, and it leads us back to Hutcheon's (1988) query earlier in this chapter: Can historical documents be equated with the past they are intended to represent? Postmodern historiography foregrounds these questions, for "it can often enact the problematic nature of the relation of writing history to narrativization and, thus, to fictionalization, thereby raising the same questions about the cognitive status of historical knowledge with which current philosophers of history are also grappling" (Hutcheon 1988, 92–93).

Can we relate the textualization of history, the critique of language to represent the past, with the images that we have already seen at work in Murakami's literature? It is the author's own structure that requires us to do so. From his earliest writing Murakami has suggested as one constant in his literature that words (and by extension, language) are living things, and that his images are words, something the author states explicitly in "The Story of the Poor Aunt," as noted before. The "poor aunt" who appears in that story may be taken as an early attempt on Murakami's part to represent the notion of the "writerly text," one which, in the Barthesian sense, encourages or even requires the reader's active participation.[5] Murakami invites us to reinvent his open image each time we read the story and thus to keep the text alive. At the same time, he critiques the notion of a grounded, universal, *knowable* reality, just as historiographic metafiction critiques (I do not say *denies*) as irreconcilable the idea of a grounded, universal history or past. In place of universals, we have instead the specificity of discontinuous history, and with it the discontinuous sign, that which has no universal or absolute grounding, but instead is individually grounded and whose referents are specific. Totalizing, universal narratives are replaced with relativized, local ones.[6]

5. See in particular "The Death of the Author" in Barthes 1977, 142–48. It is, Barthes argues, language that takes over the task of narrating once the author has finished writing, but at the same time, the final fruition of the text occurs when it is *read*, an act that implies the logical conclusion of the linguistic process, the reception/interpretation of the narrative. Thus, "*writing* can no longer designate an operation of recording, notation, representation, 'depiction' (as the Classics would say); rather, it designates exactly what linguists . . . call a performative, a rare verbal form . . . " (p. 145; Barthes's italics).
6. Foucault makes a very similar argument concerning our historical discourses on specific areas of human knowledge. Rejecting the notion of a general, universal historical narrative by which we can grasp the totality of a given historical moment, Foucault argues

This is the kind of historiography that we encounter in *A Wild Sheep Chase*, one that may appear to be expressed through traditional metonymical tools (symbol, metaphor, etc.), yet whose "symbols" also play real characters in Murakami's historiographic relief narrative of the late 1960s. It is easy, for instance, to read the sheep that supposedly inhabits people's bodies and minds as a transcendental symbol of political power. To ignore this reading would be, in fact, to miss one of the more obvious and important elements in the text. But to suggest that the sheep is *only* a metaphor, a symbol, or an allegory for something else is to deny its reality in this case.

Instead, it is crucial to see the sheep not only as a symbol of political power, which it certainly is, but as part of a larger whole: Murakami's construct of the period of the late 1960s. In other words, while the sheep is without question a transcendent symbol of a much larger entity—political power, corruption, controllers of society, even the Symbolic Order itself, all depending upon what social or political lenses one chooses to look through— it is also a literary character in the larger scheme of history, and in this role it is not a transcendent symbol, but a very real creature.

Other characters also embody this multidimensional functionality, as symbols of a larger entity, and as real—if metaphysical—characters in the larger historiography that Murakami constructs of the 1960s, 1970s, and 1980s. Rat, as we have already seen, enacts several important roles, each occupying a "layer" of temporal space: he is the enigmatic "Sheepman" in the layer of the present; he is the protagonist's real friend in memory— the layer of the past; and he *is*, metonymically, the student movement of the late 1960s, symbolically and actually straddling *both* temporal layers via the textual position he occupies in the author's historiography. This last function is his symbolic one, but the previous two—one historical, the other historiographic—are concrete representations, not abstract ones. That is to say, as a symbol of the student movement, Rat is an abstract, but as a memory, or even as a nostalgic image, he is concrete. The sheep, too, maintains this triple identity: first as the image of the Sheepman, which it shares

---

for an archaeological approach that will appreciate the discursive and evolutionary distinctions between various bodies of human knowledge. Thus, "Archaeology . . . will show that the general area of knowledge is no longer that of identities and differences, that of non-quantitative orders, that of a universal characterization, of a general taxinomia, of a non-measurable mathesis, but an area made up of organic structures, that is, of internal relations between elements whose totality performs a function; it will show that these organic structures are discontinuous, that they do not, therefore, form a table of unbroken simultaneities, but that certain of them are on the same level whereas others form series or linear sequences" (Foucault, 1994 [1970], 218).

with Rat, in the present; second as itself, known only through a photograph, a legend, and the memory of the Sheep Professor; and finally, in its role as transcendent symbol, as political power.

A close reading of *A Wild Sheep Chase*, then, demonstrates that historical representation for Murakami operates on two levels, the present and the past, always linked by layers of metonymical signification. We recall that the novel begins with two deaths, one historically "significant," the other not. The latter concerns the sudden death of a girl the protagonist knew in college, known only as "the girl who would sleep with anyone." This is the closest we get to knowing her name, but her history—what little of it that exists in the protagonist's memory—leads us quickly back to the other, historically significant death that concerns us: that of Mishima Yukio, whose suicide by *seppuku* on November 25, 1970 has been understood by many Japanese historians as one signifier for the end of Japan's "postwar" period (see esp. Karatani 1993). Interestingly, while Murakami himself gives this away by giving the opening chapter of the novel the title "11/25/70," Alfred Birnbaum leaves this out of his English translation, perhaps because he did not expect the average American reader to grasp the significance of the date.[7] Its absence for those who do, however, actually seems to heighten the effect when Mishima's ghostly image flashes again and again on the television screen in the university student lounge. By providing the atmosphere of the moment—that "eerie afternoon of November 25, 1970" (*MHZ* 2:19; *WSC* 7)—Murakami gives us the outline of the historical moment, without quite getting to the event that makes it significant: Mishima's suicide. More importantly, he does not give us any sense of why this moment should be important to him. It could be that, like so many Japanese, he is uncertain.

In retrospect, we may argue that Mishima's death was part of the closure of an era that many were unprepared to see end. One recalls the thrilling language of Murakami's description of 1969, and its contrast with the disillusion of 1970, in *A Wild Sheep Chase*. Of the former he writes,

> The Doors, The Stones, The Byrds, Deep Purple, Moody Blues—it was that kind of era. The air crackled with an invisible tension, as though with one determined kick you could smash everything to pieces. (*MHZ* 2:15; *WSC* 4)

Contrasted with this, the autumn of 1970 is bleak, empty and meaningless. "Hard rock played on as before, but the crackling tension in the air was gone. Only the girl and the tasteless coffee were the same" (*MHZ* 2:17;

7. Birnbaum does, however, note the date within the body text (*WSC* 7).

WSC 6). Mishima's death seems particularly apt as part of this overall description, as though he had simply died of boredom rather than *seppuku*. To judge from Murakami's text, the reader is uncertain whether Mishima killed the 1960s, or the 1960s killed him.

In light of this historical contrast, I would like to bring the discussion back to the matter of the radical transformations of identity discussed in the previous chapter on the unconscious Other. These transformations are, as we have seen, brought about by magical experiences that drive an inexorable wedge between the self and its unconscious Other. Note, for instance, that in *Hard-Boiled Wonderland and the End of the World* the fate envisioned for the protagonist is perpetual banishment to the inner mind, severing the lines of communication between consciousness and unconsciousness. In *The Wind-Up Bird Chronicle*, Cinnamon experiences a kind of out-of-body experience during a dream, and awakens to find that he is no longer himself, the transformation marked by the fact that he is now mute. Similarly, Myū in *The Sputnik Sweetheart* is cut off from her outer self and lives out her days feeling like a half-person, while Sumire is so utterly transformed by her desire for Myū that she can no longer live in the conscious (external) world and retreats into her inner mind to commune with her memories, real and imaginary.

I raise these images again because their common root, I believe, lies in Murakami's exploitation of Japan's political moment of transition from 1969 to 1970. The author's attempt to write a historiography of the 1969/1970 split, grounded in the intensely personal experiences of his protagonist—modeled on himself—reflects his desire to show how the very identity of Japan itself was transformed at this moment in time.

Of course, it is easy to accuse Murakami of radically reducing via allegory a historical progression that is actually quite drawn out and complex. To begin with, the 1960s did not simply "die" in 1970, either through the dawning of a new decade, the death of Mishima, or with the renewal of the U.S.-Japan Security Treaty. Rather, the 1960s—the Japanese counterculture movement in general—died a slow and painful death that began, arguably, with the escalation of violence in 1968, was confirmed by the renewal of the Security Treaty and the return of Okinawa to Japanese sovereignty, and ended with the conclusion of the Vietnam War in 1975. Viewed in terms of major international events, the political implications of the late 1960s through the mid-1970s in Japan go far beyond the scope of anything Murakami describes in his loose allegorization of this period.

And yet, as historiographic narrative Murakami's approach is valid. One may see in some sense a similar dilemma to that posed by Saleem Sinai in his historiographic exposition of India via his own subjectivity: that connections with "real" history are lost, left incomplete or unspoken. In *Midnight's Children* Saleem wonders often if he is "getting it right," and now and then feels compelled to acknowledge that he is not; no matter, however, for his version of history is honest within the parameters of his self-identification as spokesman of his postwar generation. Can the same be said of Murakami's vision of the 1969/1970 transition? Unquestionably it can. Although the specific elements of the dilemma differ somewhat—Murakami does not so much err, necessarily, as oversimplify and mythologize—we still wrestle with the same fundamental questions: what are the conditions under which "events" are selected (or excluded) to piece together a history, what are the political stakes in their selection, how are they represented, and how does the author's stance toward the process and function of history strike the reader as a result?

Taking this into account, certain observations about Murakami's historiography of 1969/1970 suggest themselves: first, that he wishes to present a version of history that is both concordant with "official" history—major events like Mishima's suicide *are* included—yet that also acknowledges the brief history of his generation's political activities, a narrative that has been not so much suppressed as *repressed*, by the participants themselves. It seems equally clear that Murakami focuses on the 1969/1970 transition because he desires earnestly to remind his contemporaries that they were a part of this transition, and thus encourage them to recuperate *and account for* their silent history. Second, Murakami's historiographic depiction of this moment is accusatory, directing our attention not only to the mainstream consumerist culture of the present, but to the role played by that system in the past. In other words, by casting works like *A Wild Sheep Chase* into a clearly political mode, the author incriminates the social establishment that guided Japan down a path of almost unmitigated emphasis on economic prosperity, smoothed over critical questions about Japan's modern history, and homogenized Japan's dissidents into "good" citizens. At the same time, by implication, he incriminates the dissidents themselves for the ease with which they were so homogenized.

STATE IDEOLOGY AND CLASS STRUGGLE IN MURAKAMI

This leads us quickly back to the notion of the Japanese state and its *modus operandi* for reclaiming the mass of Japanese counterculture in the early 1970s. Arguing much as Lacan did that the subject is created out of a response both to "an other" (anonymous, an object) and to "the Other," an imposing yet internally originating structure of power and authority (Lacan's Symbolic Order), Louis Althusser asserts that the modern subject is drawn into a system in which his relationship to production is maximized, in return for which he is given concrete assurance that he exists and is meaningful. Terming this imposing structure "ideology," Althusser likens it very closely to the structures of the mind we saw in Lacanian theory, but unlike Lacan (yet very like Murakami) he assigns a willful, managerial quality to the ways in which this ideology is conveyed to (or imposed upon) mass society. Ultimately its purpose is the maintenance of a vibrant, self-reproducing economic system.

> "So be it! . . ." This phrase proves that it *has* to be so if things are to be what they must be and let us let the words slip: if the reproduction of the relations of production is to be assured, even in the processes of production and circulation, every day, in the "consciousness," i.e. in the attitudes of the individual-subjects occupying the posts which the socio-technical division of labour assigns to them in production, exploitation, repression, ideologization, scientific practice, etc. (Althusser 1970a, 249)

Althusser's Marxist perspective naturally leads him to cast any theory of selfhood into the modes of production, labor, and class struggle in a way that Lacan does not, but it is interesting to note that Murakami has done the same thing, as we have seen, in works like *Dance Dance Dance*, which takes the position that identity (but only that as participant in the consumerist system, at the expense of subjective, individual identity) is bestowed by the state in exchange for loyalty, obedience, and productivity. As before, I do not suggest that this is new, nor even perceived as particularly oppressive; only that the most recent manifestation of that system seems to go further than ever at repressing an essential selfhood while covering up the fact behind the facade of an "open society."

In some ways an ideological critique of Murakami's work might yield more definitive results than did the psychological analyses performed in the previous chapter, though I believe those analyses, too, offer important insights to the role external society (fed by ideology, the symbolic, etc.) plays in the development of the self. By casting the question into the context of ideology, on the other hand, we lend it the distinctly political tone with which Murakami himself consistently underscores his fictional portraits of contemporary society. Ultimately, as I have suggested in various ways before, Murakami is concerned with exposing the true nature of the struggle fought out between reformists and the conservative government in the 1960s, and in later works with exploring the potential ramifications of continuing that struggle.

To term this a "class struggle" admittedly evokes the Marxist dialectical, complete with its assumptions of teleology and social evolution, and this is something I still earnestly wish to avoid, for Murakami's model of history is anything but deterministic. At the same time, there is an obvious affinity between Althusser and Murakami: both clearly view ideology—its production and dissemination—as tied to a struggle between classes, whether of capital and the proletariat, as in the former case, or between the instruments of political power and the student dissidents in the latter. In Althusser's somewhat simpler terminology, ideology emerges from a struggle between the "ruling class" and the "ruled class."

> In fact, the State and its Apparatuses only have meaning from the point of view of the class struggle, as an apparatus of class struggle ensuring class oppression and guaranteeing the conditions of exploitation and its reproduction. But there is no class struggle without antagonistic classes. Whoever says class struggle of the ruling class says resistance, revolt and class struggle of the ruled class. (Althusser 1986, 249–50)

Applied to contemporary Japan, we may say that the current structure of consumerism, control, and the media is the result of a similar class struggle, one that the Japanese elite clearly won. In similar terms, Murakami's agenda of exploring, probing, questioning, and finally undermining the dominant ideology in contemporary Japan—an ideology grounded in state-controlled economic policies and national goals—is based on his perception that Japanese society is defined by this sort of demarcation of ruler and ruled, his belief that, as Andrew Barshay (1988, 231–32) notes, the Japanese masses have in fact been objectified by the state, which now manipulates their desire. More important, however, is that the sort of antagonistic relationship Althusser describes between those classes has largely failed to develop since 1970, despite the widespread perception among many Japanese that their politicians are corrupt.[8]

Althusser refers to such ideologies as the product of "apparatuses" of the state, by which one may interpret him to mean something similar to the various "compensations" Lacan claims are offered in exchange for the surrender of one's desire for the Other. Actually, in moving our discussion

---

8. See Honda 1993, 27. See also Williams 1994, 29–30, who argues that the Japanese have come to expect a certain level of corruption in their politicians.

beyond the model of desire, repression, and substitution into the realm of politics, we may more clearly see some of the actual social mechanisms—Althusser's apparatuses—that maintain control over the individual and transform him or her from a free individual into a part of the organized system of production/reproduction. What forms do these apparatuses take? One could include, among the more conventional examples, organized religion, which carries and imposes its own moral code and motivations for following it. More recently, and consonant with the notion of the industrialized world as "post-religious," we might note (only half-facetiously) the so-called "secular religions." These include capitalism, democracy, and science, whose respective groundings (wealth, liberty/equality, empirical truth) are bound up in concepts no less mythical or constructed than those of religion.

This is not meant to suggest that these mechanisms are in themselves a bad thing, nor does Murakami wish to convey such an opinion in his writing. He seeks to expose not so much that ideological mechanisms like this exist, but that various ideological systems such as these have gradually congealed, combined to form a single ideology, what he terms "rapid capitalism," essentially synonymous with Hidaka's (1984) "economism." Moreover, Murakami would probably agree with Althusser's contention that such mechanisms dominate society not by accident, but through the manipulation of the ruling (or soon-to-be ruling) class. "The ideology of the ruling class does not become the ruling ideology by the grace of God, nor even by virtue of the seizure of State power alone. It is by the installment of the ISAs [Ideological State Apparatuses] in which this ideology is realized and realizes itself that it becomes the ruling ideology" (Althusser 1986, 250).

Nevertheless, as I argued in the previous chapter, such control mechanisms are not constructed without the cooperation of those they control; rather we willingly submit to them in exchange for an opportunity to participate, to be given intrinsic value within the system that surrounds us. But surely there must be a middle ground between the model Lacan constructs, in which we imprison ourselves, and Althusser's model, in which the dominant ideology is produced through a process of struggle between "ruler" and "ruled." In fact, the contemporary Japanese state portrayed in Murakami's writing, in which mass desire is closely controlled by a coalition of politicians, bureaucrats, industrialists, and the mass media, occupies that middle ground.

Althusser's model of ideology and its power to enfold mass culture helps us to cast into a clearer context the fate of dissidents in Japan, whose resistance was followed by their absorption into the very system they sought to topple. But what is the purpose of that system? Roland Barthes responds rhetorically: "Is it not the characteristic of reality to be *unmasterable*? And is it not the characteristic of system to *master* it?" (quoted in Hutcheon 1989, 37). In the case of Murakami's fiction we might replace "master" with "manage," and reiterate that "reality" is always acknowledged in these works as a construct, not a given. As such, it is not for the "system" operated by the Boss to master an externally existing reality, but rather to constitute a new reality that may be alternatively represented this way or that. In *A Wild Sheep Chase*, "reality" is symbolized in the form of the all-empowered sheep, and represented to the protagonist *fait accompli* as an irresistible power syndicate against which struggle is useless. Here, too, Murakami's allegorical "version" of events—Rat's futile struggle against the Sheep, for instance, is a mirror image of Zenkyōtō's struggle against the conservative establishment—suggests also a desire to revisit the past in order to recover alternative perspectives (here, that of the students who did *not* accept absorption by the system). In Kawamoto's terms, Rat "symbolizes the countless victims, forever silent, who died for a revolutionary ideal" (1986, 56).

    A Wild Sheep Chase is, then, a kind of recuperative history, an attempt to demarginalize, or revive, the generation that committed political mass suicide between 1968 and 1970. It is also about power, the control of historical realities that feed social, cultural, historical ideologies. However, Murakami's protagonist—and one could almost certainly say this of the author himself—seeks through these narratives not control over others, but to regain control over himself and his own destiny.[9]

    In this sense Murakami's work bears resemblance to that of non-Japanese writers of historiography and historiographic metafiction. The impulse to control knowledge, balanced by the acknowledgment of helplessness in doing so, is always present in these works. Hutcheon notes the gesture of helplessness in *Midnight's Children*, for instance, but minimizes the almost megalomaniac drive of Saleem Sinai to control the events he narrates. It is, of course, inherent in the structure of the text: Saleem attempts to show us how India's history is grounded in *his* life, rather that the other way around. He takes responsibility for events whose scope goes far beyond that of his immediate surroundings (and even beyond his compre-

---

9. Wendy Faris (1995, 111) creates an interesting link between the magical realist and historiographic texts that is relevant here when she writes: "In many cases, in magical realist fictions, we witness an idiosyncratic recreation of historical events, but events grounded firmly in historical realities—often alternate versions of officially sanctioned accounts."

hension at times), implying a power that is at once, paradoxically, omniscient and god-like, yet accidental in its results. Thus, Hutcheon is probably right when she argues that *Midnight's Children* is not intended to force a historical interpretation on us, but merely to force us to question our own "understanding," and, in the process of questioning it, seek new readings and perspectives (1988, 180).

Hutcheon, then, celebrates the open-ended nature of postmodern historiography, whose enhanced sense of liberation in its approaches to the world is born, I think, partially out of the tendency that began in the 1960s to question authority, to question "truth" as a singular concept. That is to say, contemporary historiography developed very much along similar lines as the "New Journalism" that emerged in response to the perceived program of misinformation concerning the findings of the Warren Commission in 1964, and the escalation of the Vietnam War from 1965. As John Pauly (1990, 111) argues, "In the name of New Journalism, critics once condemned the corporate caution of newswork, reporters' overreliance on official sources, the increasing concentration of media ownership, and biased news coverage of political concentrations." Pauly goes on, however, to bewail the fact that New Journalism has lost its critical edge, having suffered, over time, the same fateful canonization that Huyssen (1986) claims befell 1960s postmodernist expression. "Even the sense of newness has diminished," writes Pauly, "for [Tom] Wolfe and his cohorts have entered respectable middle age. . . . Our critical discourse forged [New Journalism] into a literary canon and, in the process, disarmed its politics . . . " (ibid.).

My sense of Murakami's use of the techniques of historiography—and later, of literary journalism (whether or not it can be called "New")—is that he takes a position more similar to Pauly's than to Hutcheon's in his desire to restore a critical voice for contemporary writing. That is to say, whereas Hutcheon acknowledges the political, but celebrates the liberation of voice in postmodern historical discourse, Murakami is far less content merely to accept that different "versions" of history exist. Unwilling simply to present his notion of historical events and leave it there, he is determined instead to expose a collusive effort on the part of political and media enterprises to whitewash those events in such a way as to produce a particular model of the Japanese subject, and indeed, a particular conception of the modern Japanese state to the rest of the world. Murakami, then, presents an aggressive critique of the contemporary Japanese state and its manipulative role in the invention of both historical and current events.

What, if not revolution, is the purpose of this gesture? To undermine our once cherished ontological certainties is well and good, but ultimately larger monoliths are to be undermined, exposed as artificial. In Althusser's terminology, the "ISAs" must be exposed and dealt with. I wish to argue that Murakami's attempt to reconstitute the 1960s in *A Wild Sheep Chase* is not merely an attempt to create doubt in his readers' minds concerning their memories of the events of that decade. This is without question one of the results of the text, but Murakami's purpose is more critical: he wishes to wrest control of this narrative away from the keepers of the "official history." The chapters above have demonstrated amply that the control of information and how it is (or is not) disseminated has had a constant and definitive impact on the formation of identity in Japan. The same can be said of history as information, an issue that is perhaps more crucial in Japan, where, as noted earlier, the Ministry of Education serves as the final arbiter of what is "true," and more importantly, what is passed on to the next generation as part of the dominant ideology. Murakami, while not necessarily denying the events that actually happened, rewrites conventional interpretations of them in order to reinvigorate some of the sense of dialectical (oppositional) thinking among contemporary Japanese. His method, as noted above, is to superimpose his version of events onto the events more or less as they happened.

Conventional history, of course, documents some of these instances. The revitalization of the New Left after the end of Zenkyōtō is part of the "official" history of the time. The 1972 incident at Mt. Asama, in which a handful of student terrorists made one final stand, is also well known, and Yokoo Kazuhiro, as I noted earlier, has suggested a purely allegorical link between the death of the Zenkyōtō movement (if not the activists involved, who survived!) in that incident and the death of Rat in his own mountain villa in Hokkaido (1991, 16-18).

But—and I think here we touch upon Murakami's *raison d'être* as a writer again—these "historically real" events are, in fact, *never real enough*. Let us pose a hypothetical question: Why are historiography and historiographic metafiction written? What makes these modes of writing at least potentially more powerful than ordinary history? The answer, I believe, is that it permits the (admittedly fictitious) rehumanization of the participants involved. For instance, when one reads a conventional "history" of Zenkyōtō, one catches the "facts," so to speak, but the participants, though named, never truly come to life. Even in histories of more horrendous events, such as the rape of Nanjing, the holocaust, or the atomic bombings, the impersonality of the victims—we do not truly know them—engenders the risk of our desensitization to the violence. We are horrified, but given the sublimity of the event, the impossibility of our apprehending the effects of the event on specific individuals, conventional history is incapable of showing us much beyond the reality of thousands of victims being butchered.

This is, in a sense, a "safe" way to read history, a characteristic shared with ordinary historical fiction, as well. As McHale (1992) points out, historical fiction seeks to minimize the readers' awareness of the seams between historical and fictional writing, and thus may have the same potential as historiography to draw its readers into the events of history. I would argue, however, that the purpose of such writing is more often to entertain, to create a "safe ground," so to speak, into which readers can retreat in the comfortable understanding that this is only fiction, even if based on true events.

Historiography, on the other hand, because it forces us to confront not only the events of history itself but also the seams that lie between history and fiction, may be a more effective way of both drawing the reader into the significant events of history, yet also closing some of the critical distance between reader and text. I would argue that the mechanism at work here is similar to the one seen in chapter one above, in which the very juxtaposition of the formulaic and inventive styles created an effect sufficient to draw our attention, one that encouraged us to seek a deeper reading than we might otherwise have done.

At the same time, by presenting his work as historiography, Murakami continues his agenda of subjectivizing historical events, and thus rehumanizing the participants involved. That is to say, by placing historical events into a subjective framework, the author gains the "right" to amplify the lives of those involved, even to make them up. Is this not what Doctorow accomplishes in bringing "Emma Goldman" and "Henry Ford" to life in *Ragtime*? We get a much greater sense of a *reality* (but only one possibility of many) of these people because we enter their (fictionalized) lives. This gives us a uniquely personal perspective on the various fates that befall them, as well. In this way Murakami similarly creates a "history" of the end of Zenkyōtō, embodied in Rat, that is tremendously moving, more memorable than a conventional historical text might be.

Such a personal approach is not without risks, of course. By fictionalizing characters like Rat, Murakami must accept the possibility that readers will merely write them off as fabrications—the suspension of disbelief followed by its reintroduction. I think this is less likely to occur in historiography of the type Murakami writes, however, because we are constantly made aware of the backdrop of the "real," of the actual events that happened. Thus, even as we are tempted to view Rat's fate as fabrication, we are frequently reminded that Rat is emblematic of something actual, and this permits us both the microcosmic view (Rat, as a person, dies) and the macrocosmic (a movement, known historically as Zenkyōtō, died).

Similar results are observable in *The Wind-Up Bird Chronicle*, in which the author writes a more conventional historiography based on actual events. Historical events are given more or less direct representation here, and while Murakami does superimpose historical periods on top of one another, as noted previously, we do not have the sense of allegorization or symbolization of events here.

Instead, Murakami endeavors to recreate an account of the virtually forgotten Japanese war against the Soviets in Manchuria and Outer Mongolia. Indeed, four major chapters of *The Wind-Up Bird Chronicle*, and half of a fifth, are devoted to recounting events related to that conflict. In order to give the historical narratives greater depth, moreover, they are offered in three distinct "voices:" that of Lt. Mamiya, whose terrifying account has been dealt with above; the point of view of "Akasaka Nutmeg," who recounts her father's adventures as a cavalry veterinarian, and his interaction with a young lieutenant in the closing days of the war; and finally, the narrative of Nutmeg's son, Cinnamon, who writes with authority semi-fictitious texts about the killing of Chinese prisoners, and of the various deaths of those who participate in the executions, including his own grandfather.

What is the point of these narratives? To begin with, they convey the largely forgotten story of the Japanese invasion and occupation of Manchuria and, even less known, of Japanese excursions into Mongolian territory during those years. Moreover, rather than simply providing an objective, statistically based history of those violent events, by personalizing the narratives Murakami allows us a microscopic view of them, thereby humanizing both the events and their participants. Thus, when Lt. Mamiya recounts the horror of seeing his comrade staked to the ground and skinned alive, we are able to witness the slow, deliberate care with which the flayer's knife is wielded, and in some sense we gain access to the thoughts of those who witness the event. Far from painting an impersonal landscape portrait of the war, a singular history that applies to all who were there, Murakami recuperates (or invents) the highly personalized stories of individuals, creating not a history but many histor*ies*.

This approach, among other things, permits certain relationships to emerge that would not otherwise have done so. Looked at macrocosmically, for instance, the war in Manchuria concerned the Japanese Army taking territory, setting up a puppet state known as

"Manchukuo," and protecting this new possession from the threat of military force by the Chinese, the Soviets, and so forth. Not only do complex human relationships never come into play in such a perspective, but even such essential parts of war as violence and death are rarely part of the equation, except in the cold, objective terms of statistical data and military logistics. The microcosmic perspective allowed us via personal narration, on the other hand, though fictional, brings the war alive in ways that have only rarely been possible before. It permits us to eavesdrop on the implied dissidence of the Lieutenant who is in charge of bayoneting Chinese prisoners, wherein is revealed the inner tension he feels between following orders (as an organ of the state), and his awareness that these are gratuitous killings (as an individual). That this opinion cannot be contained in any official view of the war goes without saying, partly because in the macrocosmic scheme of things it is unimportant, but also, no less significantly, because to express it could prove fatal.

It might well be noted that Murakami's depictions of the events in Asia during the war do not go far enough in elucidating Japanese war atrocities there. Indeed, some readers might even be irritated by the author's evident efforts to "balance" the score—presenting both Japanese *and* Soviet war crimes in a remarkably nonjudgmental tone (the Chinese prisoners are killed in retaliation for their own murder of a Japanese teacher at school; the man skinned by "Boris" *is* a spy). But his purpose, according to my analysis, is not to indict either the Japanese or the Soviet military establishments for war crimes. Rather, his purpose is more a determination to contrast the two extremes of "humanity" and "bestiality" that often emerge in war, and to understand that *all* the participants in this conflict (and, by extension, any other) are equally human, equally bestial, depending on the circumstances of the moment. This, too, is part of Murakami's program of focusing on participants of major events—both major and minor participants, tormentors and victims—and attempting to understand them as individuals, with real motivations and real emotions behind them. It is the same impulse, I think, that lies behind the author's desire to publish interviews with the victims of the 1995 sarin gas incident that left twelve dead and thousands injured, and his willingness to take a significant chance with his readership by doing the same with members of AUM Shinrikyō cult that was responsible. Murakami's purpose in doing this is not to approve the actions but to put a human face on both the victims *and* the perpetrators, resisting the mass media's tendency to simplify the matter to one of "good" (victim) versus "evil." "It was probably easier for the mass media to deal with these people if they did not have actual faces," writes Murakami. "It would then be a simple matter to create an archaic diagram opposing these '(anonymous) wholesome citizens' to those 'highly defined criminals'" (*Underground*, 26).

This desire to humanize victim and criminal alike is something that, arguably, is lacking in some other texts concerning violent crime in Japan recently. For instance, in the same year that Murakami Haruki's interviews with the victims of the sarin incident were released, Murakami Ryū published *In za miso sūpu* (In the Miso Soup, 1997), a disturbing novel about a serial killer that goes as far at *de*humanizing both victim and killer alike as Murakami's work does the reverse. Yet for all the obvious differences in approach, both Haruki and Ryū seem able to agree that it is the epidemic of indifference, born of rampant consumerism, that has brought about this state of affairs.

In the Miso Soup is told from the perspective of Kenji, a professional guide (usually for foreign tourists) to Tokyo's bustling nightlife and sex industry. He is hired by an American visitor calling himself "Frank" to arrange sexual liaisons for the latter. From the very start we have the impression, through Kenji's eyes, that Frank is somehow less than human.

> I had dealt with maybe two hundred foreigners in my work before this, and the majority of them had been Americans. But this was my first time to see a face like Frank's. Then it hit me what was wrong with his face: the skin had an odd, man-made look about it. It looked almost like a skillfully made artificial skin someone might wear after having been horribly burned in a fire.
> (Murakami Ryū, *In za miso sūpu*, 8)

Soon Kenji comes to suspect that Frank is the man sought by the police following two gruesome murders, one of a high-school-age prostitute, the other of a homeless man. His fears are confirmed on their second night out when, at an "*omiai* pub"[10] in downtown Tokyo, Frank hypnotizes a room full of people—including Kenji—and murders them all right in front of Kenji's eyes.

Why does Frank do this? It is because, while he never fails to accept his own criminality, he nevertheless considers himself superior to these "useless" and "degenerate" people he sees around him. Indeed, targeting prostitutes and the homeless, Frank envisions himself to be the cleanser of society's useless people—a group he sees as increasingly prominent in soci-

---

10. *O-miai* is, traditionally, the meeting between the prospective bride and groom in an arranged marriage. Today, however, it has been transformed by the sex industry into a bar where prospective sexual partners (including prostitutes) meet one another.

ety. Near the end of the novel he tries to explain this to Kenji.

> "Who do think is more dangerous to society, that homeless guy or
> me? . . . Someone like me is clearly a threat, of course; I'm like a
> virus. But you know, there are very few types of virus that cause
> illness in humans; there are a lot more that don't, whose real
> purpose is to help bring about sudden mutations that lead to the
> diversification of life. . . . I kill consciously, and I'm *trying* to shock
> people by it, to force them to start thinking. I consider myself
> necessary to this world; homeless guys like that are not."
> (Murakami Ryū, *In the Miso Soup*, 231–32)

The real shock of *In the Miso Soup*, however, lies not in Frank's attitude
about his social use-value as a killer, but Kenji's eventual agreement with
Frank's assessment of contemporary Japanese society. What are the Japanese today, Kenji wonders, except degenerate, clueless, directionless consumers who actually are as good dead as alive? After having been set free
by Frank after the killings in the "omiai" pub, Kenji ponders whether he
should report the matter to the police—in fact, there is a police box only a
few meters from him. But he does nothing. The victims he has left behind
in the pub are, after all, worthless. They do not even merit the trouble of
answering questions at the police station. Kenji finds he can feel no emotion for them at all.

> Awful as it might sound, I couldn't feel sympathy for them. Those
> people in the club were like robots, like dolls. . . . Not one of
> them had been living a serious life. They were there because they
> had nothing better to do. None of them was there because his life
> depended on it. Even the owner and his waiter had just been
> killing time there, fighting off loneliness. That was all that had
> died there. I couldn't see myself going through a lot of half-assed
> questioning by the police for the likes of them. (Murakami Ryū,
> *In the Miso Soup*, 168–69)

The term *sabishisa*—perhaps best translated as "desolation" here—
is one that comes up over and over in this novel. The characters in Ryū's
version of Tokyo seem almost fatally afflicted with this kind of desolation,
a sense of total hopelessness, utter uselessness. It really does not matter in
the least to them or anyone else what they do. The world will not improve
because of them, nor will it miss them if they are gone.

Unlike Murakami Haruki, whose young heroes are usually chic and
sophisticated, if a little muddled, Ryū's interest tends to fall on the lower
depths of Japanese society, and perhaps this is why his characters are darker,
more cynical, than Haruki's tend to be. Nevertheless, the two writers ap-

pear to agree (certainly their characters do) that the Japanese today lack moral, spiritual, and intellectual depth—what I have alternately cast into the terms of the symbolic, of ideology, and so forth—and this has left them directionless and lost. *In the Miso Soup*, expresses this as a total lack of knowledge of spiritual origins on the part of the Japanese, a situation both Frank and Kenji abhor. Catching up with Kenji late in the novel, Frank tells him about a Peruvian prostitute he has been talking with, whose sense of cultural awareness and purposefulness, even as a prostitute, contrasts for him with the lack of purpose and cultural awareness in the Japanese. She is here in order to provide a better life for her family in the mountains of Peru, and she understands her mission, and her occupation as a prostitute, to be morally correct. However, seeking to connect with the spiritual side of her host country, the woman finds there is nothing there.

> "She said she wanted to learn about the gods of Japan, but couldn't find any books in Spanish on the subject. She has no English, so she tried asking her customers. But it seems there isn't a Japanese alive who knows a thing about them. She was appalled at the idea of a country where people don't think about such things." (Murakami Ryū, *In the Miso Soup*, 185–86)

Eventually Kenji's own survival depends upon his ability to explain to Frank the meaning of the 108 ringings of the bells of New Year, and in the end he manages well enough to convince the killer that his life is not as pointless or empty as those around him. Kenji, on the other hand, is left to think very hard about the fate of the Japanese now that all sense of spirituality and historical grounding has been lost. On what are the Japanese to blame this loss of grounding, this failure of ideology to inform them of who they are, or to help them find a point to their lives? The answer is the same as we have seen in Murakami Haruki's fiction: the single-minded pursuit of money and consumer goods. Kenji's angry self-reflection cannot but remind us of parts of *Dance Dance Dance*, and also of Shimada's "Kubi" in *Dream Messenger*:

> The young had no basis for judging what was important. Adults lived for money, for things whose value had been fixed already—for brand-name goods. The young were bombarded with announcements on television, on the radio, in the papers and all other media, that their only interest, their only need, was for these same brand-name goods. From politicians to bureaucrats, from the lowest corporate lackey sucking down cheap sake at the local stand to the boss himself, their lifestyles declared the same truth: all they wanted was money. They might say otherwise, but their lives proved them liars. (Murakami Ryū, *In the Miso Soup*, 217–18)

Like Murakami Haruki, then, Ryū depicts a social system that perpetuates itself, yet in which those who have lost their direction willingly participate in that system, deluding themselves that their lives have meaning. And while he may share Haruki's belief that the mass media is responsible for drawing individual Japanese into this system, his characters are far more cynical in their assumption that the Japanese, in their present state, are not worth saving.

And also like Haruki, Ryū suggests something generational in the disillusionment of contemporary Japanese youth. Blaming their parents' generation for giving themselves over to consumerism, the pursuit of brand-name products, Kenji expresses the embitterment of a generation that has little or nothing of significance to live for. They have been given everything, yet nothing, by their parents. "We were always told, 'we had nothing to eat but yams; we gave everything we had to give you a rich country!' And we all knew that we would become just like them. But it was too cruel. The old men would die off soon enough, but we still had another fifty or sixty years to live in this rotting place" (Murakami Ryū, *In the Miso Soup*, 218).

The point we may take away from *In the Miso Soup*, I think, is that the depersonalization of the contemporary Japanese is without question a part of the consumerist ideology that has been imposed upon them. It is an ideology that, as I have noted repeatedly above, encourages even the Japanese themselves to view their sense of individual self as secondary to the perpetuation of a strong, growing economy. Thus, we find that neither Kenji nor the people murdered at the "omiai pub" are capable of assigning any meaning to their existence. This is the trend that Murakami Haruki's most recent writing has sought to reverse through his campaign of "rehumanization."

The importance of this kind of rehumanization cannot be overemphasized, particularly at a time when so much information is disseminated that every news story must be limited to thirty seconds on the evening news, when the persons involved are no longer persons at all, but statistics.[11] Murakami reveals a similar concern near the end of *The Wind-Up Bird Chronicle* in which Tōru, in the unconscious hotel, hears a story on the news about a truck driver who was killed in a mountain accident. He wants

---

11. Ironically, this is one of the aspects of the postmodern that Newman (1985, 130) finds so egregious, as well. "[T]he perniciousness of television is not that it serves up vulgar entertainment, that as sensory deprivation it functions as a mass sedative, that it incites violence in children, or even that it fires 25,000 volts of phosphorescent light per second into our endocrine systems; it is that it treats all events as a *story*. TV is *total* Aristotle, and it is *story at all costs*, not realism *per se*, which becomes the characteristic expression of contemporary bourgeois society."

to feel something, but without personal knowledge of the man this is impossible. Anyone who reads the newspapers or watches television news has experienced this, but to Murakami it represents a dangerous trend in an increasingly depersonalized world.

LITERARY JOURNALISM AND CURRENT EVENTS

As I noted in the chapter on magical realism, Murakami's true aim as a writer increasingly has been to humanize those who have suffered what he terms the "double injury" of being victims of accidents or terrorism, and then being reduced to the level of so much newspaper print. This is certainly visible in the way the newspapers present the death of "the girl who would sleep with anyone" in *A Wild Sheep Chase*; "It was an ordinary sort of story. The kind of piece that would have been written for practice by some cub reporter fresh out of college" (*MHZ* 2:13; *WSC* 3). Murakami's protagonist feels the urge to share some sense of this girl's humanity with us. Irritated by a friend who asks if she had a family, he retorts to himself, "Of course she had a family" (ibid.). What follows, fueled perhaps by the protagonist's sense of duty, is a kind of eulogy of the dead woman, for, as he himself seems to realize, it is the only one she is likely to get.

This is also the impulse behind the author's two recent works of nonfiction, *Underground* and *The Place that Was Promised: Underground 2*. As noted above, both of these works seem to aim at the recovery of a sense of humanity for the victims and, later, the perpetrators of the Tokyo poison gas incident of March 20, 1995. At the same time, they urge us, the readers, toward a fuller and more realistic understanding of the events of that day. As Murakami writes in the "Preface" to *Underground 2*,

> What made me want to write this book was my sense that the reality of the victims of the poison gas incident in the subways had been presented to the world only in the most cursory way, as information. . . . As a novelist, I wanted to grasp the reality of what it meant to be sprayed, without any warning at all, with poison gas on a subway car, and how this changed (or did not change) the life and consciousness of each victim of it. I felt that we urbanites . . . needed to have a more vivid understanding of what that meant. Not as knowledge, but as reality. The searing of their flesh, the sadness that gripped their hearts. (*Underground 2*, 9).

Such an approach, obviously, cannot lay claim to objectivity, and Murakami does not mean for us to read *Underground* or its sequel as "objective" truth.

Rather, as I noted briefly above, he seeks to revive the narratives of the victims, and later the perpetrators, of the sarin incident in such a way as to force readers to confront the fact that these events were generated by ordinary people like themselves, and that such events must be understood in that context before there can be any hope of preventing their repetition.

This leads us, naturally, back to the question of journalism, and whether the tropes of "literary journalism" of the late nineteenth and early twentieth centuries, or of the "New Journalism" of Norman Mailer, Tom Wolfe, and Hunter S. Thompson that emerged in the 1960s might be applied to this kind of writing. In the final analysis, readers of *Underground* and *Underground 2* will probably come away with the impression that such works lie somewhere in between the parameters of these two journalistic genres.[12]

As I noted briefly above, the primary goal of literary journalism was to shift focus in the story from the events that made up the news to the people who were involved in those events. In this sense, literary journalism would probably bear some affiliation with historiographic metafiction, one of the purposes of which is to recover "peripheralized" narratives. The literary journalist, too, was concerned with showing motivations, providing explanations for why things happened, understanding the human element involved in, for instance, a crime of passion. As Norman Sims points out, writers of this type tended to break with orthodox journalism, whose objectivity rested always on the "classical formula of who, what, where, when, and how, with a superficial nod to why" (Sims 1990, 14). For the literary journalist, in contrast to this, it was precisely the *why* that took on such important dimensions.

Obviously, this reflects an effort not merely to report "the facts" but to get at the "human dimension" of the story, to go into some depth as to what led to the events in question and what it might have felt like to be a part of them. One means to this end was to include large segments of interviews with principal participants.

> [I]t was common in the 1890s to let a speaker tell his or her own
> story, so that many articles would consist of paragraphs of quo-

---

12. A word or two may be in order here about the legitimacy of including works such as these that deal with current events in a chapter on history and historiography. Certainly I do not mean to claim that historiography and journalism are the same thing, any more than history and current events are to be conflated. However, inasmuch as Murakami's goal in writing historiography is, ultimately, closely related to his goal in writing his journalistic accounts—the rehumanization of the subject—I feel that these genres cannot be wholly separated in the overall analysis of his work.

tations, allowing the narrative movement of the piece to be provided by the speaker. Although that made the story another step
removed from the reader, it was effective, perhaps even more real
than if the speaker had been concealed in a third-person narration because the writer thus conveyed to the reader that he or she
had actually talked to the speaker. This technique gave the ar-
ticles a stronger basis in fact, yet, if used properly, could create
the "literary" approach. . . . (Sims 1990, 11)

The above, as we can readily see, is readily consonant both with Murakami's
method, which is almost solely interview, and with his self-stated purpose,
noted above, in publishing *Underground* and *Underground 2*.

At the same time, however, we must not ignore one of the most
important political motivations behind the author's desire to compile these
works: his perception that the Japanese mass media have failed to bring
these stories to the public in such a way that the average Japanese reader
will comprehend the human dimension behind the events described. Murakami's comments in the foreword and afterword sections of both *Underground* and *Underground 2* reveal, for instance, his belief that the press
has oversimplified the incident into two "sides": "The perspective of the
mass media in disseminating information about this incident has taken the
form of an opposition, consisting of 'our side,' meaning 'victims=purity=
justice,' and 'their side,' meaning 'perpetrators=befoulment=evil'" (*Underground*, 691–92). At the same time, he is apprehensive about the evident
lack of interest in the individual identities of the victims (or, later, the cult
members), the tendency to focus on them as victims of an atrocity, but to
ignore them as ordinary people. Looked at in a slightly different way, one
might say that the mass media had no interest in these people until the
events of March 20, 1995 had taken place. This is not to imply that they
are mere statistics in the Japanese mass media; indeed, a number of moving narratives concerning the victims have been produced, including the
airing on the Tokyo Broadcasting Service of a brief follow-up piece on one
of the victims, a woman disabled since the incident.[13] But Murakami's interest in the incident is to bring out a much greater depth, a greater degree
of detail, to the characterizations of the victims of the sarin incident through
lengthy interviews, either with the victims or, when the victims were dead,
with their surviving families.

Yet as with so much of his writing, Murakami's approach is eclectic. While he maintains for the most part an effort to be hidden, a mere

13. Aired on March 20, 2000 as part of the television media's observance of the fifth anniver-
sary of the incident.

mouthpiece through which the victims might tell their stories in their own words (carefully recorded on tape and, according to Murakami, faithfully transcribed), his "removal" from the narrative is suspect for two reasons: first, because as a novelist taking up a subject that has already been "done" in the popular press over and over, Murakami clearly has an agenda; and second, because his predilection toward the "underground world" is so explicit, both in his fiction and his afterword, that we cannot assume his interrogation of the victims amounts to nothing more than letting them "tell their own stories." In fact, Murakami asks a remarkable variety of questions, from the mundane ("What were your [dead] husband's interests and hobbies?") to the speculative ("Had you thought of changing trains [after smelling something peculiar on the train]?"), to the interpretive ("Why have you avoided speaking of the lingering symptoms to your family?"). What he really hopes to gain is some in-depth, intensely *personal* understanding of the people he interviews, and in this sense his work *is* interpretive, it *is* creative, a narrative construction, yet also real, grounded in fact, genuine experience, and actual events. This is even more pronounced in the sequel. "In many instances," he writes of *Underground 2*, "I have interposed my own thoughts among those of the persons I interview. Sometimes I have expressed my doubtfulness, or even argued with them" (*Underground 2*, 15). The reasons for this are clear: while Murakami intends to present a personal, human image of the AUM Shinrikyō cult members *and their motivations* to his readers—something the Japanese media have yet largely failed to do—he also has his own political agenda in conveying this "history"; to express his very public belief that Japanese society as it stands is—or at least ought to be!—a powder keg of tension waiting to explode.

This is where I am inclined to characterize both *Underground* and *Underground 2* as having something in common with New Journalism, particularly in its resistance to the dominant narrative concerning historical and current events. Murakami seems determined to deal with the violence he sees in contemporary Japan as something that arises naturally out of the conditions of Japanese life, a notion that can only contrast with the exported images of Japan as a peaceful, homogeneous, prosperous, stable society. That violence erupts, he argues, out of the tension that builds up between the needs of individualistic types who do not find satisfaction in this "stable" society (and here, we may imagine, he includes himself), and the pressures that a strictly conformist society must produce.

> Our reality is that beneath the main system of Japanese society there exists no subsystem, no safety net, to catch those who slip through the cracks. This reality has not changed as a result of the

sarin incident. There is a basic gap in our society, a kind of black hole, and no matter how thoroughly we stamp out the AUM Shinri-kyō, similar groups are certain to form in the future to bring about the same kinds of disasters. (*Underground 2*, 12)

Using terms like "system" and "subsystem," Murakami speaks of an identity drawn from one's integral role in society. But Japan's social "system" today is one in which individuals are defined according to their role in economic/industrial mechanisms—Althusser's ISAs again. As such, there can be very little room for deviation in this society, and thus the lack of a "subsystem"—an alternative means of defining oneself outside the parameters of ordinary life as a *sarariiman* (white collar worker), wife/mother, or some other predefined role—becomes highly problematic for those who wish simply to be different. Moreover, as I have suggested above, the "system" in its present form no longer includes provisions for the spiritual, philosophical, or even intellectual welfare of the individual, an intolerable condition for anyone even slightly inclined to be curious about other possibilities. This sensation must be especially acute, one imagines, at a time when technology such as the internet and satellite communications make the world so visible and, seemingly, accessible. In a rigidly defined society, taunted by images from abroad, Murakami argues, the outbreak of violence is inevitable.

Here, too, the author's comments on Japanese society run counter to the official lines that emerge from more "official" spokesmen. That is to say, while the Japanese media can hardly pretend that the poison gas incident did not occur, they can and do draw portraits of the cult members as aberrant, unusual, somehow mentally deformed. There can be little question of the strategy that leads to this conclusion: no society finds it advantageous to project a cultural identity of mayhem either domestically or internationally (there are too many relevant examples even to list here). To report such incidents as anything but the work of madmen and monsters might give the impression, as it has done in the United States, of a serious flaw in the dominant social system—in Japan's case, it might even undermine the myth of the stable homogeneous society itself. Thus, incidents of terrorism and antisocial behavior must, of necessity, be treated as something "outside the system." Violence, when it erupts, must be treated as an aberration.[14]

---

14. One notes even now the reluctance of the Japanese press to provide detailed accounts of the *ijime* (bullying) problem in Japanese schools (particularly against the physically and mentally handicapped), despite the number of lives it has claimed.

Murakami's portrayal, then, suggests just the opposite: that the AUM Shinrikyō is a group of ordinary people led by the very extraordinary Asahara Shōkō. What his portrayals of terror suggest more than anything, to return to Roland Barthes comment above, is that Japan's social "system" is not *mastering anything*, but is instead creating pockets of "ex-centrics," peripheralized types who somehow slip through the cracks of Japan's homogeneity and express their disillusionment, fear, and rage through acts of terror—hearkening back to Hidaka Rokurō's contention that Japanese youth today lacks an outlet for self-expression, and thus becomes either very timid, or very violent (Hidaka 1984, 151). Murakami's depiction of these types is also an intensely personal, subjective act for, as he himself admits, "I could not escape the sense that there were points in common between what I sought through writing and what they sought through religion. There was something extremely similar there" (*Underground 2*, 16).

What is this "something similar" between religion and the act of writing? Here Murakami is careful not to suggest a link between himself and terrorism, but I believe that what both he and Japan's other "ex-centrics" seek are answers to some very basic questions about life that are altogether too philosophical, too metaphysical, for a culture based on rapid capitalism. They seek to know who they are, why and how their lives might have meaning, and what their role in society can or should be. These are age-old questions, by no means products of the contemporary or postmodern moment, but we may well conclude, with Murakami, that the present is less equipped than any other time in history to deal with such questions. We live today in a postreligious era—one in which our epistemological and ontological questions are no longer necessarily grounded in a concept of God. More important, however, is the fact that nothing has come along to fill the breach, or rather, nothing but affluence. In all likelihood it was this realization in 1979 that led Murakami to seek himself, and evidence of his existence, through writing (and to declare once that if he ever stopped writing he would cease to exist).[15] It was also, I think, part of the impetus for the actions of the AUM Shinrikyō. This is suggested in the comments of one cult member, who told Murakami that "For me, learning was supposed to be getting smarter. But all they wanted to do in school was rote memorization like, 'How many sheep are there in Australia?' No matter how much of that you do, you can never get smarter" (*Underground 2*, 25). When he asked questions, either of his father or his teachers, "they just got irritated with me" (ibid.).

15. Interview with the author in Cambridge, Massachusetts, October 22, 1994.

This is certainly consonant with the comments of Honda (1993) and Hidaka (1984) earlier, and supports the basically true assertion that Japan's education system is rigid in what it teaches and also in what it does not. Yet, it would be oversimplifying the matter to state that what is taught is just rote memorization; rather, as argued earlier, Japanese public school curriculum supplements regular academic studies with classes in life guidance and morality (*dōtoku*), all that is needed to produce "good" citizens. What the Japanese education system does not teach, however, is a means of establishing self-identity without resorting to conventional participation in Japan's megacomplex of industrial production.

HISTORIOGRAPHIC RELIEF METAFICTION: *ALL THE GODS' CHILDREN DANCE*

It is, perhaps, appropriate to close out this final chapter with some relevant comments about Murakami's most recent work of fiction, *Kami no Kodomotachi wa mina odoru* (All the Gods' Children Dance, 2000). This is a difficult work to categorize, both in terms of its layout (is it a novel or a collection of stories?) and its genre (one is uncertain whether the work is journalistic fiction, historiography, or just a set of stories organized [very loosely!] around the 1995 Kobe earthquake). In fact, *All the Gods' Children Dance* is vaguely interposed between journalism and fiction: its journalistic impulse lies in its attempts to view another side of the Kobe earthquake—this time entirely from the perspective of those who *weren't* there—and yet the work clearly consists of fanciful characters (in some cases, fairy tale characters) and contrived plots. Its most distinguishing feature is that it presents us with a view of the Kobe earthquake so oblique as to prevent our ever really confronting the event directly; it is a vision we see only in outline, in relief, and for this reason may be the best example by Murakami yet of what I have above termed "relief historiography." Very much like Oda Makoto's presentation of bigotry and political deceit in *Hiroshima*, *All the Gods' Children Dance* uses the Kobe earthquake as a unifying device by which to describe alienation and despair. Its characters are all linked in the fact that, like their author, none of them was in Kobe at the time of the earthquake. They are also linked by a sense of traumatization, but not by the earthquake itself; rather, in every case the characters involved suffer from a kind of latent trauma that is triggered, brought to life, by the earthquake's destruction. Perhaps it is for this reason that Murakami titled the earlier, serialized version of this collection *Jishin no Ato de*: "*after* the earthquake." His interest, as with the sarin gas incident, lies in exploring the ways in which this event irrevocably changed the lives of those who experienced it, either directly or indirectly, after the fact.

Of course, we may certainly surmise that part of the author's desire to approach the Kobe earthquake lay in the fact that the epicenter was very close to Ashiya, his hometown. Kawamura Minato (2000), however, offers an additional insight to this: in the short story "Go-gatsu no Kaigansen" (The Waterfront in May, 1981 [*MHZ* 5:101–11; originally published in *Torefuru*, April 1981), Murakami's protagonist sits on a beach near Ashiya, surveying the high-rise apartment buildings that have arisen to form the skyline of his hometown. Feeling nostalgic for the once uncluttered landscape he remembers from his youth, the protagonist wishes that these buildings would simply collapse into nothing. In this brief passage, Kawamura believes, Murakami fatefully prophesied the destruction of Kobe, a fact that has perhaps shaken the author more than he has previously admitted.

> In "The Waterfront in May," Murakami wrote of Ashiya, the town in which he was raised, with a certain animosity, almost as though he were putting a curse on it. And in a certain sense his curse became reality. One cannot help believing that this is why he wrote the present collection of stories, perhaps feeling that he needed to revisit this ground. (Kawamura and Ōsugi 2000)

Whether indeed Murakami wrote out of a desire to redress some perceived wrong in an earlier text, it seems clear that he is deeply concerned with the potential of such an event to cause massive, permanent change in the individual identity—even in those who were not present in Kobe at the time of the earthquake.

Taken with the evidently similar underlying theme of *Underground*—the inability of one to go back to the way one was—we might even view these works as a shift in the author's perspective on returning to the unconscious. Whereas in previous texts the protagonist has sought his answers by re-engaging imagistic memories lurking in the darkness of his unconscious, the characters presented in *All the Gods' Children Dance*, especially, seem to have given up on such a recourse, and instead declare over and over that "there is no going back to the way things were" (*moto ni wa modoranai*). This must surely be the same sense of "origins" (*moto*) as in *Pinball, 1973*, in which the Twins, upon departing, declare that they will now return to their *moto no tokoro*, or "place of origin," already established above as the unconscious. By contrast, characters in this latest text do not even bother trying to seek answers to their problems in this way.

Each story, rather, is about an irrevocable change. In the first, a man named Komura watches helplessly as his wife is transfixed by the televised news reports of the Kobe earthquake. For several days she neither eats, sleeps, nor even relieves herself, but merely stares at the television screen. Finally, she leaves the house altogether—reminiscent of Kumiko's departure in *The Wind-Up Bird Chronicle*—leaving a note in which she tells Komura "I will not be coming back. There is nothing else you can do for me" (*AGCD* 14). Komura comes to realize this himself: "No matter how long he might wait, or how much thinking might go on, *things could never go back to the way they had been*" (*AGCD* 14; my italics). Another character near the end of the book, a writer who has been estranged from his parents since his decision to become a novelist rather than run the family business, explains in similar terms his reason for not attempting to contact his family in Kobe after the earthquake. "The rift between himself and his parents was too deep, and had continued for too long. He couldn't see any possibility of salvaging the relationship" (*AGCD* 189). In the same story, the novelist's best friend, a woman whose husband has had an affair and who seeks to divorce him, uses almost the same expression about her husband: "He has another lover, and there is no way to make things go back to the way they were" (*AGCD* 184).

Such estrangements fill this depressing, hopeless book. The protagonist of the title story, Yoshiya, has the peculiar experience of being the son of a divine being (or so he is told), a deity worshipped by the religious group to which his mother belongs. Having thus no possibility whatever of reconnecting with his father (revisiting an important theme of *The Sputnik Sweetheart*), Yoshiya distances himself from the group and its beliefs on account of "the limitless coldness, the dark, heavy, stone-hearted silence of his father" (*AGCD* 83). The only connection this story might claim with the earthquake is that his mother goes to Kobe after the fact to give aid to the survivors.

At the same time, flashes of the earlier Murakami are to be found in these stories, several of which contain magical (or at least dream) elements. Such elements are, however, more or less universally terrifying. In "Mr. Frog Saves Tokyo," a loan collector named "Katagiri" is visited by a gigantic frog who enlists his help in defeating the efforts of "Mr. Worm," a massive earthworm supposedly responsible for major earthquakes. According to the frog, "Mr. Worm" normally sleeps, but occasionally awakens to satisfy his urge to cause mass destruction. The frog's plan is to go underground and battle the worm, with Katagiri there to cheer him on when he tires. At the appointed hour of their showdown, however, Katagiri collapses (believing he has been shot by a hold-up man) and is unable to keep his promise. "Mr. Frog" finally appears to him in his hospital room, battered and near death, but victorious, and thus Tokyo has been spared its fate, at least for the moment.

In the final story, "Honey Pie," the earthquake takes on a similarly sinister personification: a young girl dreams repeatedly of the "Jishin-otoko," or "Earthquake Man," who tries repeatedly to force her into a box. By the story's end he has told her that he has a box prepared for her and everyone in her family, but that she must being them to him. Here, as in "Mr. Frog Saves Tokyo," Murakami seems both to revisit Kobe and also to foresee the inevitable earthquake that will strike the Kantō region that surrounds To-kyo in the coming years.

But *All the Gods' Children Dance* is really about darkness, alien-ation, and flight from Kobe. With exceptions like Yoshiya, whose mother goes to the ruins of Kobe to minister to the survivors, many protagonists in these stories are refugees from that region (Osaka, Kobe, Kyoto), having escaped *before* the earthquake struck. Each lives a solitary existence, sepa-rated from, yet inevitably tied to, Kobe and those they left behind there. "Miyake," the protagonist of "Iron-laden Landscape," admits to a girlfriend that he left a wife and two children in Kansai before wandering on to his present location, and yet he is tormented not by concern for their safety after the earthquake, but by a recurring dream of suffocating in a refrig-erator that has become latched from the outside (foreshadowing the dreams of the "Earthquake Man" in the final chapter). His description of his death by suffocation, however, is not merely to be read as a way of dying; it is a symbolic rendering of his position in the world, his isolation as a man. It is, indeed, not dissimilar to the constriction felt by Rat at the end of *Hear the Wind Sing* when he is left behind, alone and in despair, by the protagonist's departure to Tokyo for college.

> I'm stuck in this cramped, pitch-black place, slowly dying. Of course, if dying were that simple I would have no problem with it, but it isn't that easy. Just a little air always gets in from some-where, so I can't just suffocate and be done with it. It takes for-ever to die. No matter how much I scream, no one hears me. No one even notices that I'm there. It's so cramped that I can't move a muscle. And however much I struggle, there is no way to open the door from the inside. (*AGCD* 59)

This description might also be read as a metaphorical depiction of death in a collapsed building, the fate of many in Kobe. Like the other characters in *All the Gods' Children Dance*, Miyake suffers from a kind of indirect trauma, the trauma born of a kind of prescience of impending doom. At the same time, this trauma is infiltrated by a vague sense of guilt—perhaps a sense felt by the author himself—for having gotten out when others did not. Miyake ultimately elects to die. Why should he? We can only guess, but a plausible reading is that his death is to be an atonement, a means of ending the nightmarish visions he sees of dying trapped in a refrigerator.

As I noted above, this work is intriguingly difficult to classify. The collection was serialized, much as a novel might be, in *Shinchō* from August through December of 1999 under the general title, *Jishin no Ato de*, suggesting the work's common theme. Yet the work is no novel; there is no unity of plot, the characters, as the book jacket also notes, are entirely unrelated to one another. Rather, we deal here with what might be termed a series of variations on a theme, the theme of trauma triggered by—but not grounded necessarily in—the Kobe earthquake.

All the Gods' Children Dance does, however, have something in common with works like *Underground* and *Underground 2*, and not merely in its focus on current events. Rather, like those earlier texts, this latest collection is focused on offering readers radically new ways of looking at those events presented in the media as events. This is, however, probably not intended as an indictment of the mass media as *Underground* and *Underground 2* were; rather, Murakami simply wants to explore some of the ramifications of the Kobe earthquake that no one else has thought of yet, and he does so from, perhaps, the only perspective he can: that of a distant observer, for like the writer at the end of this collection, Murakami was abroad when the earthquake struck. Yet there is value, he seems to argue, in the outsider's perspective, something to be learned from the expatriate who can only stand by helplessly and watch. This, we may imagine, is Murakami's atonement, his assurance that the event *did* matter to him, even if his only way of approaching it was from the periphery. We may recall in this regard the author's resistance to telling the story of the sarin gas incident in his own words, as well; instead, he merely acted as an organizer of the accounts, permitting the principals their say.

But Murakami's commitment to bringing a potentially more subjective perspective to the Kobe earthquake is clear from the very opening pages. We catch reminiscent tones of his earlier project of "rehumanization" in the opening of the book, a quote from Jean-Luc Godard's *The Mad Jester*:

> *Radio News* *U.S. forces suffered heavy casualties, but 115 Vietcong were also killed.*
> Woman: "It's horrid to be nameless like that."
> Man: "What do you mean?"

Woman: "What do we really learn from the fact that 115 guerrillas died in combat? We know absolutely nothing about any of them. Did they have wives and children? Did they prefer plays to movies? We know nothing; only that 115 people died in combat." (Quoted in *All the Gods' Children Dance*)

Does this not sum up, as perhaps no other words could have done, Murakami's persistent urge, sometimes overtly political, other times merely humanist, to revisit the traumatic events of our recent past in order to reinvigorate the sense of human dimension that is frequently lost in conventional mass media reportage? Murakami might just as well be saying that the statistics attached to the Kobe earthquake—the numbers of dead, injured, homeless, and so forth—are meaningless when separated from the context of the human factor. That is to say, he urges us to consider not the temporary aspects of the event—lost homes, extent of damage, and so forth—nor even the dead, necessarily, but rather the ways in which the lives of the living were permanently scarred by the events. Such trauma, his book seems to argue, cannot be assumed to limit itself to those who were actually present in Kobe on that day. By presenting us with a radically alternative view, the author enables readers to understand, perhaps in the only way an outsider possibly could, what the earthquake meant and continues to mean for them. This, as Ōsugi also argues, may be read as a confirmation that "since *Underground* we sense clearly a performative commitment to the times in Murakami Haruki's writing . . ." (Kawamura & Ōsugi 2000, 129). In the terms of this chapter, we might simply say that Murakami is committed to recuperating related stories that are intrinsically peripheral, or have been peripheralized by the workings of the mass media. And in all cases, he is deeply concerned about the potential for damage to the sense of individual identity that such events can bring about, either by design or by accident.

THE HISTORICAL CRISIS OF IDENTITY IN CONTEMPORARY JAPAN

What I have sought to show in this chapter is the link, highly politicized, between history (or, alternatively, current events), representation, and ideology. There can be little question of the seriousness of the stakes involved in the appropriation of any notion of "reality" or "truth value" in the process of writing history, and this is why the issue of representation is so critical. I have sought to demonstrate that control over the historical past, the practice of seeking out a new means of representing that past, must be reasserted by the periphery in order to present an alternative, oppositional voice to the dominant ideological paradigm. At the same time, I feel we have come to realize that efforts of this type in Japan are almost always futile, a struggle against an ideology whose material attractions mask its perceived consequences, and whose tendency is to paint over the more unpleasant elements of the past. It is an ideology, then, that enjoys the support not only of the organs of control—education, government, industry, and the media—but, generally speaking, of the Japanese people themselves. As many have pointed out over the years, this has led to a level of historical denial that has reached alarming levels. Honda calls the Japanese "irresponsible" because of their reckless unwillingness to confront their own responsibility for the Second World War, particularly in light of Japan's more recent efforts to be taken seriously as a peacemonger in other parts of Asia (1993, 57). We see both attempts to deny events and (as evidence to the contrary is built up) efforts to reinterpret them more favorably. (In an unnerving development, a new historical society was formed in Japan a few years ago with the express purpose of declaring Japanese war atrocities in China "fabrications" or, alternatively, asserting that this was merely part of an overall culture of brutality that had dominated in China for centuries.)   This raises an interesting dilemma, however, one that seems to intersect morality and philosophy. That is, if history *is* a matter of perception, representation, and language, then this admonition must cut both ways. Ultimately, we cannot *know* the historical past except as it is represented to us, and cultural factors seem—especially in Japan—to prove more powerful in many cases than memory, visible evidence, or testimonials. One observes in this an interesting phenomenon: the opposing impulses to revisit, and yet to avoid confrontation with the historical past. It is simultaneously the urge to re-engage history, in the sense of rethinking *and rewriting* it, and the urge to flee from what is perceived to be the truth.

This urge to run backwards, to rediscover, yet obscure who we are and where we have been is not specific to Japan, of course. Baudrillard (1994a) writes of a worldwide trend, at least among the industrialized nations, to reverse the trajectory of history until time actually moves backward, giving us both the opportunity to redress the errors of the twentieth century and also to avoid the reckoning that the *fin de siècle* must inevitably bring.

> Are we condemned, in the vain hope of not abiding in our present destruction . . . to the retrospective melancholia of living everything through again in order to correct it all, in order to elucidate it all. . .do we have to summon all past events to appear before us, to reinvestigate it all as though we were conduct-

ing a trial? A mania for trials has taken hold of us in recent times, together with a mania for responsibility, precisely at the point when this latter is becoming increasingly hard to pin down. We are looking to remake a clean history, to whitewash all the abominations: the obscure (resentful) feeling behind the proliferation of scandals is that history itself is a scandal. (Baudrillard 1994a, 11–12)

Baudrillard expresses a cautionary note similar to Rat's in *A Wild Sheep Chase* that even with its imperfections the past should be preserved as accurately as possible, because that is who we are, and to give up the "glory, character, meaning and singularity" (1994a, 12) of our historical past is to give up ourselves and whatever sense of identity remains to us. Interestingly, like Murakami, Baudrillard too makes reference to the past as a "shadow," arguing that we seek to reverse history in order "to leapfrog our own shadows, leapfrog the shadow of the century" (ibid.).

Ironically, this is precisely the gesture of which Ōe (1989) accuses Murakami: a refusal to engage dialectically with the past, to face "reality" and to contribute to the discursive debate of the postwar, thus forging a new theoretical groundwork, a new intellectual ideology for his generation. I would argue in response, however, that in so saying, Ōe reveals his affinity with Jameson and Althusser in the assumption not only that "reality" exists outside of a cultural context, but that our project should be an attempt to recover that reality and pass it on, repaired and intact, to the next generation. One recalls Althusser's self-assurance in declaring that ideologies, illusory though they may be, are built on the "obviousness" of certain things, including "the obviousness of the 'transparency of language'" and "the 'obviousness' that you and I are subjects . . ." (Althusser 1986, 244–45). Ōe, too, writes of an "obviousness"—that of man's historicity, a matter with which few would have cause to complain. But when Ōe (1989, 193) declares that "man is obviously a historical being," he fails to consider the question of what is historical, how we can know and represent what is historical, and thus how we are to engage it and critique it dialectically. This is, I think, a fundamental difference in thinking between Ōe and Murakami, and it will probably never be reconciled.

From this perspective Ōe's contention that Murakami does not engage history is partially correct; by reconstituting history subjectively, Murakami denies history and declares histor*ies*. But this denial of a singular history is not gratuitous, and his fiction should be read, as the above amply demonstrates, not as an attempt to ignore historical reality, but to challenge the truth value of predominant historical paradigms—a particularly important agenda in Japan, where such paradigms are often grounded in wishful thinking that blatantly contradicts the collective memories of the rest of Asia. Indeed, it is remarkable how much of Japan's political energy in the past several decades has been expended on attempts to whitewash the historical past in such a way that confrontations over "old" issues may be avoided, leading to ever greater levels of homogenization, of "harmony" across Japanese society.

Murakami's fiction confronts these attempts to whitewash history. His retrieval—and even construction—of the lesser-known events of the Second World War, for instance, reminds us of the tendency since the postwar years to rewrite the history of this period in more desirable language. Interestingly, Murakami's efforts as historiographer, as with his efforts as formulaic writer, prove unorthodox, for embedded in his retrieval of the virtually forgotten war at Nomonhan, or in his description of the Chinese student massacre, are narratives containing not the "lost voices" of the victims, but those of the demonized aggressors, the soldiers who actually did the killing. As noted above, these perspectives may surprise us with their comparative humanity. As in *Underground 2*, Murakami succeeds, at least to a point, in rehumanizing these aggressors as men, yet acknowledging their transformation into beasts by the events around them. The army lieutenant in charge of executing the Chinese students expresses this tension succinctly when he notes to Akasaka Nutmeg's father, "We've already killed enough Chinese, and I just don't see the point of adding to the body count" (*NK* 3:320; *WUBC* 522). Nevertheless, soldier that he is, the lieutenant ignores his personal inclinations and carries out his orders to the letter. Murakami's interest in the war is based on this tension, for, as he told interviewer Ian Buruma several years ago, he is interested in how war "stretches the tension between individuals and the state to the very limit" (Buruma 1996, 62).

It would be accurate to say that Murakami's focus on the peripheral events in Manchuria in *The Wind-Up Bird Chronicle*, events that few have heard of and even fewer care much about, is a challenge to "official" history, just as his literature has consistently proved a challenge to the sense of identity the system has "officially" bestowed upon the Japanese. His work offers an opportunity to reevaluate the hypocrisy of a national history that annually commemorates the atrocities of Hiroshima and Nagasaki but still refers to the massacre of Chinese civilians at Nanjing as an "incident." It speaks to the self-delusion of a nation that, in Kuroko Kazuo's estimation, dedicates itself to peace and prosperity but supports its affluence by tacitly participating in the destruction of the environment in the Third World (Kuroko 1990, 15).

I noted at the beginning of this book that Murakami Haruki's appearance on the Japanese literary scene in 1979 was no accident, that the historical moment was exceptionally conducive to the emergence of such a writer. It is probably also true that his first intended audience was his own generation, those who were between 17 and 20 years of age in 1969, in other words those who led or participated in the doomed Zenkyōtō movement as a vehicle to establish their sense of subjectivity. This would explain two things: first, why a novel as vaguely written as *Hear the Wind Sing* would prove so popular, and second, why the Gunzō Prize committee found it so difficult to explain its preference for the work.[16] The members of this committee were not insensitive in their reading; rather, separated from Murakami by the experiential generation gap I noted earlier, they simply found it difficult to grasp the vacuum of post-Zenkyōtō disillusionment in which Murakami's protagonist seeks his identity. Whereas Japanese of the prewar and war years, despite their hardships, gained a sense of purpose and identity through their participation in the process of Japan's emergence as a modern state, and whereas those who participated in Japan's recovery after the war found a clear purpose in rebuilding the physical, economic, and ideological structures of the nation, the aftermath of the counterculture movements of the 1960s left a void of disillusionment that was enhanced by the apparent success (symbolized in the conspicuous affluence of the 1980s) of the establishment.

As I have sought to demonstrate at various points in this book, Murakami's concern for identity, his desire to recover the past in order to rediscover the sense of identity lost in 1970, is echoed in the works of other writers of his generation. Murakami Ryū (b. 1952), as noted above, attempts to recover the violent, angry atmosphere of counterculture in his first work, *Almost Transparent Blue*, but achieves a more sensitive nostalgia in *69 sixty-nine* (1987), a work that recalls Ryū's activities as a seventeen-year-old high school student in 1969, his gang's attempts to create a "miniature Zenkyōtō" movement of their own on the high school campus. Similarly, Nakagami Kenji's (1946–92) short story "Jūhassai" (Eighteen,

---

16. Among the five-member panel, only Maruya Saiichi felt that the work, representing significant understanding of the style of American popular literature, pointed to the new direction Japanese literature was taking. Of the others, Sasaki Kiichi and Sata Ineko liked the work, but found it difficult to articulate their reasons; Yoshiyuki Junnosuke ranked it "somewhere between sixty and eighty-five" out of a hundred on his first reading, and after rereading it decided it was "a good work," and Shimao Toshio selected *Hear the Wind Sing* as the least objectionable of the choices. See "Gunzō Shinjin Bungakushō Senbyō," in Murakami Ryū 1986, 36–40.

1980), which the author claims to have begun writing at around that age, presents the self-assurance of teenagers on the verge of graduating from high school in the mid-1960s.

But the writer who most closely resembles Murakami's approach to the past via magical realism is probably Shimizu Yoshinori (b. 1947). Like Murakami, Shimizu's characters live in a world that is realistic but tinged with the magical and look to their past experiences to rediscover themselves. One sees this especially in Shimizu's "Guroingu Daun" (Growing Down, 1989), in which time is suddenly reversed. No one can say why, but as time goes backward the dead rise and grow younger, while the living gradually make their way toward infancy and birth, the end of the line. Yet the experience is not frightening to the narrator/protagonist; rather, it is a pleasant one, for there is a sense of anticipation as he draws steadily nearer to the magical era of the 1960s and gradually regains his childhood innocence. And why did time suddenly reverse? The protagonist's speculation echoes the concern of Baudrillard above:

> "There were those who saw the Year 2000 as a kind of wall. It seems that people were afraid of going beyond the Year 2000."
>
> *   *   *
>
> It suddenly occurred to me that it was the uneasiness of our time that had made this happen. We used to think that all the time. I had completely forgotten.
> That time had been awful. It was widely believed that humans were rapidly approaching their destruction. (Shimizu 1989, 28–30)

Time, then, reverses because people sense their doom in the *fin de siècle*, for in a sense the "project of modernity," to return to Habermas' terminology, will at the end of the century be proved a failure.

Yet, in its seemingly utopian reversal of time, the work also contains a caveat: after the sophistication of the 1980s, can one really return to the comparative simplicity of the 1960s and 1950s? Shimizu's protagonist notes that at one time there had been intellectuals who studied the problem, but as time went onward (backward) they grew younger and more ignorant, and eventually there was no one left with sophistication enough to think the problems through. Technology, he also notes, especially computers, has gone steadily backward, making the task of studying the *fin de siècle* increasingly difficult. With symbolism that is perhaps a little too obvious, his protagonist reads *Flowers for Algernon*, suggesting that his characters, too, are stepping away from knowledge, from the *savoir-faire* of contemporary urban Japanese and the cool savvy of Tanaka Yasuo's *Somehow, Crystal*, to rediscover their innocence.

One must not permit terms such as "innocence" or "simplicity" to give the sense that the nostalgia in Murakami (or even Shimizu) is naive, however, that it simply "misses" the past. Particularly in reading Murakami one recalls that the author, like his protagonists, has generally denied any particular fondness for the 1960s, for Zenkyōtō or the issues it represented. What he seeks through his nostalgia is not to "whitewash" the past, as Baudrillard suggests, but to use it as a means to seek the identity that he and his contemporaries lost between 1969 and 1970. One hardly need add that the realities of the 1980s and 1990s have as yet given little evidence that those in the twenty- to thirty-year-old age group in today's Japan have much more on which to build their sense of identity than did Murakami's generation, which helps to explain why his readership remains chiefly in that age group.

There is no real solution to the social and historical dilemma Murakami presents in his fiction. Despite the persistent recession that slows Japanese economic expansion outward, Japan's cultural movement, like that of other industrialized states, remains largely without direction or purpose. The quest for economic domination abroad and affluence at home has been largely achieved, perhaps more evenly in Japan, where the vast majority of the population considers itself "middle class," than anywhere else in the world (Williams 1994, 140–42). What is left? Murakami implicitly questions whether this goal of affluence by itself is sufficient, whether it can adequately replace a true sense of self, and what will happen to those who find it unsatisfactory.

Perhaps these questions are too philosophical for some, too prosaic for others, but the author's strong readership, one that cuts across the boundaries that normally divide popular writers from the more serious sort, suggests that he is not alone in his sense of foreboding about Japan's economic obsession and its consequences for the individual. As Murakami suggests in *Underground* and *Underground 2*, anyone who doubts the existence of a serious philosophical and spiritual gap in contemporary Japan has not yet considered the real significance of the events of March 20, 1995.

Conclusion

The Reluctant Postmodernist

> People can read my books, or books by my contemporaries, and they can say, "Hey! I could do this!" That's my role, what I want my readers to learn from me. Not theories and rules, just an example to follow.
>
> —Murakami Haruki

Throughout this book, I have sought above all to demonstrate my contention that Murakami Haruki's *raison d'être* as a writer lies in certain key questions he raises about the nature (and ultimate fate) of individual identity in contemporary Japan. As we have seen, his basic thesis, perhaps more accurately termed his fundamental ideological principle, is that under the best of circumstances individual identity emerges on its own through a process of discursive engagement with other people, through the pursuit of goals, and through a process of overcoming hardship; in contemporary Japan, however, as a result of the hyper-commodification of late-model capitalism, the total focus on economic prosperity, and the need in such an economy to control the desire of the consumer, individual identity has been gradually lost, replaced by what might be termed a "manufactured" subjectivity, a "ready-made" identity. This "manufactured" identity, according to my reading of Murakami's fiction, is created and imposed by a consortium of major power groups in Japan: political, industrial, financial, and the mass media. As has been noted by a variety of commentators, from academics (Ivy, Treat, Karatani, and Jameson among many others) to journalists (Honda, Hidaka, Kawamoto, van Wolferen), this system of controlled desire is very much consonant with the parameters of postmodernism, particularly in its tendency to seek out new markets, its gradual assumption of control over the collective unconscious, and its reliance on a complex web of power structures, all of which combine to form the so-called "empty center" of power in Japan.

Because of this, it has been necessary to cast the author's search for identity into the terms and the historical moment of the postmodern, despite some interesting dilemmas to which this has led. Among the more perplexing questions is that of the author's own attitude toward the postmodern tendencies that so frequently show up in his writing. What is revealed there, I think, is a highly ambivalent stance toward the postmodern on the author's part, one we might even choose to term "opportunistic." In short, while Murakami frequently borrows from the trappings of postmodernism, if he is himself "postmodern" in any respect, he is so reluctantly, with reserve. In fact, in terms of narrative content, Murakami finds the postmodern useful for presenting his message; in cultural terms—particularly but not exclusively the economic—he sees the postmodern as a harmful factor, suppressing the impulse to establish meaningful identity. Similar to Jameson and Althusser, he sees real-world manifestations such as "late-model capitalism," and his own "rapid capitalism," as dictatorial and intrusive—perhaps even as the result of a kind of ideological "class struggle" between materialism and idealism. As we have seen, this argument can be cast in Marxist terms as a kind of induced fetishism, one that replaces individual desires with those supported by the needs of the market; it can also be presented in Lacanian terms as the suppression of the desire for the individual, internal self (the Other) in favor of the terms and conditions of the symbolic, now almost wholly given over to powering the economic needs of the state.

The issue can also be presented as an expression of artistic resistance, however, and this is what I have attempted to show in the first chapter of this book, where, as we have seen, Murakami tests the limits of literary identity. His play with the literary formula, and more importantly, his subversion of the very expectations that define the formula, are themselves challenges to the fixed identity of literary forms, most particularly the traditional distinctions that have existed between "pure" and "mass" literature. It is unlikely, however, that Murakami involves himself in this debate for the sake of aesthetics in and of themselves; rather, his hostility is inevitably directed toward all attempts to fix identity in any uniform or predetermined way. If the above examinations of Murakami's fiction tell us anything, it is that the author is committed to the preservation of a uniquely constituted identity, one developed through a discursive process, through action, reaction, and interaction of distinctly determined units. In the case of the literary formula, this amounts to the interaction of literary elements previously thought to be incompatible with one another: the inventive and the formulaic.

We have seen a similar impulse in the production of works like *Underground* and *Underground 2*, which are clearly journalistic in their efforts to discuss an event that is more or less "current," recent enough to remain imprinted on the collective consciousness of Japanese society, yet that is also "historical" in the far-reaching implications of the event—one that dispelled in part the myth of Japan as a society that miraculously combines spectacular economic dominance with a happy, stable, controlled society. But in approaching this event through these two texts, Murakami has again disrupted not only the methodology of orthodox journalism, but indeed that of nonorthodox journalism, by combining together the tropes of the politically resistant "New Journalism" and the equally subjective, but decidedly more humanistic (if anachronistic) "literary journalism." In both cases he succeeds in producing texts that are at once "true" (the events happened), subjective (each "voice" is but one tiny part of a very large whole), and interpretive (the author plays an active role in guiding the discussion, and occasionally adding his own comments). In so doing, Murakami implicitly attacks the binary opposition of "fact versus fiction," "journalism versus fiction/literature," "subjectivity versus objectivity," and even that of the center (mainstream journalism) versus the periphery (subjective journalistic accounts). In other words, his approach is again "postmodern" in its methodology, if not in its agenda of expressing his contention that both victims and perpetrators alike of the sarin incident have been abstracted, reduced to mere symbols ("good" and "evil"; "purity" and "defilement").

This, as noted above, is part of the reason certain elements of the literary establishment have judged Murakami's fiction to bode ill for the future of Japanese literature in general. Such concerns are reasonably well founded, for certainly Murakami's writing does not necessarily conform to what we would normally consider *belles lettres*; nor, in fact, does it even aspire to produce the sense of "newness" or "differentiation" that the Formalists and the avantgarde hold in such high regard. For Murakami and many of his fellow contemporary writers, the story is everything, and all aspirations to Art must be subordinate to this. At the same time—and the analyses in this book support this—there can be no question of Murakami's commitment to the potential of the story to share new insights about the nature of reality and the need for change. In this sense, Murakami's fiction demonstrates the same didactic potential as other writing of the postwar. It is, then, the lack of an active aesthetic, of an aspiration to create Art, in the author's work to which the literary establishment—I am still thinking primarily of Ōe here—will object.

It is, of course, also an issue of recent postmodern writing in general, for many of the writers mentioned in the analyses above share Murakami's rejection of fiction as Art (literature). But then the issue arises again, how are we to characterize the postmodernism of Murakami Haruki? More to the point, his rejection of fiction as Art aside, can one who views so negatively late-model capitalism, who so obviously sees the contemporary moment as less free rather than *more* free, be termed a postmodern writer at all? Murakami unquestionably embodies many of the attributes most commonly associated with postmodern expression: his writing crosses boundaries between genres and styles; he works in an ever-changing "no man's land" between the real and magical; his settings are always marked by shifting boundaries between real and unreal; his thematics is constantly aware of the limitations of language in the representation of those realities and unrealities; he is concerned with offering new perspectives, new ways in which to look at the world already around us.

And yet, he is no apologist for the postmodern. Unlike Hutcheon, who sees the postmodern as liberating, an opportunity for the recovery of a lost periphery, Murakami seems perfectly willing to explore these possibilities, but not to follow them through to their logical conclusions. In other words, his protagonists *fail* in their quests to rediscover what has been lost or peripheralized. For them, the peripheral is always hidden in the dark recesses of the unconscious, always in the mode of memories, represented through language—a chain of metonymical signification—that permits the protagonist a certain freedom of interpretation (which is to say, the invention of nostalgic images), but prevents direct contact with the object of desire. Thus, Murakami offers a "reading" of the unconscious that is consonant with the Lacanian understanding of the inner and outer minds as connected always by language, chains of signification, the displacement of desire by the Symbolic Order (or, in Murakami's terms, the state, authority), and thus always marked by the inevitable frustration of the quest for the other. Unlike Lacan, however, as noted earlier, Murakami is unprepared to view the intervention of the symbolic as "neutral," preferring instead to assign a persona to this authority in the form of the state.

Murakami's fiction suggests a determination to view this intervention as a willful, calculated attempt to subvert the "free" development of the self in order to transplant a more easily controlled version of identity into each individual subject, transforming them from *thinking* subjects into *consuming* subjects. Moreover, as the allegory we have already outlined in

A Wild Sheep Chase would seem to suggest, this authority, this intervention on both an individual and a collective scale, is represented in the confrontation between materialism (mainstream) and idealism (counterculture) in the 1950s and 1960s. This is admittedly an oversimplification, but Murakami's allegories *are* simple—they do not reflect the true complexity of what Zenkyōtō was or was not, but rather seek to reduce the conflict down to individual entities—entities we can comprehend, like, dislike, and so forth. (We cannot help noting then, perhaps, that *A Wild Sheep Chase*, from one point of view, does what Murakami seems to reject in *Underground* and *Underground 2*—the reduction of the conflict into simplified binaries of "good" and "evil." There is no denying this, but Murakami's purpose in *A Wild Sheep Chase* is clearly to make Zenkyōtō *more* human through its identification with Rat, whereas in the case of the sarin incident, the mass media's approach to the victims and perpetrators as a thing of the moment—as *disposable*—has the opposite effect of *de*humanizing them.)

This conflict can certainly be read in terms of a kind of class struggle; if not the classic Marxist model of capital versus the proletariat, then at least the conservative right against a reformist-minded left. This is the link, not so tenuous, between Althusser and Murakami, for while Murakami is by no means a Marxist in the common sense of the term (despite his baleful view of fetish consumerism), he does seem to view the ascendancy of the conservative right, and the attendant growth of "rapid" capitalism, as the result of a kind of class struggle—one that ended in the defeat of the left, and the rise of the conditions of the postmodern I have described above.

In terms of the postmodern as it is manifested in social conditions, then, Murakami's work demonstrates a greater affinity with the thinking of Althusser, and even Fredric Jameson, than with that of Linda Hutcheon (even though his experiments with different literary methodologies could almost be read as a summary of Hutcheon's *Poetics of Postmodernism*!). While Murakami does not necessarily share Jameson's belief that the postmodern moment poses a threat to a stable identity—his work suggests more the concern that the state replaces individual identity with an equally stable, but more "ready-made" variety—he *does* echo Jameson's contention that the previously autonomous realm of the cultural has been infiltrated by capitalism, and that this has resulted in the commodification of areas of our personal lives that had hitherto been considered sacrosanct.

Indeed, we may be forced to conclude that, but for the determinism of the dialectical model of historical progress, the author does in fact seem to have a greater affinity with the Marxist camp than with those who celebrate the postmodern as ushering in a period of previously unimagined awareness of the realities that surround us. His texts are filled with nostalgia, but for Murakami the nostalgia of the present for the past is not couched in terms of pleasure and rediscovery, but of crushing sadness and loss. His characters do not express their nostalgia through "retro" fetishism but by their stubborn refusal to engage in the commodity fetishism that surrounds them. Pressed to join this economy, they retreat to the unique, private space of the unconscious, where they (partially) satisfy their desire by "consuming" their own memories, only to find, however, that there can be no true satisfaction from such recourse, nor is there to be any permanent escape from the system that surrounds them.

NEW DIRECTIONS

These characters represent, of course, the contemporary Japanese subject. At various points in the text above it has become clear, I believe, that Murakami's commitment as a writer lies in a project to break down some of the walls that isolate this subject, to resuscitate it through a sense of humanity, and induce others to recognize it as such. This is an impulse that appears as early as *A Wild Sheep Chase*, and comes to full fruition in *The Wind-Up Bird Chronicle*. As the chapters above have hopefully shown, Murakami's expression of this agenda has varied over the course of his first twenty years as writer, from focus on his protagonist's attempts to rediscover himself early on, to later attempts to save others. The methodologies taken to this end have also varied over time (formulaic fiction, magical realism, historiography, literary journalism, etc.). The central *raison d'être* of Murakami, however, has not in itself altered much.

This book has been admittedly limited in the breadth of texts it is to cover; for the most part I have deliberately looked only at the first twenty years of Murakami fiction, 1979 to 1999, partly out of a need to bind the scope of my work somehow, but also because Murakami himself seems ready, with the recent *fin de siècle*, to look at different modes of expression. To look very closely at his work since *The Sputnik Sweetheart*, in my opinion, is to open a whole new study. It is my intention to avoid this. I have also held myself, with just a couple of exceptions, to examining Murakami's fiction, because I sense that the surest way to the heart of the author's most critical agenda is through his purely imaginative writing. This is not to say, however, that studies of Murakami's translations of Carver or Fitzgerald, or indeed his numerous travelogues, or his "guides" to reading modern Japanese fiction, will not yield interesting results that may corroborate or refute the observations made in the present text. Indeed, I hope that such studies will be forthcoming in the near future.

Readers will perhaps have noticed that my methodology in writing this study has been historical and theoretical rather than aesthetic. In fact, this is not even what might be termed in Japanese a *sakka-ron*, a study of Murakami Haruki and his works first and foremost. Instead, I have tried to walk a fine line between a text that approaches the complexities of the Murakami fictional universe, while at the same time maintaining a level of accessibility that the casual reader will find comfortable. For this reason I have elected to deal with challenging concepts, yet to focus on texts by Murakami that are exemplary of the questions and ideas I have raised above, and at the same time available to readers in translation.

Some readers may object to the limited number of texts discussed in the pages above; indeed, several of the novels are covered in more than one chapter, while many of the short stories have been left out altogether. But my methodology throughout this book has been to focus on the major thematic and methodological points of interest in the author's writing, and these appear with the most clarity and profundity in the novels. The short stories, on the other hand, while often containing single images or concepts that appear more fully in other texts (the image of the worlds reflected in "The Mirror" comes to mind, or that of water in "Kanō Crete"), taken singly do not impart the same sense of development in the author's writing and worldview as we see in the longer fiction. One might say that Murakami experiments with individual images and ideas in his short stories, which are then given much more critical and considered treatment in the expanded versions.[1]

My focus on the historical and theoretical rather than the aesthetic may also call for a comment or two. If my attention has been more focused on the historical and theoretical parameters that shape Murakami than on examining each of his hundreds of works individually, this is because, in my opinion, Murakami's value as a writer (if we seek this) does not lie in his variety. While prolific and skillful, Murakami's fictional output does not demonstrate much diversity. His plots, in fact, are remarkably similar, and his characters are even more so. If one has encountered the Murakami

---

1. At least two of the author's novels began this way: *Norwegian Wood* was based on an earlier story called "Hotaru" (Fireflies, 1983); *The Wind-Up Bird Chronicle* grew out of "Nejimakidori to Kayōbi no Onnatachi" (1986; trans. Jay Rubin as "Wind-Up Bird and Tuesday's Women"), and the characters Kanō Malta and Kanō Crete appear in the story "Kanō Kureta" in *TV People*.

hero in one novel, one knows something about most other Murakami protagonists, as well.

Yet there is inventiveness to Murakami as well; one feels he has grasped intuitively the tropes of postmodern expression, and chosen to explore these within the fictional world he envisions. That world itself, once established, has remained more or less regular and predictable. Murakami's inventiveness lies in the subtle, often difficult to discern variations he introduces, a talent he shares with the better formulaic writers. But Murakami is no formulaic writer, as I have demonstrated above. A more appropriate analogy might be found in the terminology of music; Murakami's strength lies in his ability to compose variations on a theme. This is by no means a negative reflection on his talent; indeed, among the great composers, Bach, Schubert, Tchaikovsky, and particularly Mozart, are known for their innovative variations.

It would not be inaccurate, however, to suggest that the relative lack of variety in Murakami fiction is a reflection on the author's worldview, his perspective as an individual looking outward. Most of his protagonists, for instance, are merely variations on the author himself, who is less interested in external human nature than how he himself might internally respond to specific circumstances. At times these circumstances are absurdly prosaic; as Murakami struggled to give up cigarettes in 1982, for instance, his sheep-chasing protagonist was also compelled to quit smoking. But these changes also occur on a more life-altering scale. We certainly notice that as Murakami matures, so, also, do his protagonists grow up. Murakami's reaction to the 1995 Kobe earthquake was real—its epicenter, in fact, was directly under his neighborhood in Ashiya—and the AUM Shinrikyō incident later that year struck him equally hard. When the author returned to Japan from his years of travel abroad shortly thereafter, he did so with a newfound desire to explore the potential for a more active stance toward the world—more or less as Ōe once wished he would do—and at the same time his protagonists became more militant, more demanding, more insistent on having answers to the pressing questions in their lives.

As the text above has shown, the question that most often concerns him is one of identity—how it is formed, how it may be maintained, how it can be lost due to traumatic circumstances, and what its loss might mean to contemporary society. Indeed, to judge from the analyses of his literature above, I think one would have to conclude that Murakami's interest in the near total focus on economic interests in Japanese society during the past two decades stems directly from the supposed and real effects he believes this has had on individual Japanese. Certainly works such as *Underground*,

The Wind-Up Bird Chronicle, The Sputnik Sweetheart, and *All the Gods'
Children Dance* leave us in no doubt about Murakami's increasing convic-
tion that major traumatic events, as well as the general malaise of the era,
are closely connected to the loss or radical transformation of identity among
contemporary Japanese.

Where, exactly, the author's work will take him in the years to come
is anyone's guess, and I will not hazard to do so at this stage. I will make a
mild objection to Ōsugi Shigeo's assertion not long ago that a new Japanese
"political correctness" in the 1990s has brought an end to Murakami's importance in contemporary writing. The new focus of Japanese postcolonial
studies on other Asian cultures rather than on "things American," he argues, means that the age of writers like Murakami Haruki, and perhaps
more especially, Murakami Ryū, has passed.

> This has been the time to be working on "the Korean problem,"
> or on "the Asian problem." This is also part of a trend, but I
> think very few people were really conscious of America during
> the 1990s. Instead everyone turned to postcolonialism, to culture
> studies.
>   In that sense, this is no longer the age of Murakami Haruki
> or Murakami Ryū. . . . It is the age of "political correctness" . . .
> an age when you have to adopt a certain political stance or you
> won't make it as a writer. So how are we supposed to explain the
> continued vitality of these two? (Kawamura and Ōsugi 2000, 133)

But this is too narrow a view of either Haruki or Ryū as a writer. To sum up
Murakami Haruki's entire career in terms of some kind of era-bound longing for things American is absurd, as the analyses above should make quite
clear. In fact, if the existence of works like *Underground, Underground 2*,
or for that matter *All the Gods' Children Dance* tell us anything, it is that
Murakami Haruki has shown himself capable of moving on with the times.
Rather, one cannot help feeling that Ōsugi, among others, has critically
missed the point of the last six years of Murakami fiction, has failed to
grasp that behind the hard-boiled "American" flavor of Murakami's prose
style (though this has changed too!), the author's sights are squarely on
Japan and have been for quite some time.

As I have striven to show repeatedly above, the most important
thing we should "get" from Murakami Haruki and his fiction is that the
face and expression of Japanese literature have changed, and Murakami
has spearheaded that change. Kawamoto Saburō said in 1985 that Murakami
was a "totally *un*-political" writer whose works nevertheless always made
us think of politics. This is one way to phrase the matter. Another would be

to say that Murakami is a totally political writer who always pretends he is not. In that regard his literary style is capable of obscuring the political content of his work, but only so far; his political agenda never fails to emerge at some point. Thus, if Ōsugi is correct that no writer can survive without a political angle, herein may well lie the secret of Murakami's continued success (even Ōsugi grants him this): that he is capable of combining the political, the formulaic, the magical, and the deeply psychological, with a style of expression so entertaining as to make the dull seem fresh, the serious seem fun, and the frightening seem a little more familiar.

Bibliography

Abe Kōbō. 1966. *The face of another* (Tanin no kao). Translated by E. Dale Saunders. New York: Knopf.

Althusser, Louis. 1986. Ideology and ideological state apparatuses. In *Critical theory since Plato*, edited by Hazard Adams and Leroy Searle. Tallahassee: Florida State University Press.

_____. 1983. *Writings on psychoanalysis: Freud and Lacan*. Translated by Jeffrey Mehlman. New York: Columbia University Press.

_____. 1972. *Politics and history*. Translated by Ben Brewster. London: New Left Books.

_____. 1971. *Lenin and philosophy and other essays*. Translated by Ben Brewster. New York: New Left Books..

_____. 1970. *Reading capital*. Translated by Ben Brewster. London: New Left Books.

_____. 1969. *For Marx*. Translated by Ben Brewster. New York: Pantheon.

Aoki Tamotsu. 1996. Murakami Haruki and contemporary Japan. Translated by Matthew Strecher. In *Contemporary Japan and popular culture*, edited by John W. Treat. Honolulu: University of Hawaii Press.

_____. 1985. *Karuchā, masu karuchā* (Culture, mass culture). Tokyo: Chūō Kōronsha.

Aoyama Minami. 1994. Murakami Haruki no *Zō no Heigen* (Murakami Haruki's *The Elephant Vanishes*). Parts 1 and 2. *Subaru* (September–October).

Arima, Tatsuo. 1969. *The Failure of freedom: a portrait of modern Japanese intellectuals*. Cambridge, Mass.: Harvard University Press.

Ashley, Robert. 1989. *The study of popular fiction: a source book*. London: Pinter Publishers.

Bailey, Paul J. 1996. *Postwar Japan: 1945 to the present*. Oxford and Cambridge, Mass.: Blackwell Publishers.

Barnaby, Karin, and Pellegrino D'Acierno. 1990. *C.G. Jung and the humanities: toward a hermeneutics of culture*. Princeton: Princeton University Press.

Barshay, Andrew E. 1988. *State and intellectual in imperial Japan: the public man in crisis*. Berkeley, Los Angeles, and London: University of California Press.

Barthes, Roland. 1982. *A Barthes reader*. Edited by Susan Sontag. New York: Hill and Wang.

_____. 1977. *Image—music—text*. Translated by Stephen Heath. New York: Hill and Wang.

_____. 1975. *The pleasure of the text*. Translated by Richard Miller. New York: Hill and Wang.

_____. 1967. *Elements of semiology*. Translated by Annette Lavers and Colin Smith. New York: Hill and Wang.

Baudrillard, Jean. 1994a. *The illusion of the end*. Translated by Chris Turner. Stanford: Stanford University Press.

_____. 1994b. *Simulacra and simulation*. Translated by Sheila Faria Glaser. Ann Arbor: University of Michigan Press.

_____. 1988. *Selected writings*. Edited by Mark Poster. Stanford: Stanford University Press.

Bennett, Tony. 1990. *Popular fiction: technology, ideology, production, reading*. New York: Routledge.

Birnbaum, Alfred. 1991. Introduction. In *Monkey brain sushi*, edited by Alfred Birnbaum. Tokyo: Kodansha International.

Buruma, Ian. 1996. Turning Japanese. *The New Yorker*. 23 December and 30 December, pp. 60–71.

Carpentier, Alejo. 1995. Baroque and the marvelous real. In *Magical realism: theory, history, community*, edited by Lois Zamora and Wendy Faris. Durham, N.C.: Duke University Press.

Cawelti, John G. 1976. *Adventure, mystery, and romance: formula stories as art and popular culture*. Chicago and London: University of Chicago Press.

_____. 1969. The concept of formula in the study of popular literature. *Journal of Popular Culture* 3: 381–90.

Derrida, Jacques. 1978. *Writing and difference*. Translated by Alan Bass. Chicago: University of Chicago Press.

Dower, John. 1992. Peace and democracy in two systems. In *Postwar Japan as history*, edited by Andrew Gordon. Berkeley and London: University of California Press.

Faris, Wendy. Scheherezade's children: magical realism and postmodern fiction. In *Magical realism: theory, history, community*, edited by Lois Zamora and Wendy Faris. Durham, N.C.: Duke University Press.

Foucault, Michel. 1984. *The Foucault reader*. Edited by Paul Rabinow. New York: Pantheon.

_____. 1972. *The archaeology of knowledge*. New York: Pantheon.

_____. 1970. *The order of things: an archaeology of the human sciences.* New York: Random House. Reprinted: New York: Vintage, 1994.

Freud, Sigmund. 1961. *Civilization and its discontents.* Translated by James Strachey. New York and London: Norton.

_____. 1924. *A general introduction to psychoanalysis.* Translated by Joan Riviere. New York: Horace Liveright, Inc.

Fromm, Erich. 1950. *Psychoanalysis and religion.* New Haven: Yale University Press.

Frye, Northrop. 1957. *Anatomy of criticism.* Princeton: Princeton University Press.

Fukuda Kazuya. 1994. Sofutobōru no yō na shi no katamari o mesu de kirihiraku koto (Cutting through the hardness of softball-like death with a scalpel). *Shinchō* 91.7.

Furui Yoshikichi. 1997. *Child of darkness: Yōko and other stories.* Translated by Donna George Storey. Ann Arbor: Center for Japanese Studies, University of Michigan.

Fuse Hidetoshi. 1995. Murakami Haruki no "Shitai" (The "Corpses" of Murakami Haruki). *Subaru* (December).

Gitlin, Todd. 1987. *The sixties: years of hope, days of rage.* New York: Bantam.

Habermas, Jürgen. 1983. Modernity: an incomplete project. In *The antiaesthetic: essays on postmodern culture.* Port Townsend, Wash.: Bay Press.

Haipātekusuto: Murakami Haruki (Hypertext: Murakami Haruki). 1998. Special issue of *Kokubungaku* 43.3.

Hatanaka Yoshiki. 1989. Murakami Haruki no namae o meguru bōken (Murakami Haruki's wild name chase). *Yuriika* 21.8 (August): 138–39.

Hidaka, Rokurō. 1984. *The price of affluence: dilemmas of contemporary Japan.* Translated and edited by Gavan McCormack et al. Tokyo, New York, and San Francisco: Kodansha International.

Hisai Tsubaki. 1994. *Nejimakidori no sagashikata* (How to search for the wind-up bird). Tokyo: Ōta Shuppan.

Honda Katsuichi. 1993. *The impoverished spirit of contemporary Japan.* Edited by John Lie. Translated by Eri Fujieda, Masayuki Hamazaki, and John Lie. New York: Monthly Review Press.

Hukami Haruka. 1990. *Murakami Haruki no uta* (The song of Murakami Haruki). Tokyo: Seikyōsha.

Hutcheon, Linda. 1989. *The politics of postmodernism.* New York: Routledge.

_____. 1988. *A poetics of postmodernism: history, theory, fiction.* New York: Routledge.

_____. 1980. *Narcissistic narrative: the metafictional paradox.* Ontario: Wilfred Laurier University Press.

Huyssen, Andreas. 1986. *After the great divide*. Bloomington: Indiana University Press.

Imai Kiyoto. 1990. *OFF no kankaku* (The OFF sensation). Tokyo: Kokken Shuppan.

Inoue Yoshio. 1999. *Murakami Haruki to Nihon no "kioku"* (Murakami Haruki and Japan's "memory"). Tokyo: Shinchōsha.

Irigaray, Luce. 1981. This sex which is not one. In *New French feminisms*, edited by Elaine Marks and Isabelle de Courtivron. New York: Schocken Books.

Ivy, Marilyn. 1993. Formations of mass culture. In *Postwar Japan as history*, edited by Andrew Gordon. Berkeley and London: University of California Press.

_____.1989. Critical texts, mass artifacts: the consumption of knowledge in postmodern Japan. In *Postmodernism and Japan*, edited by Masao Miyoshi and H.D. Harutoonian. Durham, N.C. and London: Duke University Press.

Iwamoto, Yoshio. 1993. A voice from postmodern Japan: Murakami Haruki. In *World literature today* (Spring).

Jameson, Fredric. 1991. *Postmodernism, or the cultural logic of late capitalism*. Durham, N.C.: Duke University Press.

Jung, Carl. 1970. *The collected works of Carl Jung*. 10 vols. Princeton: Princeton University Press.

_____. 1957. *The undiscovered self*. Translated by R.F.C. Hull. Princeton: Princeton University Press.

Kamijō Kiyoshi. 1994. Review of Yokoo Kazuhiro's *Murakami Haruki: kyūjū nendai* (1994). *Shin Nihon Bungaku* 49.9.

Karatani Kōjin. 1997. *Shimpojiumu* (Symposium). 2 vols. Tokyo: Ōta Shuppan.

_____. 1993a. The discursive space of modern Japan. Translated by Seiji M. Lippit. In *Japan in the world*, edited by Masao Miyoshi and H.D. Harootunian. Durham and London: Duke University Press.

_____. 1993b. *Origins of modern Japanese literature*. Translated by Brett de Bary et al. Durham, N.C. and London: Duke University Press.

_____. 1990a. *Kindai Nihon no hihyo: Showa-hen*. 2 vols. Tokyo: Fukutake Shoten.

_____. 1990b. *Shūen o megutte*. Tokyo: Fukutake Shoten.

_____. 1987. *Daiarōgu* (Dialogues). 3 vols. Tokyo: Daisan Bunmeisha.

_____. 1980. *Nihon kindai bungaku no kigen* (Origins of modern Japanese literature). Tokyo: Kōdansha.

Katō Hiroichi. 1989. Ishō no mori o aruku (Walking the forests of vision). *Gunzō* 44.11.

Katō Norihiro. 1997. *Haisengo-ron* (A post-defeat study). Tokyo: Kōdansha.

_____. 1996a. *Murakami Haruki: ierō pēji* (Murakami Haruki: yellow pages). Tokyo: Arachi Shuppansha.

_____. 1996b. Natsu no jūkyūnichikan: *Kaze no uta o kike* no dokkai (Nineteen summer days: a critical reading of *Hear the wind sing*). *Kokubungaku* 40.4 (March).

_____. 1994. With Nakazawa Shin'ichi. Yūrei no ikikata (How spirits live). *Shisō no kagaku* no. 515.

_____. 1991. *Murakami Haruki o meguru bōken* (A wild Murakami Haruki chase). Tokyo: Kawai Shobō.

_____. 1988. "Masaka" to "Yareyare" ("Masaka" and "Yareyare"). *Gunzō* 43.8: 106–28.

_____. 1986. Jihei to sakoku (Self-absorption and national isolation). In *Siiku & fuaindo Murakami Haruki*, edited by Murakami Ryū. Tokyo: Seidōsha.

Kawamoto, Saburō. 1986. Murakami Haruki o meguru kaidoku (Deciphering Murakami Haruki). In *Siiku & fuaindo Murakami Haruki*, edited by Murakami Ryū. Tokyo: Seidōsha.

_____. 1985. "Monogatari" no tame no bōken (A wild "story" chase). *Bungakukai* 39.8: 34–86.

Kawamura Minato. 2000. With Ōsugi Shigeo. Murakami Ryū to Murakami Haruki: 25-nen no bungaku kūkan (Murakami Ryū and Murakami Haruki: 25 years of literary space). *Gunzō* 55.7 (July).

Kawamura, Nozomu. 1990. Sociology and socialism in the interwar period. In *Culture and identity: Japanese intellectuals during the interwar years*, edited by J. Thomas Rimer. Princeton: Princeton University Press.

Kazamaru Yoshihiko. 1992. Emuputii setto: Murakami Haruki to bokutachi no sedai (Empty set: Murakami Haruki and our generation). *Gunzō* 47.5 (May): 204–32.

Kerrane, Kevin, and Ben Yagoda. 1997. *The art of fact: a historical anthology of literary journalism*. New York: Scribner.

Kolker, Andrew, and Louis Alvarez, prod. 1991. *The Japanese Version*. New York: Center for New American Media, Inc. 56 minutes.

Kondo, Dorinne. 1992. Multiple selves: the aesthetics and politics of artisanal identities. In *Japanese sense of self*, edited by Nancy Rosenberger. Cambridge: Cambridge University Press.

_____.1990. *Crafting selves: power, gender, and discourses of identity in a Japanese workplace*. Chicago: University of Chicago Press.

Konishi Keita. 1995. *Murakami Haruki no ongaku zukan* (Music in the world of Murakami Haruki). Tokyo: Japan Mix.

Koschmann, J. Victor. 1996. *Revolution and subjectivity in postwar Japan*. Chicago and London: University of Chicago Press.

_____. 1993. Intellectuals and Politics. In *Postwar Japan as history*, edited by Andrew Gordon. Berkeley and London: University of California Press.

Kurata Mitsuhiro. 1995. Reitōko no pinbōru (Pinball in a freezer). *Shisō no kagaku* no. 521.

Kuroko Kazuo. 1997a. *Ōe Kenzaburō to kono jidai no bungaku* (Ōe Kenzaburō and the literature of this age). Tokyo: Benseisha.

_____. 1997b. *Tatematsu Wahei: shissō suru bungaku seishin* (Tatematsu Wahei: the racing literary spirit). Tokyo: Zuisōsha.

_____. 1993. *Murakami Haruki: za rosuto wārudo* (Murakami Haruki: the lost world). Tokyo: Daisan Shokan.

_____. 1990. *Murakami Haruki to dōjidai bungaku* (Murakami Haruki and contemporary literature). Tokyo: Kawai Shuppan.

Lacan, Jacques. 1988. *The seminar of Jacques Lacan.* Edited by Jacques-Alain Miller. Books 1 and 3. New York: W.W. Norton.

_____. 1978. *The four fundamental concepts of psychoanalysis.* Translated by Alan Sheridan. New York: Norton.

_____. 1977. The mirror stage as formative of the function of the I as revealed in psychoanalytic experience. In *Écrits: a selection,* translated by Alan Sheridan. New York: W.W. Norton.

Leal, Luis. 1995. Magical realism in Spanish America. In *Magical realism: theory, history, community,* edited by Lois Zamora and Wendy Faris. Durham, N.C.: Duke University Press.

LeBlanc, Robin. 1999. *Bicycle citizens: the political world of the Japanese housewife.* Berkeley: University of California Press.

Lyotard, Jean-Francois. 1984. *The postmodern condition: a report on knowledge.* Translated by Geoff Bennington and Brian Massumi. Minneapolis: University of Minnesota Press.

MacCannell, Juliet Flower. 1986. *Figuring Lacan: criticism and the cultural unconscious.* London: Croom Helm.

Marshall, Brenda K. 1992. *Teaching the postmodern: fiction and theory.* New York: Routledge.

Maruya Saiichi. 1995. With Miura Masashi. Motoori Norinaga kara Murakami Haruki made (From Motoori Norinaga to Murakami Haruki). *Bungakukai* 49.1.

McGee, Patrick. 1992. *Telling the other: the question of value in modern and postcolonial writing.* Ithaca and London: Cornell University Press.

McGowan, John. 1991. *Postmodernism and its critics.* Ithaca and London: Cornell University Press.

McHale, Brian. 1992. *Constructing postmodernism.* New York and London: Routledge.

_____. 1987. *Postmodernist fiction.* New York and London: Methuen.

Mead, George H. 1956. *On social psychology.* Edited by Anselm Strauss. Chicago and London: University of Chicago Press.

Mitgang, Herbert. From Japan, Big Macs and Marlboros in stories: review of *The Elephant Vanishes. New York Times,* 12 May 1993.

Miyoshi, Masao. 1993. With H.D. Harootunian. *Japan in the world.* Durham and London: Duke University Press.

_____. 1991. *Off center: power and culture relations between Japan and the United States.* Cambridge, Mass., and London: Harvard University Press.

_____. 1989. With H.D. Harootunian. *Postmodernism and Japan.* Durham and London: Duke University Press.

Modleski, Tania. 1982. *Loving with a vengeance: mass-produced fantasies for women.* New York: Routledge.

Mukai Satoshi. 1993. Shudai ni shisshite monogatari o ushinau (Sacrificing the story to a theme). *Bungakukai* 47.1.

Mulhern, Chieko Irie. 1989. Japanese Harlequin Romances as transcultural woman's fiction. *Journal of Asian Studies* 48.1.

Murakami Haruki. 2000a. *Kami no kodomotachi wa mina odoru* (All the gods' children dance). Tokyo: Shinchōsha.

_____. 2000b. *South of the border, west of the sun.* Translated by Philip Gabriel. New York: Vintage. Originally published 1999 by Alfred A. Knopf.

_____. 1999a. Jishin no ato de (After the earthquake). Serialized in *Shinchō* (August-December).

_____. 1999b. *Spūtoniku no koibito* (The Sputnik sweetheart). Tokyo: Kōdansha.

_____. 1998. *Yakusoku sareta basho de: Underground 2* (The place that was promised: Underground 2). Tokyo: Bungei Shunjū.

_____. 1997a. *Andāguraundo* (Underground). Tokyo: Kōdansha.

_____. 1997b. *The wind-up bird chronicle.* Translated by Jay Rubin. New York: Knopf.

_____. 1997c. *Wakai dokusha no tame no tampen shōsetu annai* (A guide to short fiction for young readers). Tokyo: Bungei Shunjū.

_____. 1995. *Dance, dance, dance.* Translated by Alfred Birnbaum. New York: Vintage.

_____. 1994-96. *Nejimakidori kuronikuru* (Wind-up bird chronicle). Tokyo: Shinchōsha.

_____. 1994. *Yagate kanashiki gaikokugo* (Ultimately, a sad foreign language). Tokyo: Kōdansha.

_____. 1993. *The elephant vanishes.* Translated by Alfred Birnbaum and Jay Rubin. New York: Knopf.

_____. 1992. *Kokkyō no minami, taiyō no nishi* (South of the border, west of the sun). Tokyo: Kōdansha.

_____. 1991. *Hard-boiled wonderland and the end of the world.* Translated by Alfred Birnbaum. New York: Vintage.

_____. 1990-91. *Murakami Haruki zensakuhin, 1979-1989* (Complete works of Murakami Haruki, 1979-1989). 8 vols. Tokyo: Kōdansha.

_____. 1990. *Terebi piipuru* (TV people). Tokyo: Bungei Shunjū.

_____. 1989. *A wild sheep chase.* Translated by Alfred Birnbaum. New York: Plume.

Murakami Haruki. 1998. Edited by Kimata Satoshi. Tokyo: Wakakusa Shobō.

Murakami Haruki. 1997. Special series: *Gunzō* Japanese Writers no. 26. Tokyo: Shōgakukan.

Murakami Haruki no sekai. 1989. Special issue of *Yuriika* 21.8.

Murakami Ryū. 1997. *In za miso sūpu* (In the miso soup). Tokyo: Yomiuri Shimbunsha.

_____, ed. 1986. *Siiku & fuaindo Murakami Haruki.* Tokyo: Seidōsha.

_____. 1976. Kagirinaku tōmei ni chikai burū. Tokyo: Kōdansha.

Murakami Tomohiko. 1990. Mada shinenai de iru "Kōbe" no tame ni (For the Kobe that cannot die). *Shisō no kagaku* no. 135.

Nakagami Kenji to Murakami Haruki (Nakagami Kenji and Murakami Haruki). 1985. Special issue of *Kokubungaku* 30.3.

Nakamura Mitsuharu. 1998. Yukue fumei jinbutsu kankei (Missing human relationships). *Kokubungaku* 43.3.

Napier, Susan. 1996. *The fantastic in modern Japanese literature: the subversion of modernity.* London and New York: Routledge.

_____. 1995. The magic of identity: magic realism in modern Japanese fiction. In *Magical realism: theory, history, community,* edited by Lois Zamora and Wendy Faris, 451–75. Durham, N.C.: Duke University Press.

Newman, Charles. 1985. *The postmodern aura.* Evanston, Ill.: Northwestern University Press.

Noda Masaaki. 1997. Kakusareta dōki (The hidden motive). *Gunzō* 52.5.

Noruwei no Mori no himitsu (The secret of *Norwegian Wood*). 1989. *Bungei Shunjū* 67.5.

Numano Mitsuyoshi. 1995. With Suzumura Kazunari. "Nejimakidori" wa doko e tobu ka? (To where will the "wind-up bird" fly?). *Bungakukai* 49.10.

_____. 1994. Murakami Haruki wa sekai no "ima" ni tachimukau (Murakami Haruki faces the "now" of the world). *Bungakukai* 48.7.

_____. 1989. Dōnatsu, biiru, supagetii (Donuts, beer, spaghetti). *Yuriika* 21.8 (August).

O'Brien, Tim. 1985. *The nuclear age.* New York: Knopf.

Ōe Kenzaburō. 1993. With Kazuo Ishiguro. The novelist in today's world: a conversation. In *Japan in the world,* edited by Masao Miyoshi and H.D. Harootunian. Durham and London: Duke University Press.

_____. 1989. Japan's dual identity: a writer's dilemma. In *Postmodernism and Japan,* edited by Masao Miyoshi and H.D. Harootunian. Durham, N.C., and London: Duke University Press.

Oka, Yoshitake. 1982. Generational conflict after the Russo-Japanese war. In *Conflict in modern Japanese history: the neglected tradition,* edited by Tetsuo Najita and J. Victor Koschmann. Princeton: Princeton University Press.

Painter, Andrew. 1993. Japanese daytime television, popular culture, and ideology. *The Journal of Japanese Studies* 19.2 (Summer).

Radway, Janice. 1984. *Reading the romance: women, patriarchy, and popular literature*. Chapel Hill and London: University of North Carolina Press.

Ragland-Sullivan, Ellie. 1991. With Mark Bracher. *Lacan and the subject of language*. New York: Routledge.

_____. 1986. *Jacques Lacan and the philosophy of psychoanalysis*. Urbana: University of Illinois Press.

Roberts, Thomas. 1990. *An aesthetics of junk fiction*. Athens, Ga., and London: University of Georgia Press.

Rubin, Gayle. 1975. The traffic in women: notes on the "political economy" of sex. In *Toward an anthropology of women*, edited by Rayna Rapp Reiter. New York: Monthly Review Press.

Rubin, Jay. 1999. Murakami Haruki's two poor aunts tell everything they know about sheep, wells, unicorns, Proust, elephants, and magpies. In *Ōe and beyond*, edited by Stephen Snyder and Philip Gabriel. Honolulu: University of Hawai'i Press.

_____. 1992. The other world of Murakami Haruki. *Japan Quarterly* 39.4.

_____. 1990. Deep sheep dip. *The World and I* (April).

Rushdie, Salman. 1981. *Midnight's children*. London: Jonathan Cape.

Saitō Eiji. 1993. Gendai no gōsuto sutōrii (A modern ghost story). *Shinchō* 90.2 (February).

Sekine Makihiko. 1994. Aimu natto raiku eburibadii erusu (I'm not like everybody else). *Shisō no kagaku* no. 511.

Sengoku Hideyo. 1991. *Airon o kakeru seinen: Murakami Haruki to Amerika* (The youth plying the iron: Murakami Haruki and America). Tokyo: Sairyūsha.

Shimada Masahiko. 1990. *Rokoko-chō* (Rococo-ville). Tokyo: Shūeisha.

_____. 1989. *Dream messenger*. Translated by Philip Gabriel. Tokyo, New York, and London: Kodansha International.

Siegle, Robert. 1986. *The politics of reflexivity: narrative and the constitutive poetics of culture*. Baltimore and London: Johns Hopkins University Press.

Sims, Norman. 1990. *Literary journalism in the twentieth century*. Oxford and New York: Oxford University Press.

Sims, Norman, and Mark Kramer, eds. 1995. *Literary journalism*. New York: Ballantine Books.

Sklovsky, Viktor. 1991 (1929). *Theory of prose*. Chicago: Dalkey Archive Press.

Snyder, Stephen. 1996. Two Murakamis and Marcel Proust: memory as form in contemporary Japanese fiction. In *In pursuit of contemporary East Asian culture*, edited by Xiaobing Tang and Stephen Snyder. Boulder: Westview Press.

Stalph, Jürgen. 1995. Doitsu no Murakami Haruki (Murakami Haruki in Germany). *Kokubungaku* 40.4 (March): 104–8.

Strecher, Matthew. 1999. Magical realism and the search for identity in the fiction of Murakami Haruki. *Journal of Japanese Studies* 25.2.

_____. 1998a. Beyond "pure" literature: mimesis, formula, and the postmodern in the fiction of Murakami Haruki. *Journal of Asian Studies* 57.2.

_____. 1998b. Murakami Haruki: Japan's coolest writer heats up. *Japan Quarterly* 45.1.

Suzumaru Kazunari. 1990. *Mada/sude ni: Murakami Haruki to "hādoboirudo wandārando"* (Encore/Déjà: Murakami Haruki and the "hardboiled wonderland"). Tokyo: Yosensha.

Takagi Masayuki. 1985. *Zengakuren to Zenkyōtō* (Zengakuren and Zenkyōtō). Tokyo: Kōdansha Gendai Shinsho.

Tatsumi Takayuki. 1998. *Nihon henryū bungaku* (Japanese slipstream literature). Tokyo: Shinchōsha.

Treat, John. 1995. *Writing ground zero: Japanese literature and the atomic bomb*. Chicago and London: University of Chicago Press.

_____. 1993. Yoshimoto Banana writes home: shōjo culture and the nostalgic subject. *Journal of Japanese Studies* 19.2.

Ueno Chizuko et al. 1992. *Danryū bungaku-ron* (A theory of men's literature). Tokyo: Chikuma Shobō.

Uno, Kathleen. 1993. The death of "good wife, wise mother"? In *Postwar Japan as history*, edited by Andrew Gordon. Berkeley and London: University of California Press.

White, Hayden. 1987. *The content of the form: narrative discourse and historical representation*. Baltimore and London: The Johns Hopkins University Press.

_____. 1973. *Metahistory: the historical imagination in nineteenth-century Europe*. Baltimore: The Johns Hopkins University Press.

Williams, David. 1994. *Japan: beyond the end of history*. New York and London: Routledge.

Wolfe, Alan. 1989. Suicide and the Japanese postmodern. In *Postmodernism and Japan*, edited by Masao Miyoshi and H.D. Harutoonian. Durham, N.C. and London: Duke University Press.

Wolferen, Karel van. 1989. *The enigma of Japanese power: people and politics in a stateless nation*. New York: Knopf.

Yamawaki Ayako. 1997. Tachiagaru jijitsu no "monogatari" (Real "stories" that stand up). *Aera* 10.13.

Yokoo, Kazuhiro. 1994. *Murakami Haruki: kyūjū nendai* (Murakami Haruki: the nineties). Tokyo: Daisan Shokan.

_____. 1991. *Murakami Haruki to Dosutoēfusukii* (Murakami Haruki and Dostoevsky). Tokyo: Kindai Bungeisha.

Yoshida Haruo. 1997. *Murakami Haruki, tenkan suru* (Murakami Haruki, about face). Tokyo: Sairyūsha.

Index

Made in the USA
Middletown, DE
24 April 2021